Early Childhood Field Experience

Learning to Teach Well

SECOND EDITION

Kathryn Williams Browne
Skyline College

Ann Miles Gordon
Consultant

PEARSON

Boston   Columbus   Indianapolis   New York   San Francisco   Upper Saddle River   Amsterdam
Cape Town   Dubai   London   Madrid   Milan   Munich   Paris   Montreal   Toronto
Delhi   Mexico City   São Paulo   Sydney   Hong Kong   Seoul   Singapore   Taipei   Tokyo

Vice President and Editorial Director: Jeffery W. Johnston
Senior Acquisitions Editor: Julie Peters
Editorial Assistant: Andrea Hall
Senior Marketing Manager: Margaret Waples
Marketing Manager: Christopher D. Barry
Senior Managing Editor: Pamela D. Bennett
Production Manager: Susan Hannahs
Senior Art Director: Jayne Conte
Cover Designer: Bruce Kenselaar
Cover Art: Comstock Images/Jupiterimages/GettyImages (top); Mel Yates/Cultura/Getty Images (center);
   SOMOS/SuperStock (bottom)
Full-Service Project Management: Nitin Agarwal, Aptara®, Inc.
Composition: Aptara®, Inc.
Printer/Bindery: LSC Communications
Cover Printer: LSC Communications
Text Font: 11/15 Meridien

Credits and acknowledgments borrowed from other sources and reproduced, with permission, in this textbook appear on the appropriate page within the text.

Every effort has been made to provide accurate and current Internet information in this book. However, the Internet and information posted on it are constantly changing, so it is inevitable that some of the Internet addresses listed in this textbook will change.

Photo Credits: © michaeljung/Fotolia.com, pp. 4, 40; © Photo_Ma/Fotolia.com, p. 7; © micromonkey/Fotolia.com, p. 10; Krista Greco/Merrill, pp. 14, 63, 71, 109; © Dorling Kindersley, Courtesy of the Nordoff Robins Music Therapy Centre London, pp. 28, 151; © Marc Dietrich/Fotolia.com, p. 43, © auremar/Fotolia.com, p. 46, 211; © darko64/Fotolia.com, p. 57; © Kalim/Fotolia.com, p. 76; © SergiyN/Fotolia.com, p. 85; Annie Fuller/Pearson, pp. 87, 216; © diego cervo/Fotolia.com, p. 94, Eddie Lawrence © Dorling Kindersley, p. 98, © Neo Edmund/Fotolia.com, p. 108, © Cheryl Casey/Fotolia.com, p. 116; © Monkey Business/Fotolia.com, pp. 122, 179; Ruth Jenkinson © Dorling Kindersley, p. 130; © Jane September/Fotolia.com, p. 134, © Claudia Paulussen/Fotolia.com, p. 139; Katelyn Metzger/Merrill, p. 162; Vanessa Davies © Dorling Kindersley, p. 167; Lori Whitley/Merrill, p. 174; © Rob/Fotolia.com, p. 187; © Andy Dean/Fotolia.com, p. 192, Annie Fuller / Pearson Education, p. 198, © Ella/Fotolia.com, p. 201, © mangostock/Fotolia.com, p. 211; © Shutterstock, p. 226; Dave King © Dorling Kindersley, p. 229.

Library of Congress Cataloging-in-Publication Data
Browne, Kathryn Williams.
   Early childhood field experience : learning to teach well / Kathryn Williams Browne; Ann Miles Gordon, consultant. —2nd ed.
      p. cm.
   Rev. ed. of: To teach well: Upper Saddle River, N.J.:Merrill, c2009.
   ISBN-13: 978-0-13-265706-8
   ISBN-10: 0-13-265706-6
   1. Early childhood teachers—Training of.   2. Student teaching.   I. Gordon, Ann Miles.   II. Browne, Kathryn Williams. To teach well.   III. Title.
   LB1775.6.B76 2013
   371.1—dc23   2012022294

6 2019

ISBN 10:   0-13-265706-6
ISBN 13: 978-0-13-265706-8

To the student teachers of Skyline College 2005–present, of Canada and De Anza-Foothill Colleges 1995–2000, and Stanford University 1980–1995. They have taught me what it means to be stellar "beginner educators" and shown what early childhood students need to understand to become professionals.

Kate Williams Browne

To K. Eileen Allen, my first and foremost mentor and lifelong friend.

Ann Gordon

preface

··

D o you remember how you felt the first time you walked into a classroom as a child? It was an exciting time, filled with expectations and aspirations of success. Yet it was also a time of uneasiness and uncertainty. Now you are a student teacher. Here comes the surprise and the anxiety again! How do you learn to be competent? Too often the real world of teaching young children seems overwhelming.

Early Childhood Field Experiences: Learning to Teach Well, Second Edition, offers a successful, accessible, and lively introduction to student teaching. Chapters with real-life situations and features that illustrate teaching practices will help you connect your fieldwork experiences with the knowledge and theory you are learning in the courses that have prepared you for this moment. This text is appropriate for student teaching, practicum, or other fieldwork placement for students getting hands-on experience in an early childhood program. Whether you are practice teaching in a family child care home, infant–toddler center, preschool, kindergarten, or school-age program, you can use this text to help you master the key components of teaching. Welcome to the field of early learning and care for our youngest citizens, their families, and your fellow teachers!

New to This Edition

- Expanded content on working with infants and toddlers
- Expanded strategies for adapting teaching practices with children with exceptional needs and atypical development
- *Ethical dilemmas* in every chapter enable student teachers to better understand the importance of developing and using both a professional code of ethics and high personal behavior standards when working with children, family, and staff
- *Student Learning Outcomes* have been added at the beginning of each chapter, and thus follow into the major headings of the chapter, giving readers a clear sense of what they are to know and be able to do upon mastering the content as well as providing them with a helpful clue about how to read for understanding and review the content.
- Expanded content in Chapter 1 on program types and the wide range of programs that serve young children in the field of early

childhood education to helps students become familiar with the setting in which they will have a field experience.

- Expanded content in Chapter 3 includes guidance strategies for infants, toddlers, and children with special needs.

- A thorough update and expansion on curriculum in Chapter 6 takes into consideration the special challenges novice teachers face when trying to develop master planning and implementing a curriculum. New content on curriculum for infants, toddlers, and children with special needs enlarges the range of student knowledge. The inclusion of large- and small-group activities for infants/toddlers, preschoolers, and school-age children will help the student teacher plan age-appropriate experiences

Features of This Text

A successful student practicum is one that presents a realistic view of what it takes to be a teacher in today's educational settings and helps student teachers come to know their own capacities and attitudes. Our book is an informational text that encourages reflective thinking while also offering content about concepts and application. It allows faculty instructors to use the book in many different ways to augment the fieldwork experience. Throughout the book, contributions from student teachers and mentor supervisors give the text relevance and authenticity. Developmentally and culturally appropriate practices are woven throughout the text to ensure that students become aware of national standards for programs and practices.

This book introduces student teachers to the fundamental principles of teaching and professionalism so that they have a strong base on which to build the knowledge and skills they learn through their practicum. We guide students from the first days of getting started in their fieldwork through the many areas of responsibility they will encounter as they teach. Each chapter stresses thoughtful consideration—both in the chapter content and throughout multiple activities—that helps students gain insight into their teaching experiences. A "top 10" list in each chapter either highlights basic principles or offers the student concise and relevant tips for teaching.

Teachers' self-awareness is one of the most important elements in effective teaching; it keeps them grounded and present for their children, thus helping them gain a healthy attitude toward understanding themselves, their actions, and their attitudes. In a way, the subtitle of the text could be "It Begins with Me." The book promotes the process of reflective teaching from the beginning of a student's classroom experience in each chapter through the following features:

Reflective Incident: The reader responds to a real student teacher's classroom incident or a chapter topic by answering the following questions: How would I feel? What would I do? What might the results be? How does my experience in ECE so far help me? What professional standards can I use as resources?

My Reaction: This feature gives specific examples of situations that other student teachers have experienced and how they felt and responded, offering students a realistic and sympathetic look at other new teacher–student struggles and triumphs.

Lessons from the Field: An experienced teacher describes an area of teaching from the point of "what I know now that I wish I'd known then," suggesting that teaching is a lifelong learning process as well as echoing the need for self-reflection.

Ethical Dilemma: Each chapter raises an ethical issue that students may experience during their field experience. In this way, the student becomes familiar with solving ethical dilemmas by using the NAEYC Code of Ethical Conduct as their guide.

Practicum Activity: Students apply their on-site learning to questions that encourage critical thinking and problem solving. Their responses then can be discussed in their student teaching seminars.

Journaling Assignment: This activity serves as a prompt for student's journals, or an online discussion board, or a talk with the supervising teacher, again bringing home the point that reflection equals growth. Students are encouraged to consider "What do I bring to the current situation?" and then to write, which helps them move from divergent thinking to problem solving while summing up their journey to become a teacher.

Format and Chapter Focus

Each chapter has a specific focus and offers basic information and strategies for making the student teaching experience as productive and valuable as possible. Theory evolves into practice through the enhancements noted previously that are woven throughout the chapter. Instructors are given multiple ways to interact with students, reinforcing the chapter content. Relevant photographs and charts further illuminate theory and implementations of key concepts.

Chapter 1, "Getting Started," begins with an overview of the top 10 fundamentals of teaching and the roles and responsibilities of teaching. Fieldwork guidelines include preparing students for a successful start and some of the situations they may encounter. Types of early childhood programs are described so student teachers can understand the various settings available for their fieldwork.

Chapter 2, "Becoming a Professional Teacher," focuses on professionalism. Professional standards and goal setting are discussed along with assessment and evaluation. The top 10 reasons for teacher assessment and evaluation help students understand the value of assessments as avenues for growth and give them specific examples of teacher assessment tools. This chapter also introduces students to a professional code of ethics, with exercises, by using the National Association for the Education of Young Children (NAEYC) Code of Ethical Conduct to problem-solve real scenarios faced by student teachers. Students also explore career options and learn to create their own professional portfolio. Student teachers can then demonstrate their understanding of professional standards, goal setting and assessment of one's teaching experience, and the Code of Ethical Conduct, as they relate to teaching proficiency.

Chapter 3, "Understanding and Guiding Behavior," reviews the important concepts of guidance, which can be a source of confusion and insecurity for new teachers. Basic guidance beliefs and the differences among guidance, discipline, and punishment are clearly defined, as are developmentally and culturally appropriate guidance. The top 10 guidance techniques offer students an overview of strategies, ranging from the least intrusive to those requiring the most teacher intervention. Students will be able to identify effective guidance strategies that are developmentally and culturally appropriate, based on respectful and supportive relationships with children.

Chapter 4, "Observing and Assessing Children," covers the critical areas of observation and assessment of children with attention to NAEYC standards and school readiness. The top 10 characteristics of quality child assessment along with sample assessment tools help the beginning student learn the value of observing children and using authentic assessment to create positive interactions, learning environments, and curriculum. The ethical dilemma of observing children who may have atypical development is addressed. Student teachers will then be able to identify methods of observation, interpretation, documentation, and assessment to positively influence children's development and learning.

Chapter 5, "Environments and Schedules," demonstrates ways to consider children's needs through the use of appropriate environments and schedules. The top 10 tips for building developmentally appropriate schedules and basic space-planning considerations give student teachers insights into behavior management as well as meeting program goals. Student teachers will then be able to identify the components of effective environments and schedules to create positive learning experiences for children.

Chapter 6, "Curriculum," explains how children learn and how play as the learning medium provides the basis for developmentally appropriate curriculum. The top 10 questions when creating curriculum serve as guidelines for developing age-appropriate, culturally responsive, integrated, emergent, and inclusive curriculum. The how-to of written lesson plans and planning and leading group times gives student teachers the necessary tools to master these important tasks. Student teachers learn several different ways to design, implement, and evaluate meaningful curriculum that is play based, integrated, and grounded in active learning for children with typical and atypical development and for all three age groups.

Chapter 7, "Team Teaching," explores the common practice of sharing teaching responsibilities with other adults. The chapter offers specific examples of the challenges of team teaching along with top 10 tips for team teaching to help beginning teachers learn to work well with other adults. Students will come to understand the essentials of team teaching and the challenges of developing positive working relationships with colleagues.

Chapter 8, "Collaborating with Families," explores family–school connections and discusses why they are important. The diversity and definition of today's family set the tone for understanding the parent–school relationship. The top 10 tips for positive family–school relationships help students begin to make the important links to the families of the children in their classroom. Students will examine how to understand families, the various family-school connections, and communication issues.

Chapter 9, "The Dynamics of Diversity," addresses equity, inclusion, early intervention, accommodations for disabilities, and the antibias approach. Students are asked to reflect on the many facets of diversity. The top 10 strategies for addressing diversity contain practical suggestions and reflective exercises that help students employ what they have learned and encourage student teachers to examine their own feelings and responses to the meaning and expressions of diversity today. Student teachers come to an understanding of the many facets of diversity and the skills for interacting collaboratively with children and adults with various cultures, languages, and abilities in group care and education settings.

Acknowledgments

Good teachers continue to learn throughout their careers. To all the Mentor and Supervising Teachers of the San Mateo and San Francisco areas, we express our sincere appreciation for your generosity of spirit and time: *Xiè-xie!* From student teachers Yuji to Azhar and everyone in between, whose practicum voices are heard throughout the text: *Gracias por todo!* The comments, reflections, reactions, and questions from the students in early childhood courses at Skyline College in San Bruno, California, gave us insights that can only come from new and fresh minds. The smart minds of our colleagues at California Community College Early Childhood Education (CCCECE) Faculty Association have been invaluable, as have our State University and Community Colleges colleagues of the Competency Integration Project (CIP) Steering Committee. Truths about teaching and myriad teaching resources and wisdom helped us offer here the best experiences for student teachers.

The Pearson staff offered encouragement and sometimes gentle nudges along the way. Julie Peters, whose knowledge of the field and feedback pushed us forward, and her assistant, Andrea Hall, asked and answered questions and sent appropriate resources. We appreciate the concerted efforts of project managers Linda Bayma and Sheryl Langner.

Sometimes authors are too close to the subject matter to see what is missing or what needs to be changed. We thank the team of reviewers whose helpful comments enhanced the content: Mary Elizabeth Ambery, Southwest Missouri State University; Rachel Bernal, San Jacinto College Central; Joan Campbell, Santa Fe College; Martina Ebesugawa, De Anza College; Ellie Salour, Montgomery College; and Mary Barbara Trube, Ohio University–Chillicothe. This book is by far a better text thanks to their efforts.

brief contents

contents

chapter 8   **Collaborating with Families**   **185**

chapter 9   **The Dynamics of Diversity**   210

chapter 1

Getting Started

LEARNING OUTCOME

Integrate an understanding of the fundamentals of teaching with the student teacher's roles and professional behavior.

Why Become a Teacher?

Winona became a Head Start teacher's aide when her children were enrolled in the program on their reservation. As she taught, she realized how much of the children's learning was based on her own Native American values, especially the ability to connect with others through storytelling. This inspired her to take classes, further her education, and continue to teach. For Winona, it was important to give back to her community by passing on its culture to her students.

Olga is a 23-year-old working as an assistant in a child care center sponsored by her church, where she also teaches Sunday school. She likes to feel useful to families, so she babysits regularly within her church community. Olga is challenged by the opportunity to learn how to care for and educate children in a group setting and has already adapted some of her insights to her Sunday school class. She likes being a member of a teaching team.

LeAnne's mother ran a family child care home while she and her brother were growing up. They often helped out their mother after school. Now that LeAnne has children, she too has started a family child care home. This work gives her an opportunity to stay at home with her own young children, help out with the family finances, and do work that she enjoys. LeAnne has been taking some courses at the local community college as time permits and will continue to work toward an associate degree in early childhood.

Sam comes from a long line of teachers. His father and grandmothers taught, and it seemed natural to Sam to go into teaching. He got a degree in early childhood education (ECE) and has been teaching first grade for 6 years. He has become a mentor teacher in a local program and enjoys working with people who are just beginning their teaching careers. For Sam, teaching is part of the commitment he takes on as a citizen of the United States. He cares deeply about the kind of future his students will have and their ability to work with people of other backgrounds, religions, and races. The school where he teaches does not have the kind of diversity he would like to see, and he hopes that in the near future he will be able to transfer to a school where changing neighborhoods are creating greater diversity.

These four teachers have different reasons for the different paths they followed to the classroom. They are motivated by any number of issues and interests. What they have in common, however, is that each of them *wants* to be a teacher. Not all adults are able to work with young children. Good teachers, like Winona, LeAnne, Olga, and Sam, understand the positive effect they can have on children and their learning. They feel that the work they do is important and that they have something to offer the field of early education. Their talent may be a desire to work with children with special needs, or a unique ability to communicate with parents, or an artistic talent that enhances the curriculum. This inner motivation gives these four people the confidence they need to become effective teachers.

As you embark on your own personal journey toward early childhood teaching, you will find yourself with countless questions, such as "Hmmm—why do I want to do this work?" or "Yikes! What am I doing here?" In preparing yourself to be a teacher in the future, take time now to think about your own *disposition* for teaching.

The National Council for Accreditation of Teacher Education (NCATE, 2011) defines dispositions as

> the values, commitments, and professional ethics that influence students, families, colleagues, and communities and affect student learning, motivation, and development as well as the educator's own personal growth. Dispositions are guided by beliefs and attitudes related to values such as caring, fairness, honesty, responsibility, and social justice.

The work of an early childhood teacher is complex, and often intense and sensitive. Consider your own dispositions of teaching as you read this introductory chapter.

Fundamentals of Teaching

A number of factors help create an effective teacher. In combination, they can be guidelines for personal and professional growth throughout a lifetime. Individually, each defines an aspect of the role and responsibility of teaching young children, and outlines a critical function in becoming an effective teacher. Together, they form the essential elements in preparing to

1. Have a passion for the work.
2. Master knowledge of development and learning.
3. Adhere to professional and ethical standards of teaching.
4. Engage in reflective teaching.
5. Create positive relationships.
6. Respect family individuality and diversity.
7. Be an effective communicator.
8. Observe and assess children's development and behavior.
9. Manage the classroom and guide children's behavior.
10. Plan and execute appropriate curriculum and environments.

Figure 1.1
Top 10 Fundamentals of Teaching
As you read the top 10 list, make a note of which fundamentals are already on your list and which you will work on during your student teaching.

become a teacher. The 10 fundamentals enhance your ability to practice reflective teaching, so that you learn as much about yourself as you do about children, environments, and curriculum. You will find these guiding principles in the chapters that follow. Figure 1.1 lists the top 10 fundamentals of teaching.

Have a Passion for the Work. Do you remember some really good teachers you had? Surely one of the factors that made them memorable is that they had a passion for teaching and were able to communicate the excitement of the subject matter to you. It was clear they loved their job and couldn't imagine doing anything else. That teacher would never say "I drag myself to work every day just to pay the bills" or "My job is so boring." The teachers you remember knew the demands of their work in the classroom as well as the deep satisfaction it provided them, renewing their enthusiasm.

Teachers who are passionate about teaching have a strong, persistent interest in the way children grow and develop. The subject of human growth and development is very exciting to them. They enjoy watching children change throughout the school year and how their life circumstances affect them. They are challenged by how their own teaching may enhance or diminish what and how children learn.

Someone who loves to teach has a disposition for wanting to communicate the joy of learning. Teachers are in an exciting position as they watch the world unfold before the eyes of their students. Awe and wonder, curiosity, and imagination are evident in the many teachable moments in a child's life.

Master Knowledge of Development and Learning. An indispensable part of any early childhood teacher's background is to have a working knowledge and understanding of child development and early education. What can be expected developmentally from the particular age group with which the teacher is working? What are the teacher's goals for the group?

The joys of teaching are communicated in many ways.

How do these children learn best? What is each child's preferred learning style based on what has been observed? A teacher's knowledge of these questions and their answers leads to good judgment and wisdom about teaching in the early childhood classroom.

Each classroom is filled with children who are at various levels in their overall development. When teachers are aware of the cycles within human development, they see that children's growth and maturity follow an uneven path; therefore, teachers are prepared for a diverse mix of abilities. Through developmentally appropriate methods and techniques, the teacher helps children consolidate their gains through rehearsal, practice, and repetition until they gain mastery over a skill, whether it be pouring juice, buttoning a sweater, or doing double-digit addition. The teacher has faith in the knowledge that children will learn and grow at their own pace and according to their own time.

Adhere to Professional and Ethical Standards of Teaching. Through the National Association for the Education of Young Children (NAEYC), the early childhood profession has a set of professional guidelines and a code of conduct that express the values and beliefs of those who teach in the field. The standards for early childhood professional preparation include promoting child development and learning; building family and community relationships; observing, documenting, and assessing children; teaching and learning; becoming a professional; and field experiences. The code describes a teacher's responsibilities to children, to families, to their colleagues, and to the community at large. Both Professional Preparation Standards and the Code of Ethical Conduct will be elaborated in Chapter 2.

Why have professional standards or a code of ethical conduct? Standards outline what it means to be a professional teacher, describing the components of the work. In addition, each day teachers are faced with conflicts that range from the use of punitive discipline with children, to teacher misbehavior, to parent pressure. Beginning teachers need to know the importance of making decisions based on a code of ethics. A specific set of values is not just about what one teacher would do in a situation; it is about what *all* teachers should do.

Through experience and insights over the first few years in the classroom, teachers gain confidence to formulate their own philosophy of learning. Teachers' educational philosophies are based on their own values and beliefs about what is best for young children, their own experiences with groups of children, and the code of ethical conduct.

Engage in Reflective Teaching. Reflect on the four teachers described at the beginning of this chapter. In one way or another each made the connection between wanting to teach and finding personal meaning in what they do. They were able to make that link because they engaged in *reflective teaching*.

When you participate in reflective teaching, you set aside lesson plans and guidance strategies in order to look at the broader meaning of teaching. You take time to think about your role, your attitude, and your behavior. You look at the classroom as a community of learners—and realize that you are one of them. This goes to the very core of teaching: the relationship between self-understanding and its impact on educational practices.

Working with young children challenges teachers to look at and consider changing their own attitudes and behaviors. Because teachers spend a great deal of time observing children's growth and development, they understand that changes continue throughout the life cycle and that learning is a lifelong process. Adults grow, learn, and change as well. Those who view themselves as learners become successful teachers whose lives are meaningful and who have confidence in themselves and their teaching.

Each chapter of this text will encourage you to practice reflective teaching throughout your student practicum experience. Figure 1.2 begins this process. The questions will stimulate you to watch yourself grow, learn, and change. Also, each chapter features a Reflective Incident to prompt the process of self-knowledge. The longer you teach, the more you will be confronted with questions about your attitudes, biases, beliefs, knowledge, and understanding of the world in which children live.

Create Positive Relationships. To work effectively in an early childhood setting, teachers need to develop positive relationships with other adults as well as with the children. These relationships, based on trust and respect, begin when you and your supervisor set goals together for your teaching experience and he or she becomes a guide for your growth and development as a teacher. Maintaining a positive attitude throughout the process is key.

- *How do I deal with differences?*
  Which of my beliefs about child rearing differ from the way my parents raised
    me? Which practices have I already changed? How?
  How do I feel about talking with and discussing early childhood care and
    education with families whose child-rearing practices differ from mine?

- *How do I best address these issues with myself and others?*
  Do I respect those who are different in some way from my values and beliefs and
    how do I show it? What do I need to work on?
  What are some of the differences I enjoy about my friends, colleagues,
    family, and all children? What are some of the differences in them that I am
    uncomfortable with? Who can help me address these differences?

- *How do I deal with bias?*
  How and when do I examine my biases?
  Can I change my attitudes and biases? How?
  Have I passed my biases long to people I work with? When? How?

- *How do I interact with children?*
  Do I have a preference for children who most closely fit my own ethnic, cultural,
    and religious background? If so, how can I change that?
  Do I see children as capable and able to use each other as resources and do I
    communicate that to them? How?
  How do I feel about teaching children with disabilities? Where did this attitude
    come from?
  Do I need to change?
  Do I allow myself to learn from children? How and when?

One way to maintain a positive attitude and a positive relationship with those you work with is to become a good team member. Take responsibility for learning the guidelines you are given as a student teacher. Be on time, dress appropriately, do your assignments in a timely manner, listen respectfully, and ask questions as needed. These simple but necessary tasks will give you the confidence you need and will win you the respect of your co-workers.

You may already have a good feeling about working with young children from babysitting, coaching, or taking care of your own siblings or children. Some student teachers have had previous work experience in educational settings. This should certainly help you in your initial approach to children in the class where you are student teaching. At some point, perhaps even on your first day, children will begin to test you. They want to know if your boundaries are different from the rest of the teaching staff, and they may sense your insecurity or nervousness. Your knowledge of the school's philosophy and procedures will be a critical factor in your ability to relate positively to the children from the beginning.

Flexibility, acceptance, patience, encouragement, dependability, and a nonjudgmental attitude are key elements in creating positive relationships wherever you are. Chapters 3, 6, and 7 will demonstrate these elements in detail.

Respect Family Individuality and Diversity. Three of the core values in the NAEYC's (2011) Code of Ethical Conduct are to (a) recognize that children are best understood and supported in the context of family, culture, community, and society; (b) respect the dignity, worth, and uniqueness of each individual (child, family member, and colleague; and (c) respect diversity in children, families, and colleagues. These values form the foundation on which we build relationships with children and their families.

You may have already experienced living in a community with great diversity. Many student teachers have family or friends who come from ethnic, social, or economic cultures other than their own. Some may have

Student teachers learn about the context of a child's family and culture so that they are better able to understand the individual child.

worked or lived with people who have disabilities. If so, you are fortunate, because understanding and respecting individual differences is an important attribute for any teacher.

Cultural awareness and sensitivity affect the way you interact with children and their families. When a teacher has knowledge of the social and cultural context in which a child lives, the program and curriculum can be more meaningful, relevant, and respectful of the families enrolled in that setting. Insight into the family gives teachers the ability to respond positively to the individual child's unique learning style, growth, language skills, and communication style. Chapters 7 and 8 explore these issues in depth.

Be an Effective Communicator. Early childhood teachers work not only with children but also with adults. At your job site, you may meet other professionals (consultants, physicians, child psychiatrists, specialists), support staff (secretaries, janitors, cooks, bus drivers, maintenance workers), co-workers (teachers, directors, aides, volunteers), and family members (parents, grandparents, nannies). Good communication skills will help you become more effective with all of them.

The skills needed for good communication apply to working with children or adults. Your goal is to create a mutually trusting and respectful relationship within the classroom and the workplace. To do that, you need to be clear in what you want to say and to understand fully what is being said to you. Here are some ways to begin:

- *Listen carefully to what is said.* This means that you listen more than you talk so that you can get at the meaning and feelings of what you are hearing. This skill, called "active listening," is discussed in Chapter 3.

- *Ask a lot of questions.* Get as much clarification as you can on how best to do your job. Keep a notepad with you to jot down your questions so that you can ask them at the appropriate time, not while everyone is busy with children. You will use this to connect with your teaching team as seen in Chapter 7.

- *Respond to the questions, comments, and observations you hear. Be* interested, don't just *act* interested. Keep the focus on the adult or child who is talking to you, not on your next response. Chapter 4 will help you hone your observations skills.

- *Use body language.* With children, get down to their eye level and make clear, simple statements. For all, use facial expressions that indicate interest, concern, and understanding. The person with whom you are talking will likely use nonverbal clues, such as facial or hand gestures and body stance. Look for them.

- *Be culturally sensitive in your communication with others.* Remember that each person comes from a set of values fostered over a lifetime by family, culture, religion, and socioeconomic background, and it may be different from yours. Chapter 9 discusses some of the dynamics of diversity.

- *Learn to deal with conflict through effective problem-solving skills.* These are discussed in Chapters 3, 7, and 8.

Observe and Assess Children's Development and Behavior. Your eyes and mind need to be wide open when you teach. Good observation skills are fundamental tools in understanding children. As you observe how children play, how they behave, and how they interact with others, you come to know them: their needs, abilities, personalities, and concerns. You gain a picture of where the child is today. As you assess the information you observe, you can then plan for growth and learning opportunities for the future.

Learning to observe and record behavior effectively takes time and practice. We assess children's growth and abilities to establish a baseline that helps us plan curriculum, guidance measures, communication with families, and program decisions.

You will learn some techniques in Chapter 4 that will help you enhance your knowledge of individual children, the group, and child growth and development.

Manage the Classroom and Guide Children's Behavior. Classroom management is one of the most challenging aspects of teaching. Effective classroom management is based on the expectations you have for children's behavior, use of the space, interactions among people and materials, and time frames that make up the daily schedule. The routines, rules, and procedures also help determine how well the classroom is managed. Children need to know that what happens in class is predictable and consistent

The goal of effective classroom management is to maximize learning through a well-organized system that supports productive and positive behaviors. Children's behavior will be more positive when expectations are clearly communicated and supported by appropriate room arrangements.

A good guidance philosophy goes hand in hand with classroom management. The most effective methods of guiding children are clear, consistent, and fair rules that are enforced in consistent and humane ways. Successful guidance strategies emphasize the positive aspects of a child's behavior, not just the problem behavior. Guidance measures have greater meaning to children if they are encouraged to take responsibility for their own actions and are part of the problem-solving process. In Chapter 3 you will learn a number of successful methods for guiding young children.

Plan and Execute Appropriate Curriculum and Environments.
A sound curriculum is the hallmark of a quality program for children. Today's teachers ensure that young children are exposed to a developmentally and culturally appropriate curriculum that reflects student needs and is meaningful in its content. A key element to understanding curriculum in the early years is the premise that *play* is the primary medium that forms the foundation for learning (Erikson, 1963; Piaget, 1954).

Many curriculum models are available, notably the Reggio Emilia approach, High/Scope, Montessori, and Bank Street (see Chapter 5). However, many teachers develop their own curriculum using an eclectic, or blended, approach that encompasses some of these models.

To develop curriculum, you must first set goals and establish priorities. What do you want children to learn? When do they need to learn it? What is the best way to teach the material? You must take into consideration the wide range of abilities evident in a single classroom and the skills that are appropriate to learn at this age. Emergent curriculum (see Chapter 6) is built on the interests of the children in the class with the teacher helping them explore their ideas in greater depth. This often leads to a project that will engross children for week or even months. Curriculum building is also based on the knowledge of how individual children learn best. Multiple intelligence theory (Gardner, 1993) helps teachers understand how to create a curriculum that appeals to a broad range of interests and abilities.

The curriculum mirrors the goals and philosophy of the program, and so does the environment. With the intentional placement of furniture, a plan for where and how adults are deployed, and a schedule for each portion of the day, teachers demonstrate program priorities. For example, in early childhood settings where children's self-reliance is valued, the environment is created to support independent behavior. An antibias curriculum (Derman-

Sparks and Edwards, 2010) values differences in race, culture, ability, and gender, so those environments reflect that belief in the choice of curriculum, books, materials, toys, and equipment. Inclusive environments foster the participation of children with varying abilities and disabilities and adapt the facility to create a safe and challenging environment for all. Infant and toddler programs and curricula reflect the schedules and settings appropriate for very young children, which is inherently different from what preschoolers need. Chapters 5 and 6 will explore all of these issues in greater depth.

Roles and Responsibilities

What do teachers do all day? In most of early childhood education, the backbone of the program is the teacher. The teacher is a model for the children, and so teachers must focus on the quality of the child's relationship with them. Over 60 years ago, Katherine Read Baker (1950) outlined the teacher's role in her classic foundations book, *The Nursery School: A Human Relationships Laboratory:*

> She needs to have an understanding of what the child has learned, what his parents want for him and themselves, and what the child himself seems to want. For all children the goal of the teacher is to provide a curriculum that will promote the development of the individual who enjoys learning and can make good use of the available resources for learning. (p. 59)

The student teacher is experiencing one of the roles he or she will take on as a teacher.

Indeed, a teacher must be a consummate and welcoming host, storyteller, traffic cop, conflict mediator, medical examiner, psychological and academic assessor, kind but firm disciplinarian, and file clerk—not to mention plumber, therapist, poet, musician, and janitor!

Although it is true that the teacher wears many hats, the first is interacting with children in the classroom and managing the environment. This will be your initial focus as a student teacher. Setting the tone provides an emotional framework for the children, both as a group and as individuals, and handling the children's behavior is often as compelling as organizing the room and yard or assessing the children's growth and learning. You will work with adults as well, including other teachers, aides, volunteers, and administrators, and you will develop relationships with parents and other family members.

Outside the classroom, teachers have a role beyond working with children. They keep records, attend staff meetings, connect with families in conferences, make home visits, hold parent education meetings, attend school social functions, participate in workshops or other professional development opportunities, and hold student–teacher conferences. They also plan and evaluate the curriculum, often purchasing and preparing materials for the program.

As a student teacher, you will have a role in your practicum site that is unique to your position (see Figure 1.3). At the same time, you will be acclimating yourself to the world of a children's program, to the culture

Teachers . . .	Student Teachers . . .
Interact with children	Get acquainted with children
Observe and assess growth and learning	Practice observing children
Manage the classroom	Watch how the team deals with children; alert children to dangers; model themselves after the teachers
Create and maintain the environment	Clean up after themselves; ask where they can help with routine tasks
Plan and evaluate curriculum	Start implementing the ongoing activities of the program; ask when and how they can try to do some on their own
Attend meetings	Find out when they can meet with the supervising teacher outside class; see when the staff meetings, conferences, and class events take place and how they can get involved

Figure 1.3
Teachers' Versus
Student Teachers'
Responsibilities

My Reaction

"How Did I Begin?"

How did I get started? I tried getting my goals and objectives together in my journal before seeing Sarah yesterday: talking to myself out loud, in writing—a thought here and a thought there. The most persistent thought was the sense of lack of confidence; I have not worked in any preschool situation before. In spite of having two amazing semesters of coursework and being a full-time mother with two wonderful grown-up sons, I'm nervous! Sarah smiled and said, "That's how I started." She made me think we're sharing a secret. She put me at ease right then and there. This is my mentor.

—Ichun

and rhythm of the group. Over the course of time, you will move toward being part of the educational team. In short, you will become a teacher!

Supervision is a delicate and important matter, both to you and your supervising teacher. Meetings are probably the most time-consuming of all out-of-class jobs, and you will want to be sensitive to the demands on your supervising teacher's time as well as clear about getting the one-on-one time you need to improve your work. Read how Ichun felt in the My Reaction feature as she began student teaching. Making a plan for when and how long you can meet, and having an agenda (or at least a question and comment) for those times, will be helpful.

Your role and that of your supervisor can take many forms. You might see yourself as a kind of *apprentice* who is learning from an experienced teacher how to become proficient in the child care and education profession, much as young people apprenticed to merchants in the Middle Ages in order to learn their trade. Supervising teachers often see themselves as *mentors*, which has a history of its own.

The first record of mentoring comes from Homer's classic work, the *Odyssey*. In this tale, the adventurer Odysseus is about to depart on a 10-year journey and he leaves his son Telemachus with a servant/ friend named Mentor. In the father's absence, Mentor's role was to guide and inspire Telemachus as the youngster prepared himself for his future task as the ruler of Ithaca. This first story about a Mentor has a strong feminine aspect also. In the *Odyssey*, Athena (also known as the goddess of wisdom) disguises herself as Mentor and comes to Telemachus several times to guide and counsel him. (Sherk & Perry, 2005, p. 2)

At the same time, you might be thinking that you'd better hurry up and practice all the teaching experiences you can, because soon you'll be in charge yourself. Such an attitude can infuse tension and urgency into your work, spurring panic or withdrawal. This hat, more like the one in Disney's *Sorcerer's Apprentice*, may not fit you or sit well with your supervising teacher, either. Your supervisor may be dealing with competing demands, not so sensitive to your needs, or may see you as an extra pair of hands more than a learner. These expectations are not often verbalized, but they can change the teaching–learning relationship in ways that become unsatisfying.

Clear guidelines, regular communication, and responsive time together build a trusting relationship that rewards all involved. Knowing who you are and the various people and institutions that will support you will help. See Table 1.1 for key terms to clarify your role and those of

T a b l e 1.1 Key Terms for Student Teachers

Term	Definition
Mentor	A Mentor mentor provides vital day-to-day instruction that allows a student teacher to become a successful professional educator.
Field placement	The goal of a student teaching course is to find the best match of setting or supervisor with student teachers. This process involves the faculty, supervisors, and student teachers.
Student teacher, intern, practicum student, or practicing teacher	Students who are learning to become teachers often have different titles; they may be called student teachers, interns, practicum students, or practicing teachers. All will spend substantial time in program settings, learning to teach by doing the work of professional educators, with guidance from both the program supervisor and the college-based teacher educators. An intern often gets a stipend and is a professional-in-training.
Partner school	Partner schools work closely to provide interns the best learning experiences. Partner schools and colleges or universities share responsibility for preparing interns to be successful professional educators.
Master or supervising teacher	The master or supervising teacher observes, guides, and evaluates the student teacher during practicum/student teaching experience.
Faculty instructor	The faculty instructor is a college instructor who will observe and evaluate the student teacher, in addition to the mentor/supervising teacher, during the student teaching experience.

others while you are a student teacher. From the start, students begin to assume some of the responsibilities of teaching in a classroom. With more experience, the student teacher's role expands.

As a student teacher you will be under the supervision of a person who is an authority figure to you. You might reflect on what that means to you, what you want from your supervisor, how you respond to authority, and how to work together. Building a relationship with this master teacher should be one of your first tasks, even as you begin to make friends with children or to build teaching skills. Concentrate on developing connections of trust and respect. Reflect on who was a good teacher in your life, and the qualities that person had that were important to you. Now see how you can have this experience with your master teacher. Try to be open about both what you are to learn and how you are to learn it. Successful student teachers sometimes start their practicum by simply observing, shadowing their supervisor, or sitting at an activity table with a child. There are many ways to get started.

Fieldwork Guidelines

Your student teaching experience can be an exciting time. Textbook theories come alive as children live out child development concepts. Student teachers expect to learn about individual child growth and development; many are surprised to discover that they also learn how children function in groups and with adults. For some students, the practicum may be the first hands-on opportunity to work directly with children.

Student teachers learn from their hands-on experiences with children.

Preparing for Student Teaching

Planning and executing activities that fit the needs and abilities of the children are usually part of the student teacher's role. This gives you an opportunity to test curriculum ideas, and to see what happens when children use the materials. The classroom tasks you are assigned will vary according to those assigned by your faculty instructor and the goals you set with your supervising teacher. College and state requirements for student teaching will determine the amount of time you spend in the classroom. When you finish, you should have many of the tools you need to become a successful teacher.

You may have some choice in selecting a setting for your student teaching site, or you may be assigned one by the college faculty. Your practicum may take place in the college's child development center or in early childhood programs throughout the community. Ideally, your site will provide a high-quality program as determined by an external program review process or accreditation. Your faculty instructor may make on-site visits to observe and monitor your fieldwork progress.

Working with an experienced teacher who models highly polished skills is an important part of your teaching experience. Team teaching situations can be especially supportive, and identification with a number of professionals can help you find a teaching identity.

Although student teaching is enjoyable, it can also be a time for intensive self-searching and anxiety. The memory of a negative school experience of your own can undermine your confidence. You may still have doubts about being a teacher. It is uncomfortable to be evaluated by others, but this is part of the learning process. You will be assessed on, among other things,

- how effectively you participate,
- the variety and creativity in your planned activities,
- your classroom management skills,
- how well you meet timelines, and
- whether you behave professionally.

In Chapter 2 you will learn more about the student teacher assessment and evaluation process. If all this begins to feel like too much pressure, you might want to remember that even the most poised and confident master teacher was once a beginner like you. The Reflective Incident that follows tells about one student teacher's first-day experience.

Together, you, your faculty instructor, and the supervising teacher will set goals and expectations for your student teaching experience. From this you will develop by the end of the semester a concrete definition of what you will gain from the time you spend in the classroom, whether it is creating a lesson plan or leading a group time. All three of you will be working toward the same goals to ensure a successful student practicum.

Planning Before School Starts

Beginnings are important as they set the tone for what will follow. You will want to plan your first steps carefully. Here are some strategies for

Reflective Incident "First Impressions"

Wow! is how I would describe my first baby steps into student teaching. There are so many things to learn, getting acquainted and learning the names of all the children, meeting the parents, and meeting the rest of the staff. My first impression of children was that they were very open-minded and fun to work with. Even before my first day, some of the children were already coming up to me and playing with me as the director showed me around—and they don't even know my name yet. I believe I have connected with some of the children, and that moment when they approach you for a hug when they need comforting, I love it. It feels really good.

My head teacher made me feel comfortable and at ease because she gave me a tour a week ahead. Just yesterday, we had a mini meeting and discussed my goals and how to achieve them. They said that they have lots of materials and resources that I can borrow. I am also part of their weekly e-mail updates. They have a wall with each teacher's picture and bio, and mine is already posted there. The setting and my impression of the school gave me ideas for my future.

—AZHAR

Your Thoughts

1. How would I feel?

2. What would I do?

3. What might the results be?

easing the transition into the classroom that will help make your first days more satisfying and positive:

- *Contact and meet your supervising teacher.* Find out what time you are expected to arrive, where the classroom is located, what age group you will be working with, the size and makeup of the class, the daily schedule, and what hours you are expected to be on site. Ask if there are children with special needs or cultural considerations that you should know about. Find out what is expected of you the first few days as you get to know the children. If possible, meet the other faculty and staff of the school.

- *Look at this as an interview.* You will meet and interact with several people, you will have questions to ask, and it is the first impression you will all be making with one another.

- *Know the requirements.* You may already have a list from your faculty instructor, but you will need to check with the supervising teacher for special requirements, such as tuberculosis (TB) clearance, physician's report, evidence of insurance, or fingerprinting. One requirement may be criminal history and child abuse clearances.

- *Visit the classroom and building where you will be teaching.* Become acquainted with its layout. Tour the yard. Find out where the janitor's room, kitchen, bathrooms, and storerooms are located.

- *Share with your master teacher any special skills or talents you may have.* Let the teacher help you use these skills in new ways with young children.

- *Complete a student information sheet that may be provided by your college instructor.* The basic information about yourself (address, phone number, previous experience, courses) will help your supervising teacher know more about your background. (See the sample format in Figure 1.4.)

Getting Started

After the first few days of teaching, you will be familiar with the routines, you will know most of the children's names, and your presence in the program will be accepted. Your behavior is important (Browne & Dilko, 2005):

- *Dress appropriately.* Wear clothing that is comfortable, appropriate to the season, and easily covered by a smock or apron. Sturdy, waterproof shoes are good for outdoor activities. If you are uncertain about your clothing or items such as piercings or tattoos, call ahead or ask before you begin.

- *Be prompt.* Arrive on schedule and always inform the supervising teacher if you will be late or absent. If transportation is an issue for you, alert your supervising teacher before you begin.

- *Know where things are.* Find out where important equipment and materials are stored. You may be given a map or list; if not, ask if you should look in cupboards or closets before you start to work in class.

- *Use professional ethics.* Avoid discussing children and families by name outside the classroom. Children's behavior is both delightful and upsetting, but their privacy should be respected. Keep confidentiality outside the classroom and also talk to your teacher regularly about what you observe.

Figure 1.4
Student Input Form

This form provides your teaching site supervisor with important information about you.

Name _____

Address _____

City, State, Zip Code _____

Phone _____ E-mail _____

    Worksite _____

    Address _____

    City, State, Zip Code _____ Phone _____

    Supervisor _____ Teaching hours _____

Have you worked with children before? Yes _____ No _____

In what capacity: _____

_____

Other coursework (and colleges you have attended)

_____

List a few things about yourself that I should know (unique talents, hobbies, languages, relevant experiences, family information)

_____

_____

_____

In case of emergency, please contact: _____

_____

Phone _____ Relationship _____

Medical insurance plan _____

Number _____

Physician's name and address _____

Most recent TB test results _____ Date _____

(Give documentation to supervisor within a week of starting)

Do you have any important medical condition? Yes _____ No _____

Do you take medication? If yes, what? _____

Note: Permission is granted by the publisher to reproduce "Student Information Sheet" for evaluation and recordkeeping. From Browne & Gordon (2009). Copyright © 2009 by Pearson Education, Inc. All rights reserved.

Once you get started in your practicum site, you will be working directly with children, teachers, even other adults such as parents, janitors, and so on. Table 1.2 suggests guidelines to follow as you interact with children and adults during your student teaching days.

Table 1.2 Strategies for Positive Interactions

With Children	With Adults
Observe and move in only when necessary. Watch, listen, and analyze what children are doing before involving yourself. Pick up on the cues that tell you about their mood, their interests, and their intentions.	*Allow other teachers to solve problem situations between or among children.* Professional courtesy requires you to stay out of the way unless specifically invited to help.
Promote child-centered activities. Avoid making yourself or other teachers the focus of children's play. Emphasize children's attention on one another and on the activities.	*Ask questions about what you observe.* Find out why and how other teachers handled various situations the way they did. Think about how you would have handled the problem.
Allow time for children to solve their own problems. Monitor their progress and move in only when needed. Trust the child's abilities to work through solutions.	*Keep all staff members informed.* Ensure that significant events and problems and parent concerns and questions are communicated to the supervising teacher appropriately and in a timely fashion. Learn to deflect questions and comments from parents with a supportive but firm attitude.
Be alert to times when children have to wait. Have songs and fingerplays memorized, or a short book ready to read. Make a game of waiting for the next activity to being.	*Maintain a professional relationship with parents and families.* If families want to befriend you, wait until you are no longer teaching their child. Protect the confidentiality of the children, teachers, and other families in the class.
Know where everyone is. Be aware of the children and other teachers even when they are not in your immediate area. Maintain an overview of what is happening throughout the program.	*Work with your supervising teacher.* Ask for help in selecting and evaluating age-appropriate activities. Be aware of the curriculum goals that have been established for the group and the individual children.
Do not leave children unsupervised. Contact another teacher if you must leave the area. If you are alone with a group, send one of the children to get another adult.	*Let other staff members know you appreciate their support and help.* Tell them how they make a difference in your teaching experience by giving them examples. Everyone appreciates being acknowledged.
Enlist children's help in caring for the learning environment. Promote responsibility by having children clean up and organize materials and equipment.	*Acknowledge and respect all families and their efforts.* Be aware of their cultural background and let them teach you about their child's heritage.
Use a positive tone of voice. When talking to a child, bend down, and speak clearly. Do not shout from across the room or yard. Make eye contact and communicate support.	*Tell a good story.* All families appreciate hearing about their children. Help them to get to know their children more by telling them about their daily interests, friends, and activities.
Never use force. Use your knowledge of positive guidance strategies to get the child to cooperate. If that does not succeed, get help from one of the teaching staff.	*Read the handbook.* Become familiar with the policies and procedures spelled out in the guidelines issued to parents upon enrollment.

Source: Based on Gordon & Browne (2013).

The Absent Supervisor

Situation: In her weekly class with her faculty instructor Dora, student teacher Anna reports that her supervising teacher, Michelle, is often absent from the classroom when Anna is present and cancels meetings with her, saying she doesn't have time to reschedule. Anna is frustrated and concerned about her student teaching evaluation that is coming up in a month. Anna feels her attempts to contact Michelle are making Michelle angry. Dora tells Anna that she will contact Michelle.

Code of Ethical Conduct References:
Section III: Ethical Responsibilities to Colleagues: A: Responsibilities to Co-workers.

I-3A.3–To support co-workers in meeting their professional needs and in their professional development.

P-3A.2–When we have concerns about the professional behavior of a co-worker, we shall first let that person know of our concern in a way that shows respect for personal dignity . . . and then attempt to resolve the matter collegially and in a confidential manner.

Solution: Dora calls Michele to make an appointment to meet. Michelle attempts to stall her but finally gives in and sets a date. During their meeting, Dora expresses concern for Michelle, saying that she has been a highly regarded classroom teacher and student teacher supervisor, but she wonders about her recent behavior with Anna. Michelle acknowledges that she has not given Anna the time and attention she deserves, adding that a recent family situation has overwhelmed her. Her widowed father has just moved in with Michelle and her family, and they are busy sorting out the changes this requires. Michelle regrets the impact this has on her professional obligations. Dora is empathetic and suggests that Michelle might ask her assistant teacher, Jeremy, to supervise Anna's field experience. Jeremy is one of Dora's former students, and she knows him to be qualified to assume these duties. Michelle seems relieved and says she will contact Jeremy immediately and then call Anna to apologize for her behavior and, hopefully, let her know that Jeremy will be her supervisor.

Early Childhood Programs: Where Will You Teach?

"From the types available, to the numbers of children who attend . . . the name of the game in early childhood programs is diversity" (Gordon & Browne, 2014). Because the age range in early childhood is birth to age 8, and programs for children run from once a week to full days (and beyond), group care arrangements serve many needs and have varied features. See Table 1.3 for an overview. Programs in early childhood settings are defined by these elements:

- Age of children
- Philosophical or theoretical approach
- Program goals

Table 1.3 Types of Early Childhood Programs: Settings for Fieldwork

Type	Sponsor	Ages	Schedule	Key Characteristics	Settings
Nursery School/ Preschool	Public or Private	2½ to 5 years	Half day or full day	Focus on social competence, emotional well-being, and self-enrichment; teachers support learning through play; often fewer than 20 children	Churches, synagogues, community centers, elementary schools, customized buildings
Child care Centers	Community, churches, synagogues, government agencies; public and private	Infant/toddlers, preschool, and school age	Full day and half day	Subsidized by sponsoring organization or government agency, which often provides low or free rent	Community buildings, government office buildings, churches, synagogues
Laboratory schools	2- and 4-year colleges, universities	Infant/toddlers, preschoolers	Full day and half day	Students and teachers often participate in teacher training and research activities; offer model programs	Located on or near the campus
Family child care	Caregiver's home	Infancy through elementary school	Flexible; full or half day	Small and personalized; often in child's neighborhood, wide variety of age levels; may or may not have a formal curriculum	Private home
Parent cooperative	School districts, private owners	Preschoolers	Full day and half day	Parents commit to teaching in the classroom on a regular basis; scheduled parent education meetings; time-consuming, lower costs	Community centers, privately owned buildings, churches, synagogues
Kindergarten and early elementary grades	Public and private	5 through 8 years of age	Kindergarten may be half or full day; grades 1–3 are full day	Formal schooling begins, emphasizing reading and math and a variety of academic disciplines, such as social studies and science	Public and private schools; some kindergartens may be part of preschools and child care centers
Before/after schools, school care	Public schools, community organizations, YW/YMCA's, churches, synagogues	Preschool and elementary school ages	Before and after regular school hours	Safe place for children during parents' work hours; may provide holiday and vacation programs	Schools, community centers, YM/YWCA's, child care centers

Source: Based on and adapted from Gordon & Browne (2013).

- Sponsoring agency
- Teaching staff—number, composition, training
- Environment—size, shape, location
- Community makeup—culture, economic, linguistic, geographic
- Resources structure and stability

Because of this diversity—as well as the uniqueness of each student teacher—what you encounter in your practicum will also vary. Your faculty instructor has assigned you to one of the following programs for your fieldwork experience. Compare the differences and similarities in your setting with other student teachers.

Welcome aboard! Getting started in your practice teaching is an exciting, complex process. For last-minute instructions, read the Lessons from the Field feature. You are embarking on an amazing journey. Your bags are now packed, and you are ready to go.

lessons from the field

"Welcoming a Student Teacher"

by Debbie Baker-Dailey

Teacher-Director, Circle of Friends Preschool

We have a student teacher! How nice!

Your First Day. In our classroom we welcome you, our new teacher, by introducing you to everyone. You get your own nametag, just like the children and teachers. We put a picture and a few sentences about you in our classroom newsletter. It can be a little overwhelming on your first day, so many names and faces. We will give you a photo page with all the children's names and faces so you can begin to "study" them.

You will notice this is a busy place. There is a lot going on. We will ask you to observe and get to know the children. Say hello, make eye contact, and talk with them. Ask them questions and get ready to listen. There is so much to see! How is the room set up? What are the children doing? How are they interacting with each other and teachers? What are the teachers doing and saying?

The Next Step. As you spend more time here, you will start to get more settled. You can begin to greet the families as they arrive for drop-off or pickup. Some children will want you to meet their parents, grandparents, or nannies. Others may smile or hide as you introduce yourself. Know that they are all glad you are making a connection with their important "grown-ups."

Be sure to ask questions—find me, ask the teaching team, jot them down for yourself. Get on the level of the children and try to interact with them. Get comfortable with the environment and observe the children. Get familiar with the routines and habits. Remember that the best teachers are the children you are teaching.

Join In. We are glad you're here. ☺ You bring new knowledge, some expectations, fresh ideas, and perhaps some uncertainty. Teaching is a practice. Each day we reflect on our experiences, so plan to stay a little beyond your teaching time to talk with me. Every day we grow a little more as we prepare ourselves for our next day as teachers.

Practicum Activity

Look at the top 10 list (Figure 1.1). Reorder it to match your priorities, or make a list of your own. Find two other student teachers, and compare their thoughts with your own.

Journaling Assignment

Write a set of questions to ask when you get to your student teaching site. Follow up with your first impressions of the children, the setting, and your supervising teacher.

References

Baker, K. R. (1950). *The nursery school: A human relationships laboratory.* Philadelphia: Saunders.

Browne, K. W., & Dilko, P. (2005). *Guidelines for student teaching.* Unpublished manuscript, Redwood City & San Bruno, CA: Canada and Skyline Colleges.

Browne, K. W., & Gordon, A. M. (2009). *To teach well: An early childhood practicum guide.* Upper Saddle River, NJ: Pearson Education, Inc.

Derman-Sparks, L., & Edwards, J. O. (2010). *Anti-bias education for young children and ourselves.* Washington, DC: National Association for the Education of Young Children.

Erikson, E. (1963). *Childhood and society* (2nd ed.). New York: Norton.

Gardner, H. (1993). *Multiple intelligences.* New York: Basic Books.

Gordon, A. M., & Browne, K. W. (2013). *Beginning essentials in early childhood education* (2nd ed.). Belmont, CA: Wadsworth Cengage Learning.

Gordon A. M., & Browne, K. W. (2014). *Beginnings and beyond: Foundations in early childhood education* (8th ed.). Belmont, CA: Wadsworth Cengage Learning.

National Association for the Education of Young Children. (2005). *Code of ethical conduct.* Washington, DC: Author.

National Association for the Education of Young Children (2011). *2010 Standards for Initial and Advanced Early Childhood Professional Preparation Programs.* Washington, DC: Author. Retrieved June 26, 2011 from www.naeyc.org/ncate/standards

Piaget, J. (1954). *The construction of reality in the child.* New York: Basic Books. (Original work published 1937.)

Sherk J., & Perry, J. (2005). *A mentor's guide.* San Francisco: California Early Childhood Mentor Teachers Program.

Web Sites

California Early Childhood Mentor Program
www.ecementor.org

National Association for the Education of Young Children
www.naeyc.org

National Council for Accreditation of Teacher Education
www.ncate.org

chapter 2

Becoming a Professional Teacher

LEARNING OUTCOME

Demonstrate understanding of professional standards, goal setting and assessment of one's teaching experience, and the Code of Ethical Conduct, as they relate to teaching proficiency.

Congratulations! You are taking your next step in becoming a member of the teaching profession. Do you remember the four teachers you read about at the beginning of Chapter 1? They each had their own motivation for becoming a teacher. What about you? What is your incentive for joining the creative and dynamic profession of teaching? What does professionalism mean to you at this point in your student teaching?

The 10 fundamentals of teaching (see Chapter 1) are actually a roadmap you can follow on your journey toward professionalism. Two fundamentals that you will explore further in this chapter, and that are key elements in the professional life of a teacher, are these:

- Adhere to professional and ethical standards of teaching.
- Engage in reflective teaching.

Both are key elements in the professional life of a teacher. Teachers are the most important factor in determining the quality of an early childhood program. Knowing about professional standards helps student teachers in their own teaching. Therefore, an evaluation process is critical in helping teachers become the best that they can be.

Setting Professional Standards

The field of early childhood education (ECE) has grown tremendously in the last 40 years. In part, this growth is due to the increasing number of young children in settings outside the home. This has given more visibility to those who engage in the work of caring for and educating children, particularly children under 5. The National Association for the Education of Young Children (NAEYC) has undertaken several initiatives to make the work more understandable and has articulated those objectives to both those in the profession and adults outside classrooms. Writing a code of ethics, identifying developmentally appropriate practices, and developing a program accreditation process (see Chapter 5) are all efforts to make teaching a legitimate profession. Another key element is setting professional standards.

This endeavor has support from other levels of education, such as elementary and secondary teaching preparation. The NAEYC, jointly with the Council for Exceptional Children's Division for Early Childhood (CEC/DEC) and the National Board for Professional Teaching Standards (NBPTS) (2005), has identified seven standards for early childhood professional preparation. Programs that prepare student teachers are now incorporating those standards into the courses they teach. The practicum/student teaching course you are taking now may use them as well. Figure 2.1 outlines these standards.

In preparing to become a teacher, you will work on each of these standards. As you enter the field of early childhood education, you will find that these standards help you shape your ongoing professional goals and the objectives you need to reach them.

Goals and Objectives

How do student teachers develop teaching skills?

There are many proven strategies to improve your practice: observing other teachers; using a "try, reflect, try again" approach; asking advice from a supervising teacher and a faculty instructor; or talking to other student teachers. Through it all, beginning teachers set goals for themselves, and then craft objectives as a way to meet those goals.

Goals

Goals are the learning outcomes you need to attain in order to be a competent, productive, early childhood professional.

- What do you want to learn to do better?
- What would you like to work on?
- What areas would be best to stretch yourself?

Objectives

Objectives are measurable, finite steps that help you realize your goals. You can always tell if you've achieved them because you or someone else can

Figure 2.1 NAEYC Standards for Initial and Advanced Early Childhood Professional Preparation Programs

Standards for early education teaching preparation can guide you toward teaching excellence.

Standard 1: Promoting Child Development and Learning

Key elements:

1a: Knowing and understanding young children's characteristics and needs

1b: Knowing and understanding the multiple influences on development and learning

1c: Using developmental knowledge to create healthy, respectful, supportive, and challenging learning environments

Standard 2: Building Family and Community Relationships

Key elements:

2a: Knowing about and understanding diverse family and community characteristics

2b: Supporting and engaging families and communities through respectful, reciprocal relationships

2c: Involving families and communities in their children's development and learning

Standard 3: Observing, Documenting and Assessing to Support Young Children and Families

Key elements:

3a: Understanding the goals, benefits, and uses of assessment

3b: Knowing about assessment partnerships with families and with professional colleagues

3c: Understanding and practicing responsible assessment

3d: Knowing about and using observation, documentation, and other appropriate assessment tools and approaches.

Standard 4: Using Developmentally Effective Approaches to Connect with Children and Families.

Key elements:

4a. Understanding positive relationships and supportive interactions as the foundation of their work with children.

4b. Knowing and understanding effective strategies and tools for early education.

4c. Using a broad repertoire of developmentally appropriate teaching/learning approaches.

4d. Reflecting on their own practice to promote positive outcomes for each child.

Standard 5: Using content knowledge to build meaningful curriculum

Key elements:

5a. Understanding content knowledge and resources in academic disciplines

5b. Knowing and using the central concepts, inquiry tools, and structures of content areas or academic disciplines

5c. Using their own knowledge, appropriate learning standards, and other resources to design, implement, and evaluate meaningful, challenging curricula for each child

Standard 6: Becoming a Professional

Key elements:

6a. Identifying and involving oneself with the early education field

6b. Knowing about and upholding ethical standards and other professional guidelines

6c. Engaging in continuous, collaborative learning to inform practice

6d. Integrating knowledgeable, reflective, and critical perspectives on early education

6e. Engaging in informed advocacy for children and the profession.

Standard 7: Field Experiences

Key elements:

7a. Opportunities to observe and practice in at least two of the three early childhood age groups (birth–age 3, 3–5, 5–8)

7b. Opportunity to observe and practice in at least two of the three main types of early education settings (early school grades, child care centers and homes, Head Start programs)

Source: Reprinted with permission from the National Association for the Education of Young Children (2011). For full NAEYC Initial Licensure Standards, please see www.naeyc.org/positionstatements/ppp.

observe and see what you are doing that shows your work. Objectives determine how you will meet your goals, and what you will do to get there.

Student teachers are often confused about the differences between goals and objectives. A goal is the "what" you want to do to improve your teaching, and the objectives are the "how" to do it.

- The goal is the big picture; the objectives are the details.
- The goal is the forest; the objectives are the trees.

Goals	Objectives
Are broad in scope	Specify an intent of some aspect of a goal
Are general statements of ends	Detail some type of result of an action
Reflect your philosophy or priorities	Set measurable stages toward a goal
Are long term or far reaching	Are short term and narrow in scope
May not necessarily be measurable	Are specific and measurable

A goal may encompass several objectives aimed at reaching the outcome. Objectives can be for one day, week, month, or year; goals are generally for longer than a year. Figure 2.2 provides sample goals and objectives

Figure 2.2
Sample Student Practicum Goals and Objectives
Goals and objectives help professionals set reasonable expectations for themselves. Note that each of the numbered goals in this sample has several objectives that detail specific ways of accomplishing the goals.

By the end of the course, I want my students to be able to reach these goals by meeting the stated objectives.

1. *Goal:* Students can articulate teaching goals and reflect on their teaching.
   Objectives:
   a. Setting goals in class
   b. Sharing those goals and getting feedback from
      i. Another student teacher
      ii. Their supervisor at their field site
      iii. Their faculty instructor
   c. Revising the goals during the term as needed
   d. Writing about their progress toward the goals in the journal
   e. Evaluating the progress toward the goals by the end of the term

2. *Goal:* Students can define the multiple roles of an early childhood teacher.
   Objectives:
   a. Hearing and listing multiple roles in class
   b. Observing and journaling about their site teachers
   c. Interviewing their supervisor
   d. Completing a project about one of those roles

3. *Goal:* Students recognize problematic child behavior and indicate several guidance strategies to address those situations.
   Objectives:
   a. Observing children at their sites
   b. Journaling about problem behaviors and solutions tried or not
   c. Discussing situations and strategies in class

established by a college instructor for students in a student teaching seminar. Compare this list with the goals for your student teaching course. What are your instructor's objectives for helping you teach well?

Basic Teaching Skills

Goals and objectives will provide direction for the time that you spend in your fieldwork placement. Student teachers need to set reasonable goals for themselves.

First, consult your college course to see if you already have specific teaching competencies you must achieve. Many practicum courses set goals based on NAEYC teaching standards (see Figure 2.1) or follow certain community requirements. Some ask teachers to set goals based on a set of competencies. A set of *basic teaching skills* is essential for professional teaching, as outlined in Figure 2.3, both now as a student and in the future (see Figure 2.3).

Second, talk with your supervising teacher about any expectations for your placement. Some sites ask that you participate in child assessments, develop curriculum, complete a child study, or lead a circle time. Others will want you to begin by observing more than participating, then to move into more responsibilities depending on your level of expertise. Many will require you to execute a specific number of lesson plans.

Finally, consider your own stage of teacher development. Are you a beginner, who needs to first learn to establish trusting relationships with children? Are you far enough along in your own teaching that you are ready

Student teachers can learn basic skills by participating in interactions with children.

Figure 2.3 Basic Teaching Skills

Students need to know what basic teaching skills they are to work toward mastering during their fieldwork placement.

The following is a list of the basic teaching behaviors on which you will be evaluated. You will receive feedback on this list from both your supervising teacher and your faculty instructor, and you will complete a self-evaluation on this same set of skills.

I. Personal Attributes

A. Reliability

Is prompt and avoids absences

Prepares lessons carefully and age appropriately

Learns the classroom/school routine readily

B. Attitude

Is eager to learn

Has positive attitude

Is willing to seek out new experiences

Has positive work ethic

Responds professionally to feedback and suggestions

Shows initiative

Reflects on and evaluates own behavior and actions

Shows respect for people of all backgrounds and abilities

C. Grooming and Demeanor

Dresses appropriately

Is neat and clean in appearance

Uses appropriate language in written and oral communications

Behaves in an adultlike fashion

Is aware of self as role model

D. Professional Conduct

Prepares and completes work on time

Maintains privacy and confidentiality about staff, children, and families

Indicates growing understanding of professional code of ethics

Participates in class and staff meetings

Shows intellectual aptitude through written and oral assignments

II. Interactions with Children

A. Knows and Applies Child Development Theory

Understands developmentally appropriate practices

Adapts to child's learning style

Adapts to child's individual developmental needs

Is informed by observations of child

Uses variety of instructional strategies

B. Builds Relationships with Children

Learns and uses children's names

Responds warmly and attentively when approached by child

Treats children with kindness and respect

Interacts positively with all children

Encourages initiative and independence

Is sensitive to individual differences and abilities

C. Encourages Communication

Listens carefully to what children say

Responds with interest, concern, and care

Uses verbal and nonverbal communications effectively

Uses child-appropriate clear language

Uses body language well, gets down to child's level

Tempers voice and volume to suit child's needs

Applies communication skills to all children, regardless of ability

Supports peer interactions

D. Practices Positive Discipline

Fosters independent problem solving

Is alert to total classroom dynamics

Uses positive statements with children

Shows patience and understanding with children in conflict

Provides emotional support when appropriate

Uses variety of guidance strategies appropriate to the situation

Recognizes the individuality of each child in choosing guidance measures

III. Relationships with Adults

A. Builds Relationships with Families

Understands the importance of knowing family culture, values, and beliefs

Is sensitive to differences in gender, ability, culture, and language

Is pleasant and welcoming to parents

(continued)

Figure 2.3 Basic Teaching Skills (*continued*)

B. Works Positively with Other Team Members

Coordinates with team members on planning

Shows respect toward all team members

Keeps team informed of critical incidents and concerns

Feels comfortable asking others for help or information

C. Works Collaboratively

Moves in to assist team members as needed

Uses staff meetings to share information and contribute ideas

Exhibits open and frequent communication with team members

IV. Program Planning

A. Plans and Carries Out Appropriate Activities with Children

Demonstrates awareness of goals of program in planning

Shows understanding of age group, abilities, and interests

Creates experiences that provide opportunity for children to learn

Plans for children's involvement in their own learning

Fosters a hands-on approach to learning

Supports the theory that play is the medium for learning

Creates opportunities for children to make choices

Works effectively with supervising teacher in planning process

Shows skill in preparing written lesson plan

B. Evaluates Planning Process

Reflects on children's response to the activity

Shows flexibility in adapting activity as needed

Suggests ways to improve the activity

Written evaluation indicates learning from the experience

---

to take on more guidance responsibilities? Are you ready to plan activities? What about working with families or team teaching and staff meetings?

Your goal statements should be general statements on what you would like to accomplish during your field placement. For example, Philip decided one of his goals would be "to know and understand the multiple influences on development and learning." Think about how and why you selected these goals. What makes them valuable to your educational, professional, and/or personal growth? Philip identified with both Filipino and U.S. culture; by reflecting on how these two cultures had influenced him, he wanted to understand the various cultures of the children in his center.

Creating Your Plan. To help you choose your goals, think about these questions:

- What subject areas interest you the most?

- In what area do you feel you need more work, information, or practice?

- What skills do you want to develop? What approaches or techniques are you hoping to practice?

- Is there a particular child, group of children, parent or family, or staff relationship you would like to include in your goals? Are there particular strategies that you want to explore further?

- What can be reasonably accomplished in the time frame of your practicum fieldwork?

- How will you measure whether you accomplished your objectives and met or made progress on your goals?

- How can your teaching team and/or supervisor assist and support you?

Next, your objectives are the concrete, measurable steps you will take to accomplish your goals. Be specific; use action verbs and words. Then, define a time frame, and be realistic about what you can accomplish in your student teaching experience. Philip chose four objectives:

1. Do some research about family theory.

2. Learn what the children's home languages are.

3. Find out the families' wishes for their children about maintaining home language and acquiring English proficiency.

4. Learn how to bring the home languages and family traditions into the center.

Figure 2.4 outlines another student teacher's goals and objectives.

Your goals and objectives should be reviewed and shared with your site supervisor. Seek out and use your supervisor's support and guidance in working toward your objectives. To reflect, use a journal or diary to evaluate your goals along the way. (There is a journaling assignment at the end of each chapter in this book.) Figure 2.4 lists one student's work; the following suggestions help student teachers use a journal, or an online discussion board, to articulate their progress on goals and objectives. Choose the ones that make the most sense to you throughout your student teaching.

Teaching Goal #1: *To improve my large-group-time skills with children*

Objectives:

1. *Observe three teachers doing circle time for the month.*
2. *Write up five circle-time plans and get ideas from my supervisor.*
3. *Lead five circle times while my head teacher observes and gives feedback.*
4. *Lead five more group activities before the end of term.*

Teaching Goal #2: *To increase my knowledge of child growth and development*

Objectives:

1. *Learn about my center's child assessment procedures.*
2. *Choose a child to observe weekly.*
3. *Make a portfolio on that child.*

Figure 2.4 Leticia's Student Teaching Goals and Objectives

Student teaching goals and objectives should be specific; use action verbs and words to describe what you want to know and be able to do at the end of your fieldwork.

- Summarize your accomplishment of—or progress toward—each goal and objective.

- Describe any challenges or obstacles you faced and how you overcame them.

- Give examples of any successes or setbacks.

- Discuss the accomplishment you are most proud of and in which area(s) you feel you need more practice or experience.

- Explain how you worked with your supervisor and teaching team in meeting your goals and objectives.

- Discuss how your fieldwork helped you and contributed to your overall professional and personal growth

Teacher Assessment and Evaluation

Assessments and evaluations are part of the professional life of an early childhood educator (Hyson, 2003) for many reasons. In many schools, an annual performance evaluation is a professional requirement and the evaluation becomes a roadmap to follow as you work toward achieving specific goals. For the student teacher, the evaluation process helps identify strengths and areas for improvement. As your teaching improves, the skill set that you have mastered increases.

An evaluation gives you an opportunity to address specific issues and think about what they mean to your teaching. Figure 2.5 illustrates the circular feedback loop that a good evaluation can take. Figures 2.6 and 2.7

Figure 2.5
Evaluation Feedback Loop

This loop shows how evaluation feedback is used to achieve goals and improve your teaching performance.

Source: Based on and adapted from Gordon/ Browne. *Beginning Essentials.* © 2012. Wadsworth, Cengage Learning.

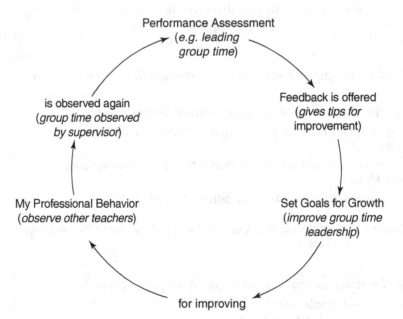

Performance Assessment
(*e.g. leading group time*)

Feedback is offered
(*gives tips for* improvement)

Set Goals for Growth
(*improve group time leadership*)

for improving

My Professional Behavior
(*observe other teachers*)

is observed again
(*group time observed by supervisor*)

Name: *Shawna F.*

Evaluator: *Marcello J., Lead Teacher*

Date: _____

Interpersonal Climate Within the Program

Indicators	Frequently	Occasionally	Not Observed
Relationships	*Stays close to children*	*More often helps children instead of encouraging peer assistance*	
Affect towards children	*Smiles and laughs with the children*		
Communication	*Verbal exchanges are enthusiastic and affectionate.*	*Expectations of children are low; Shawna assists & "does for" the children too often.*	
Respect	*Frequent eye contact, warm voice*	*Sometimes a little loud; uses slang terms [but not inappropriate language]; models sharing but doesn't encourage it among the children*	

Student Strengths: *Shawna keeps an enthusiastic attitude throughout her time with us, and has an open mind toward any new learning. She is responsive to children and shows a high degree of interest in becoming a teacher. We have come to look forward to Tuesdays and Thursdays, Shawna's teaching days with us. She has grown in her comfort in asking all of us questions before plunging into a situation, and is an enthusiastic addition to our team.*

Things to work on: *Shawna needs to study up on age-appropriate expectations of children; she does too much for them, and thus does not encourage peer cooperation, sharing, or mutual helping. We have given her some articles on "ages & stages," and she is reviewing her foundations text from college.*

Figure 2.6
Initial Evaluation of the Student Teacher
Meeting with your supervisor to discuss your progress may feel awkward at first, but the feedback you get may be the best advice you can get to improve your teaching.

Name: *Shawna F.*

Evaluator: *Marcello J., Lead Teacher*

Date: _____

Interpersonal Climate Within the Program

Indicators	Frequently	Occasionally	Not Observed
Relationships	*Stays close to children*	*More often helps children instead of encouraging peer assistance*	
Affect towards children	*Smiles and laughs with the children*		
Communication	*Verbal exchanges are enthusiastic and affectionate.*	*Expectations of children are low; Shawna assists & "does for" the children too often.*	
Respect	*Frequent eye contact, warm voice*	*Sometimes a little loud; uses slang terms [but not inappropriate language]; models sharing but doesn't encourage it among the children*	

Student Strengths: *Shawna keeps an enthusiastic attitude throughout her time with us, and has an open mind toward any new learning. She is responsive to children and shows a high degree of interest in becoming a teacher. We have come to look forward to Tuesdays and Thursdays, Shawna's teaching days with us. She has grown in her comfort in asking all of us questions before plunging into a situation, and is an enthusiastic addition to our team.*

Things to work on: *Shawna needs to study up on age-appropriate expectations of children; she does too much for them, and thus does not encourage peer cooperation, sharing, or mutual helping. We have given her some articles on "ages & stages," and she is reviewing her foundations text from college.*

Figure 2.6
Initial Evaluation of the Student Teacher
Meeting with your supervisor to discuss your progress may feel awkward at first, but the feedback you get may be the best advice you can get to improve your teaching.

Becoming a Professional Teacher

Figure 2.7 Final Evaluation of the Student Teacher

Meeting with your supervisor to discuss your progress may feel awkward at first, but the feedback you get may be the best advice you can get to improve your teaching.

Name *Shawna F.*

Evaluator *Marcello J.*

Date _____

This form is used by the supervising teacher to assess your competencies in basic teaching skills. It will be completed and given to you midterm and for a final evaluation. The faculty instructor will use it as a guide when assessing your total coursework.

Personal Qualities (reliable, positive attitude, personal characteristics)

Comments: *Shawna has come to work ready to go, with an enthusiastic focus on children every session. She keeps an enthusiastic attitude throughout her time with us, and has an open mind toward any new learning.*

Relationships with Children (child development understanding, child responsiveness, communication effectiveness, positive guidance, family sensitivity]

Comments: *Because Shawna has a 6-year-old son, she came to our preschool with some previous experience as a parent. However, she has had to widen that knowledge with our diverse group. She now says she wants to audit another child development class! As to being responsive to children, the class has really embraced Shawna and calls out for her help regularly. In particular, the children who are active and feisty like her—she is not intimidated by their energy, and doesn't get angry when they "act up." In terms of guidance, this is both an asset and area of challenge. Shawna needs to know when to intervene before a situation gets volatile, and calm it. She is working on our conflict resolution steps for the rest of the term. Building stronger family-teacher relationships is one of her special teaching goals. We had her work with our parent liaison on a monthly newsletter, and this has helped her and the families have given me positive feedback on her work in this area.*

Program Implementation (appropriate activity planning and execution)

Comments: *This was Shawna's second teaching focus. She has worked hard on literacy and music projects, bringing in beautiful high-quality picture books to go along with our monthly themes. She is learning to use the autoharp, and the children love to sing along and play it as much as she will let them.*

Working with Staff (member of the team)

Comments: *We have come to look forward to Tuesdays and Thursdays, Shawna's teaching days with us. She has grown in her comfort in asking all of us questions before plunging into a situation, and she is a thoughtful addition to our team. We have grown with her bringing in new curriculum ideas, especially the autoharp. We would like Shawna to apply for the teaching assistant opening next year.*

List the Student's Strengths and Challenges (1–3 of each)

	Midterm
Strengths	**Challenges**
Enthusiasm	*Tends to "whip up" the kids*
Responsible in attendance	*Needs to ask more questions*
	Final
Strengths	**Challenges**
Curriculum ideas	*Conflict resolution with the children*
Family connections	

1. To uphold professional standards in the field of early childhood education
2. To hold you accountable and take professional responsibility
3. To identify your strengths and limitations
4. To benefit all the stakeholders: you, the children, teachers, families, and programs
5. To promote reflective teaching
6. To help you achieve your goals
7. To increase your skill level
8. To tell you whether or not you have met your goals
9. To promote healthy change
10. To increase self-confidence

Figure 2.8 Top 10 Reasons for Teacher Assessment and Evaluation
Knowing the reasons for evaluation can help ease students' tension about being assessed on their teaching skills.

are examples of the type of performance evaluation that you may encounter. Once you have set goals for yourself, you do something that shows your work—that is, you put the objectives to work. Your mentor, observing your behavior, can offer you feedback. Then you are ready to revise your goals to have something concrete to work toward. You strengthen your abilities and increase your skill level when you try to create a lesson plan, learn a new fingerplay, or set up an age-appropriate activity. The support of your faculty instructor and supervising teacher is an important factor in reaching those goals. Goals are usually set for a certain time period, and together you can monitor your progress so that you will achieve success.

The evaluation process promotes objective assessment based on articulated criteria that are given to you as you begin your student teaching. This overview of the teaching behaviors and expectations gives you the standards on which you will be evaluated. Student teachers should have a greater understanding that the purpose in the evaluation is to be fair and to help them make the necessary changes. Figure 2.8 lists the top 10 reasons for teacher assessment and evaluation.

Two Types of Evaluations

Because a key component of good teaching is the ability to reflect and analyze one's work, it stands to reason that self-evaluation is essential. Add to that important feedback from a seasoned teacher, a peer, or eventually even a parent, and the second element of evaluation is in place.

Self-Evaluation. A critical part of any assessment of teaching skills is the involvement of the person being evaluated. That's *you*: the student teacher. You have started working in a program and have familiarized yourself with the children, teaching team, environment, schedule, and curriculum. You are starting—or continuing—to play a part in the actual teaching of the children. How are you doing? What do you bring to the enterprise? How are you faring in respect to the major responsibilities of a teacher?

An evaluation of your work is critical to your progress toward competence. Figure 2.7 is an example of a performance evaluation that a student teacher could use for a self-assessment and a supervisor could use to assess student performance. While Figure 2.3 describes a wide range of basic teaching skills, performance evaluation describes what the teacher does. The Classroom Assessment Scoring System (CLASS) is an observation instrument developed to assess classroom quality in preschool through third-grade classrooms; a revised version for infant–toddler classrooms is in progress. The CLASS dimensions are narrower than a broader basic skills list, and for good reasons, as shown in the following paragraph (Pianta, La Paro, & Hamre, 2008):

> The CLASS dimensions are based on developmental theory and research suggesting that Interactions between students and adults are the primary mechanism of student development and learning. The CLASS dimensions are based solely on interactions between teachers and students in classrooms; this system does not evaluate the presence of materials, the physical environment or safety, or the adoption of a specific curriculum.

Another way to evaluate your work is to write about your progress toward self-selected teaching goals. The My Reaction feature gives an example of a student teacher's self-evaluation.

Supervisor Evaluations. You need some feedback from your supervisor, and probably from your faculty instructor as well. Often supervising teachers give you informal feedback on a regular basis: in the moment while on the floor with children, in preparation or at the end of an activity, either before you begin or finish a session, and sometimes during weekly meetings with you or the teaching team as a whole.

Your faculty instructor may make site visits as well. All these experiences can get students feeling anxious and vulnerable, for this process opens one up to criticism. "I was worried when you set the day to visit me," writes Grace. "I thought you were there to inspect how poorly I was teaching, and I was afraid. But it didn't feel like that once you got there. You stayed in the background, and I actually forgot you were watching me! Afterward, your notes were so helpful—I have lots to think about,

My Reaction

"Self-Evaluation: How I'm Doing on My Teaching Goals"

I work with toddlers in my regular job, and with 2-year-olds at my practicum site. Sharing is not something that comes easy at either age, so my goal is *to learn to help children deal with waiting for a toy they want.* I know that sounds simple, but it's a big task. There seems to be a lot of different ways children react to their wish to have a toy—some try to take it from the other child, others start to cry, and some just look longingly for it. When a child grabs a toy, I would just give the one who lost it something else. Now I am trying to watch the child's reaction, and encourage him or her to start using words to let the other child know how he or she feels. But children don't always have the words yet!

So, I am going to work on talking to both children, helping them find the words that I give. I think I will have to be able to cope with more upsets, but if I acknowledge how hard it is to take turns, well—that's life, isn't it? Also, I am finding that we are lacking duplicate toys at my work, so I am going to talk about getting more, and trying to work on this goal at both places.

—IBEN

but I think you see me as a good beginner!" Figures 2.6 and 2.7 shows a supervisor's feedback. Supervising teachers should complete forms for the student teacher that match the same criteria the student uses for a self-evaluation.

A final note: Anticipating an evaluation can be anxiety producing, as noted in the My Reaction feature. At the same time, getting feedback helps you become a better teacher. Moreover, practicing or preservice teachers are sometimes mentored beyond their time as student teachers. In fact, you can still get help and advice to improve your work at any point in your development as a teacher. Once you become a member of a teaching team, look around for those teachers who have mastered what you still want to achieve. Katz (1995) notes that, at all four developmental stages, teachers benefit from assistance and colleague advice. The California Early Childhood Mentor program (2011) has structured the mentor teacher and director mentor elements to include opportunities for postpracticum and extended mentor–protégé relationships. Also, read Stacey James's "Lessons from the Field" article at the end of this chapter.

Ethics in the Profession

Throughout your career in teaching you will be in the position of making difficult decisions regarding children, their families, and co-workers. As a professional educator, you will have an obligation to make a responsible decision based on your knowledge and abilities. What guides you in that decision-making process? What are the values and ethics that influence you?

First and foremost, you are guided by your own ethical and moral values. These are the ideals and principles that you learned from families and friends, from your culture, from teachers, and from your religious beliefs that helped you learn right from wrong. They are a set of values that you reflect on every day when working with children, families, and other teachers.

As a member of the teaching profession, you also have a code of ethics developed by NAEYC (2011) to inform your response to moral and ethical situations. The code is important because it contains the professional standards for the early childhood field. When you are faced with an ethical dilemma, the code removes the ambiguity of "Should I do this? Or that? Or what?" and gives you the backing of all early childhood educators everywhere. The four sections of the code are as follows:

- Section 1: Ethical Responsibilities to Children
- Section 2: Ethical Responsibilities to Families
- Section 3: Ethical Responsibilities to Colleagues
- Section 4: Ethical Responsibilities to Community and Society

As an individual who works with young children, I commit myself to furthering the values of early childhood education as they are reflected in the ideals and principles of the NAEYC Code of Ethical Conduct. To the best of my ability, I will:

- Never harm children.
- Ensure that programs for young children are based on current knowledge and research of child development and early childhood education.
- Respect and support families in their task of nurturing children.
- Respect colleagues in early childhood care and education and support them in maintaining the NAEYC Code of Ethical Conduct.
- Serve as an advocate for children, their families, and their teachers in community and society.
- Stay informed of and maintain high standards of professional conduct.
- Engage in an ongoing process of self-reflection, realizing that personal characteristics, biases, and beliefs have an impact on children and families.
- Be open to new ideas and be willing to learn from the suggestions of others.
- Continue to learn, grow, and contribute as a professional.
- Honor the ideals and principles of the NAEYC Code of Ethical Conduct.

Figure 2.9
NAEYC Code of Ethics: Statement of Commitment

By committing to a professional code of ethics, teachers affirm that they will engage in professional behavior.

Source: Reprinted with permission from the National Association for the Education of Young Children. Available at www.naeyc.org/files/naeyc/file/positions/PSETH05.pdf.

Each section contains two parts: ideals and principles that inform our decisions. Here is an example:

Ideal	**Example**
The overriding philosophy and standard of behavior	To recognize and respect the unique qualities, abilities, and potential of each individual

Principle	**Example**
The guide for resolving ethical dilemmas	We shall use two-way communications to involve all those with relevant knowledge (including families and staff) in decisions concerning a child, as appropriate, ensuring confidentiality of sensitive information

The full Code of Ethical Conduct can be found on the NAEYC Web site (www.naeyc.org). Figure 2.9 is a shorter, more personal statement from NAEYC that presents the values and moral obligations set forth in the code. You might want to check back in Chapter 1 for the top 10 fundamentals of teaching and see how they relate to the Statement of Commitment and the code itself.

Using the Code of Ethics

Feeney and Freeman (1999) tell us that there are two vital aspects of ethical behavior in early childhood education. The first is to know and act on the core values as noted in the Statement of Commitment. The second is to know and use the NAEYC Code of Ethical Conduct and practice it daily as you try to participate in early childhood programs. The following scenarios offer specific examples of how to use the code of ethics in your teaching.

Ethical conduct includes maintaining confidentiality about children's behavior to families and other staff members.

Scenario #1: Ethical Responsibilities to Children

Maddy, who is 18 months old, began biting the children in her child care class after one of them bit her. Although this is typical behavior for the age group, the number of biting incidents increased to the point that another parent complained to the teacher and wanted Maddy removed from the group.

How does the Code of Ethical Conduct help? Section I, Ideal I–1.4, states that we are to "appreciate the vulnerability of children and their dependence on adults." Section I, Principle 1.4, states that "we shall involve all those with relevant knowledge (including families and staff) in decisions concerning a child, as appropriate, ensuring confidentiality of sensitive information."

These two statements guide our decisions. First of all, the teachers take the standard steps to prevent the biting. Maddy is given a rubber object to wear and told to bite it instead of the other children. Her parents are contacted, and they acknowledge that Maddy's routine and schedule had changed quite a bit at home over the past month, which might be contributing to Maddy's biting behavior. They agree to come in and meet with the teacher to talk further. The teachers start to observe Maddy to find out what seems to trigger her biting. The family of the other child is assured that appropriate measures are underway to ensure the safety of everyone, while ensuring confidentiality by not going into detail about the conversation with Maddy's parents.

Scenario #2: Ethical Responsibilities to Families

Josefina, a student teacher, has been given a small group of children to work with each day. Darrell is in her group. His cousin, Jess, is in another teacher's group. One day Jess's mother seeks out Josefina and asks that Jess be put in her group to be with Darrell. Josefina is aware that each child was assigned to the group that best suited his or her developmental abilities. She tells her supervising teacher.

How does the Code of Ethical Conduct help? Section II, Ideal I–2.7, states that we are to "share information about each child's education and development with families and to help them understand and appreciate the current knowledge base of the early childhood profession." Section II, Principle P–2.2, states that "we shall inform families of program philosophy, policies, curriculum, assessment system, and personnel qualifications, and explain why we teach as we do—which should be in accordance with our ethical responsibilities to children."

When the student teacher informed the supervising teacher of the parents' request, the staff realized it had not communicated the rationale for the small groups very well to this particular parent. The head teacher asked her for a conference and spoke with her about the wide range of developmental levels in the class. She explained that the small groups were used to enhance language development in the groups, based on the individual child's needs. The mother seemed reassured that her child was being treated fairly and according to his developmental abilities. The student teacher was commended for bringing this issue to the attention of her supervising teacher.

Scenario #3: Ethical Responsibilities to Colleagues

Laverne, a student teacher, overhears Merleen, one assistant teacher, telling Anna, another assistant teacher, that she feels Laverne is not doing her share of the work, calling her "a lazy slob." This is the second time Laverne has heard Merleen make a negative comment about her. Laverne wants to talk to Merleen but doesn't know if she should.

How does the Code of Ethical Conduct help? Section III, Ideal I–3A.1, states that we are to "establish and maintain relationships of respect, trust, confidentiality, collaboration, and cooperation with co-workers." Section III, Principle 3A.2, states that "when we have concerns about the professional behavior of a co-worker, we shall first let that person know of our concern in a way that shows respect for personal dignity and for the diversity to be found among staff members, and then attempt to resolve the matter collegially and in a confidential manner." Section III, Responsibilities to Employers, Principle 3B.4, states, "If we have concerns about a colleague's behavior, and children's well-being is not at risk, we may address the concern with that individual. If . . . the situation does not improve, we shall report the colleague's unethical . . . behavior to an appropriate authority."

Laverne decides to take this situation to her supervising teacher to ask if she should confront Merleen. The supervising teacher tells Laverne that she will speak to Merleen first. The supervising teacher talks with Merleen about her unprofessional behavior. Merleen takes it upon herself to go to Laverne and apologize for her comments. For the remainder of the semester, she becomes more supportive of Laverne. (See the Reflective Incident "My Ethical Responsibilities.")For more examples of how to use the Code, each chapter of this book contains an Ethical Dilemma related to the chapter's content. As you read them, you will come to see the breadth of issues that are covered by the Code.

Preparing for Your Career in Teaching

At this point in your early childhood education or career, you can begin to prepare for the next step in advancing your career. By the time you are student teaching, you have a good idea of why working with young children is so important, and are getting a better idea now of what early childhood educators do. Most careers in our field involve either working directly with children, or working with adults, such as families, students, or other teachers. Understanding your career options, creating a professional portfolio, and learning about teacher credentialing in your state are three ways to prepare yourself.

Career Options

Working with Children. There are many kinds of settings in which you can work with children. Related professional work includes children's librarians, child therapists or psychologists, specialists in speech and language or other special needs, and pediatricians. Each state has its own requirements for working with children, either as individuals or in groups, in public settings. Whereas most states require a bachelor's degree for kindergarten and elementary teaching, requirements vary for other teaching options. Figure 2.10 shows a kind of professional ladder that illustrates the varying levels of requirements.

Working with Adults. Many careers involve adults as well as children; indeed, most teaching positions in early childhood education require teamwork. Different kinds of professionals may work with adults on behalf of children, such as child care consultants or advocates, family services provider, or program directors. Supervisory positions may include working with children and also administering a program, although many ECE directors and home visitors work primarily with teachers and families.

Attending and presenting conferences helps teachers maintain their professional edge throughout their teaching careers.

Figure 2.10 Choices on the ECE Career Ladder

Jobs Requiring Advanced Education (College or University)

Child and Family Therapist
Kindergarten and Primary Teacher
Preschool Director and/or Site Supervisor
Child Welfare Case Worker
Bilingual Advisor/Specialist
Child Development Specialist
Early Intervention Specialist
Child Development Professor
Family Support Coordinator
Speech Therapist
Community Advocate
Public Policy & Research Specialist

Jobs Requiring Specialized Training (Postsecondary)

Parent/Family Educator
Child Health Paraprofessional
Recreation Leader
Preschool Food Service Director
Special Education Assistant
Early Intervention Aide
Art/Movement Therapy Assistant
Juvenile Court Probation Worker

Family Service Advocate
Preschool Teacher
Foster Parent
Computer/Graphic Designer of Children's Products
Welfare Child Care Worker
Infant Care Provider
Playground Designer
Bilingual Assistant

Jobs Requiring Limited Training and Experience, Entry Level (Secondary and Adult Education)

House Parent Group Home
Special Education Attendant
Bilingual Aide
Kindergarten Teacher Aide
Children's Book Author
Preschool Food Service Worker
Summer Camp Counselor
Child Care Aide
Recreation/Playground Aide
Children's Tutor
Infant Care Attendant
Home Companion
Group Home Attendant
Nanny or Au Pair

Source: Reprinted with permission of Canada College ECE/CD Department (2006).

Professors and educational journalists educate future teachers. Job responsibilities and salaries vary, although unfortunately ECE professionals usually earn relatively low salaries considering the responsibilities (and often education and training) they have.

Professionalism as a commitment to the field includes advocating for young children, for quality programs in the early years, and for support in working conditions and compensation. The NAEYC is the world's largest ECE organization. Nearly 80,000 strong, NAEYC has a network of local, state, and regional affiliates with these goals:

- To support excellent early childhood education
- To improve teaching and learning
- To build a profession
- To promote public support and policies

Ask your supervising teacher and faculty instructor about this organization, and how you can join. You also can investigate its activities on its Web site (naeyc.org), become a student member for a discount, and attend its annual conferences at both the national and state levels.

Additional state and local initiatives enhance the professionalism of the field by providing supports and program services to eligible participants. For instance, many state departments of education have a child development division or consortium that provides training, career incentive grants, or professional advising. As referred to earlier, in California the mentor program provides training and financial incentives in the form of courses for mentoring or adult supervision as well as a selection process for mentor teachers and director mentors who then receive ongoing stipends for professional growth and for supervising student teachers and director protégés. These initiatives are often coordinated through local college departments or resource and referral agencies. Check out the opportunities in your area.

Professional Portfolios

An innovative way to collect and present yourself as a professional has emerged in the last two decades. Student teachers at all levels of experience find making a professional portfolio useful and inspiring. A professional portfolio demonstrates your abilities as a developing professional. Saving student teaching artifacts can be put to use in a portfolio.

As a result of the standards movement in education, there has been growing interest in developing portfolios both for children and for teachers. "A portfolio is a tool that helps a teacher make sense of his/her own experiences that contribute to his/her competence. It helps teachers track their own professional development and provides work samples for others to review" (Campbell, Cignetti, Melenyzer, Nettles, & Wyman, 2001, p. 2). A well-organized portfolio enables teachers to document their learning and their experiences, and "presents a clear picture of yourself as a growing, changing professional. Equally as significant, it can be a convincing, effective vehicle for you to demonstrate to others in a meaningful way the skills and knowledge you have gained in something as complex as teaching" (Campbell et al., p. 9).

There are two kinds of portfolios: a working portfolio and a presentation portfolio. The former is a work-in-progress and is more inclusive than the latter. The presentation portfolio is a subset of the larger collection used in professional interactions with others. Teachers all start by creating

Creating a professional portfolio personalizes your student teaching experiences and demonstrates your growth as a teacher.

a working portfolio, and then they can pull from it what they need to present.

Include in your portfolio a collection of documents that will provide concrete evidence of your understanding of concepts, how you implemented theory, and your success in academic and teaching endeavors. There is no one standard way to create a portfolio, but you should have a system of organization. Some teachers use standards as categories (see Figure 2.1). Others prefer categories such as these:

- Academic
- Curriculum samples
- Conferences and workshops
- Leadership
- Personal statement
- References and recommendations

Take a moment to think about how to make your portfolio attractive and easy to understand and use. A cover page, table of contents, and introductory section that has a résumé and autobiography are inviting.

Creating a portfolio does not have to be difficult, but it does take time and personal reflection. Remember that you will be collecting samples, or artifacts, that show your work, so you may want to use a large file box along with a large notebook that can be divided into sections. Once you have a filing system, become a packrat! And while you collect evidence of your work, notice the gaps so you can see what to work on.

Evidence of each goal met, and a reflection piece round out the portfolio. One student teacher we know used a light bulb icon to signal her reflection; another attached large, colored sticky notes. As with children, documentation needs to be objective and accurate; a brief reflection adds your personal expertise and flavor. Figure 2.11 shows a sample list for a working professional portfolio.

Finally, remember that you will be adding to this portfolio over time. Wherever you work, be sure to get a letter of reference when you move on; for instance, be sure to keep the evaluations you get from your student teaching and, if successful, ask your supervising teacher to write you a one-page letter about what you learned and did.

Academic

Transcripts, grade reports, written evaluations from instructors, written assignments, course syllabi or summaries

Conferences and Workshops

Signed verification forms, distributed materials, notes, description of how the activity assisted in meeting your goals

Leadership

Materials you developed, meeting agenda with your contribution highlighted, letter or editorial you wrote

Creative Endeavors

Photos or special project or activity, audiotape or videotape of project or activity, letters from participants, time log

Personal Statements

Autobiography, philosophy of early childhood education, statement of your commitment, your priorities and values in the field

References and Recommendations

Letters of reference, recommendations, awards, and commendations

Figure 2.11
What Do I Save in My Professional Portfolio?

A professional portfolio is a critical element in presenting yourself as a competent early childhood teacher.

Source: Information from the San Mateo Compensation and Retention Encourage Stability (CARES) Program, 2000.

Teaching Credentials and Incentives

Each state has its own credentials and often sponsors incentive programs to recruit and/or retain teachers. Find out about this in your own state by going to your state's department of education Web site and checking the credential requirements and possibilities. For an example, Table 2.1 offers a condensed outline of the California Child Development Permit matrix for teaching in public early education programs for infant/toddler, preschool, and school-age children.

Many states offer certificate programs through postsecondary education. Either at the community college or 4-year level, these programs vary in their requirements. Many offer an ECE certificate program that verifies successful completion of particular ECE coursework; others offer associate or bachelor's degrees. Graduate programs are less common; Some universities and colleges offer master's or doctoral programs in early childhood education; others may confer graduate degrees in human development, family studies, or other related fields.

Another avenue for professionalism comes from teaching incentive programs. Again, there is great variety and availability throughout the states, so contacting your state department of education or local resource and referral agency will give you current options. One program, financed by the voters of California, established local community agencies to establish and distribute funds to teachers who stayed at their program

Table 2.1 The CA Child Development Teaching Permit

	Education Requirements	Experience Requirements	Alternative Qualifications	Renewal
Assistant teacher	6 units of ECE or CD courses	None	Accredited HERO/ROP program	105 hours of professional growth
Associate teacher	12 units of ECE or CD courses, including core courses*	50 days of 3+ hours per day within 2 years	Child Development Associate (CDA) credential	15 additional units toward teacher permit (must be met within 10 years)
Teacher	24 units of ECE or CD, including core courses*	175 days of 3+ hours per day within 4 years	AA or higher in ECE or related field with 3 semester units of supervised field experience in ECE setting (SFE/ECE)	105 hours of professional growth
Master teacher	24 units of ECE or CD, including core courses*, plus 16 general education units**	350 days of 3+ hours per day within 4 years	BA or higher with 12 units of ECE, plus 3 semester units of SFE/ECE	105 hours of professional growth
Site supervisor	AA (60 units) with 24 units of ECE or CD courses, including core "courses*, plus 6 administration units (Admin), plus 2 adult supervision units (Ad sup)	350 days of 3+ hours per day within 4 years, including at least 100 days of supervising adults	BA or higher with 12 units of ECE, plus 3 semester units of SFE/ECE; or administrative credential with 12 units of ECE, plus 3 units SFE/ECE; or teaching credential with 12 units ECE, plus 3 units SFE/ECE	105 hours of professional growth
Program director	AA (60 units), with 24 units in ECE or CD courses, including core courses*, plus 6 Admin, plus 2 Ad Sup	Site supervisor status and 1 program year of site supervisor experience	Admin. credential with 12 units of ECE, plus 3 units SFE/ECE; or teaching credential with 12 units of ECE plus 3 units SFE/ECE; or master's degree in ECE or child/human development	105 hours of professional growth

* Core courses include child development; curriculum; and child, family, and community.

** General education courses include English or language arts; mathematics or science; social science; and humanities and/or fine arts.

Source: Data from *A Guidebook for Professional Growth Planning and Documentation,* by Child Care Training Consortium of California, 2000, retrieved June 1, 2012, from www.childdevelopment.org. Used with permission. A complete copy of the CD Permit matrix is available at the California Commission on Teacher Credentialing www.ctc.ca.gov, or through the Child Development Training Consortium, www.childdevelopment.org.

of employment and continued their education through college classes or professional workshops. This compensation and retention program has been continued to help increase the educational standards for early childhood teaching in that state.

You have learned about some of the criteria that make up a professional teacher's life. Some of it may have been enjoyable, and some of it may seem uncomfortable. In either event, as you gain experience in these matters, you will be guided by experienced professional teachers who will help you meet the challenges. They can help you appreciate that this type of professional development can be a stimulating and positive reinforcement of your teaching commitment. Assessments and evaluations, ethics, and career preparation foster the reflective teaching you need to become a lifelong learner who grows and changes along with the children in the classroom (see "Lessons from the Field: Becoming a Professional").

lessons from the field

"Becoming a Professional"

by Stacey James

Mentor teacher, Geo-Kids Early Childhood Development Center

People engaged in many different types of work must participate in ongoing professional growth activities in order to remain informed, marketable, and skilled in their fields. Early childhood education is such a field. But to my mind, what makes teaching different from many other vocations is the need for ongoing *personal* growth. Personal development is professional development, and vice versa: they are inseparable and essential for us. Striving to become a more reflective, supportive, and responsive person makes me a better teacher; taking part in professional activities such as conferences, mentoring, and meaningful dialogue with colleagues makes me a better person.

I decided to become an early childhood educator at midlife, leaving a successful career in an entirely different field. The deliberateness of my choice, and the personal risk I felt I was taking, compelled me to take this career change very seriously, and I had little tolerance for people in the field who approached this work with a casual attitude. Despite my inexperience and the steep learning curve, I considered myself a "professional" from the start.

But I don't think I truly became a professional until I became a mentor teacher. Being a mentor teacher requires me to more closely examine the relationship between my theory and my practice, and to find ways to articulate both. I have become a more reflective teacher as a result, and this has made me a better teacher. I love to witness the "aha" moments as student teachers experience the richness of working with young children, and the excitement of discovering their role in the life of the classroom. These moments make my classroom experience richer, too. As my student teachers gradually take risks, I learn to become a more supportive presence. As we talk about their classroom experiences, I am drawn into more meaningful dialogue about this work. As they formulate and then succeed at achieving their goals, I feel more purposeful and hopeful about my own work with children.

"Professional development" has taken on a deeper meaning for me through mentoring. Although mentoring provides a path for my own development in this profession, it also allows me to feel that I am nurturing the development of other future professionals, as well as the development of the profession as a whole. The work that we do is too important to do less. We owe it to children, families, and ourselves to seek opportunities for personal and professional growth. Every time I stretch myself, I am rewarded with a measure of self-discovery and my practice is revitalized. I can't see how we could possibly enjoy this work if we become stagnant. After all, we clearly don't do it for the money! Speaking for myself, I do it because it is important work—endlessly fascinating, continually challenging, and frequently exhilarating. Just as the children are on an ever-expanding path of learning, so am I. I don't ever want to get to the day when I think I can stop learning—about children, myself, and teaching—because two things will happen on that day: The work will cease to be gratifying on a daily basis, and I will cease to be a good teacher.

Practicum Activity

Write two teaching goals for yourself. Now add at least two objectives for each goal. Refer to Figures 2.1 and 2.3 for help in setting and writing those goals. Compare your goals and objectives to those of a classmate and fellow student teacher.

Journaling Assignment

During the first few weeks of your student teaching do a self-evaluation based on Figure 2.6. Look at it as you finish your student teaching. See how much you've grown! Note where you would like to go next.

References

California Early Childhood Mentor Program. (2011). Home page. Retrieved June 1, 2012, from www.ecementor.org

Campbell, D. M., Cignetti, P. B., Melenyzer, B. J., Nettles, D. H., & Wyman, R. M. (2001). *How to develop a professional portfolio* (2nd ed.). Boston: Allyn & Bacon.

Canada College ECE Department (2004). *Your career* (brochure). Retrieved June 5, 2012, from www.canadacollege.edu/canece/pdfs/careers.pdf

Child Care Training Consortium of California. (2000). *A guidebook for professional growth planning and documentation.* Retrieved from June 1, 2012, from www.childdevelopment.org

Feeney, S., and Freeman, N. K. (1999). *Ethics and the early childhood educator: Using the NAEYC code.* Washington, DC: National Association for the Education of Young Children.

Gordon, A. M., & Browne, K. W. (2014). *Beginnings and beyond: Foundations in early childhood education* (9th ed.). Belmont CA: Wadsworth Cengage Learning.

Hyson, M. (Ed.). (2003). *Preparing early childhood professionals.* Washington, DC: NAEYC.

Katz, L. (1995). *Talks with teachers: Reflections on early childhood education.* Washington, DC: National Association for the Education of Young Children.

National Association for the Education of Young Children. (2005). *Code of ethical conduct.* Washington, DC: Author.

National Association for the Education of Young Children. (2011). *2010 NAEYC Standards for Initial and Advanced Early Childhood Professional Preparation Programs.* Washington, DC: Authors. Retrieved June 4, 2012, from www.naeyc.org/positionstatements/ppp

Pianta, R. C., La Paro, K. M., & Hamre, B. K. (2008). *Classroom assessment scoring system manual pre-K.* Baltimore, MD: Paul H. Brookes Publishing Company.

Web Sites

California Early Childhood Mentor Program
www.ecementor.org

Child Development Training Consortium
www.childdevelopment.org

Council for Exceptional Children
www.cec.sped.org

National Association for the Education of Young Children
www.naeyc.org

chapter 3

Understanding and Guiding Behavior

Identify effective guidance strategies that are developmentally and culturally appropriate, based on respectful and supportive relationships with children.

Basic Beliefs About Guidance

Guiding young children is a challenge for all teachers. As you observe others teach and participate more in teaching yourself, you will learn some effective ways to guide children's behavior. You will also gain insight into your own feelings about children's behavior and find that teaching young children has less to do with "love and patience" and more to do with your ability to learn how to handle situations that arise as children grow and learn to control their behavior. Figure 3.1 lists seven of the basic beliefs about guidance that will help form your attitudes toward guiding young children. Look back to these basics as you move forward in this chapter to see how well you reflect them in your own teaching experience. You may find the examples helpful as each belief is discussed more fully.

Effective guidance practices can solve many behavior issues and prevent others from occurring. Positive guidance is based on attitudes and beliefs about children, families, and the guidance process. Most are learned over a period of time through classroom experience. These seven basic guideposts can be important as you shape your own approach to effective guidance.

Help children become responsible for their own actions.

Guidance is an interactive process between teacher and child with a strong emphasis on problem solving. Our goal is to help children learn by allowing them to work out solutions without undue interference, to make judgments based on their emerging inner controls, to model appropriate behavior for them, and to use guidance techniques that are appropriate.

Example: "They won't let you play with them, Rashad, because you knocked down their block buildings. What could you say so they know you want to play?"

Figure 3.1
Seven Basic Beliefs
About Guidance

As you help children learn
the social skills they need,
these seven basic beliefs
can help you develop
more confidence in
guiding behavior.

1. Help children become responsible for their own actions.
2. Teach children to understand and respect differences.
3. Take into account a child's temperament, family, and community.
4. Learn how to apply developmental theory to guidance planning.
5. Appreciate that guidance is a system of strategies.
6. Become aware of your own potential bias.
7. Let children know you believe they are inherently good.

Teach children to understand and respect differences.

The early years are the best time to help children develop attitudes and behaviors that help them live in harmony with one other. Children learn to see each other with increasing understanding and respect for the many ways we are all different and unique. Good guidance practices teach these skills.

Example: "Takako is just learning to speak English, and that is why she pronounces words differently than you do. Her accent isn't something bad— it is just different from yours. Let's ask her if she will teach us how to say 'hello' in Japanese."

Take into account a child's temperament, family, and community.

Children's behavior is influenced by many factors. Each child has a unique style and temperament and is part of a larger community. Families, neighbors, and religious, ethnic, and cultural groups shape children's values and behavior. The essential partnership in guiding young children is between the family and the teachers and must be thoughtfully considered. In his seminal work, Bronfenbrenner (1979) called this network the "ecology of development," recognizing the influence of the child's system of family and cultural relationships that significantly affect how the child develops. The complex interactions among the child's family and community connections are probably among the most important concepts you will learn as a student teacher, for they will impact your approach to teaching in the 21st century.

Example: "Has your grandmother come back from Mexico yet, Consuela? I know you miss her a lot. When she gets back, let's see if she can visit school again and teach us the special songs she sings to you."

Learn how to apply developmental theory to guidance planning.

Child development theory teaches us about the individual nature of children; predictable patterns and stages through which they develop; variations in their growth; and what types of behaviors, fears, and interests are typical of various age groups. When we understand child development theory we gain the confidence to support the child's emerging self-control at each level of development. All teachers need to form developmental points of view so that they are able to use appropriate guidance strategies by matching theory to practice.

> *Example: "I know Ricky has been causing concern among the staff because he is taking so many risks on the climbers. Let's remember that although he has a highly developed vocabulary and is quite tall for his age, he is just 3 years old and needs more time to mature physically. When he is near the climbers, let's make sure one of us is there to support his efforts."*

Appreciate that guidance is a system of strategies.

Guidance is not a single, quick-fix response to all behavior situations. Instead, guidance is an intentional course of action based on a teacher's knowledge of the individual child, the group of children, the family, and developmental theory. (See "My Reaction" for Jane's ideas.) Teachers use the appropriate guidance strategy at each step in the process in ways that encourage and support behavior changes at various age and developmental levels.

> *Example: "I know you have trouble sitting at group time and I know how you love stories, so I am going to help you. Tomorrow, come and sit close to my chair while I am reading. You can turn the pages for me. We'll do that for a few days and see if it helps."*

Become aware of your own potential biases.

How you were raised influences the choices you make in guiding children's behavior. Teachers need to become aware of their reactions to certain behaviors and how their biases may impact their own attitudes and values. Stay open to different viewpoints of what is considered "right" or "wrong" while developing your guidance approach. This is especially important when working with families from cultures other than your own.

> *Example: "My mother taught us with the switch. I know I can't hit the children, but they need stern discipline. Don't they need me to hold onto them so they know who's boss here at school?"*

Let children know you believe they are inherently good.

Behavior is the only language children have to let us know something is bothering them until they are mature enough to use the words that will communicate their thoughts and concerns. All children will misbehave at some time; it is a natural part of growing up.

Example: "Wow, Pete. You are usually careful about other people's work. Is something bothering you? Can I help you use some words to tell me how you are feeling and why you threw Beth's papers on the floor?"

Guidance, Discipline, and Punishment: What's the Difference?

You may find that early childhood settings use the words *guidance*, *discipline*, and *punishment* in different ways. Often the meaning of each word becomes confused when used interchangeably or without clear definition. To use appropriate guidance techniques, you need to first understand the basic differences among guidance, discipline, and punishment.

What Is Guidance?

Guidance is an ongoing system by which adults help children learn to manage their impulses, express feelings, channel frustrations, solve problems, and learn the difference between acceptable and unacceptable behavior. Effective guidance strategies are based on caring, respectful, and supportive relationships among children and adults. We call this positive guidance. As trust between the child and the teacher builds, teaching and learning the skills of social interaction and behavior become easier.

Through the use of positive, appropriate guidance methods, teachers create a balance between children's emerging need for independence and their need for outer controls, such as rules and boundaries of behavior. As children achieve greater self-control, teachers allow them to make more of their own decisions and govern their own actions. Taking responsibility creates self-confidence in children as they learn to handle challenging situations while building life skills in communication and problem solving.

Classroom management becomes easier when children are independent, self-directed learners. Good guidance strategies help them see the context of their actions along with understanding the consequences of their behavior. Learning about cause and effect of one's behavior will be of value to children throughout their life.

Guidance is a way for you to be the guide, to lead children toward more positive ways of having healthy social relationships. The three elements critical to any guidance method are the child, the adult, and the situation. All three elements must be addressed as you work toward a solution. Figure 3.2 elaborates on the guidance triangle. There is not just one "right" way to solve each problem. Each child, adult, situation, and relationship is different, and the guidance triangle diagram can help clarify what is happening. Understanding is the first step toward solving a problem.

Figure 3.2
The Guidance Triangle

The guidance triangle can help teachers establish effective guidance practices by highlighting three important elements: the child, the adult, and the situation.

Source: From Ann Gordon & Kathryn Williams Browne, *Guiding Young Children in a Diverse Society*. Published by Allyn & Bacon, Boston, MA. Copyright © 1996 by Pearson Education. Reprinted by permission of the publisher.

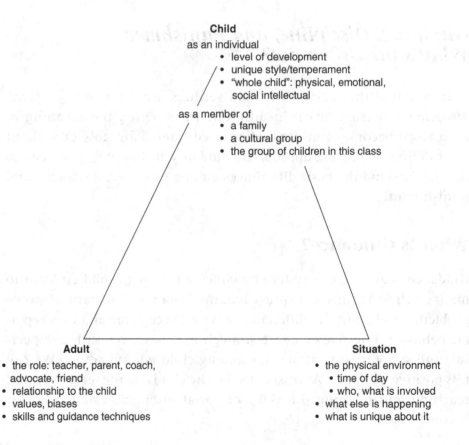

Child

as an individual
- level of development
- unique style/temperament
- "whole child": physical, emotional, social intellectual

as a member of
- a family
- a cultural group
- the group of children in this class

Adult
- the role: teacher, parent, coach, advocate, friend
- relationship to the child
- values, biases
- skills and guidance techniques

Situation
- the physical environment
- time of day
- who, what is involved
- what else is happening
- what is unique about it

Keeping Guidance Positive

Positive guidance techniques usually begin with a positive statement rather than saying "Stop!" or "Don't." Here are some strategies for creating a more positive tone:

- *Emphasize* what a child should do by making positive statements: "Put the puzzle pieces on the table, Karly, so that other children won't step on them."

- *Foster* a child's ability to think of the consequences: "What will happen if you scribble on Orlando's paper, Josh? How do you think he will feel about it?

- *Accept* a child's need for autonomy when they are being assertive, testing limits, and challenging adults: "You are so sleepy and I know you want to keep playing with your toys. But it is naptime, so I'll put you in your crib and turn on some quiet music."

- *Encourage* a sense of empathy toward others: "Kiki dropped her pencil and it rolled under her wheelchair. Can you reach it for her, Patti?"

- *Set* an example to follow: "Sometimes when I feel angry, Shantell, I find a quiet corner away from the noise and that helps me calm down. Let's see if the book nook is available."

Positive guidance is fostered by warm and caring interactions so that children can develop positive self-esteem and social competence.

- *Help* children govern their own actions: "Good for you, Rocco. You remembered to use words instead of crying."

- *Recognize* the need to be consistent. Reinforce the same rules with all children at all times: "I know you *really* want a turn on the gym mat, Julio, but it's not okay for anyone to cut."

- *Give* directions and suggestions in clear, simple statements and give reasons for your request: "Look at your feet, Eunice, and you will see how to avoid stepping on Leo's hands. Put your foot down on the next rung after Leo moves his hands."

- *Provide* ways for children to refocus: "Luz, if you sit at the table you'll be able to finish dictating your story before going outside to play kickball."

- *Communicate* support and reinforce children when they change their behaviors: "Good. You were really careful when you put away the paints. You have gotten to be a very good cleaner-upper, Todd."

By choosing your words carefully and framing them in positive ways, you help children learn that they can become more responsible for their actions.

What Is Discipline?

Discipline is an important concept and a part of the guidance system. Discipline is frequently thought of in terms of punishment and negative responses to a child's behavior, but that does not have to be the case. Good discipline is good guidance. The word *discipline* comes from *disciple*, meaning a pupil, follower, and learner. That definition suggests an important concept of following examples and having adults model the kind of behavior that they would like children to learn (Gordon & Browne, 2013).

Good or effective discipline and guidance are similar in that they have the same foundation of positive, thoughtful, nonpunitive methods. They both accept the premise that children will need time and support to learn appropriate social behavior, and they both promote children's empathy and moral reasoning. When discipline is used interchangeably with punishment, it loses its effectiveness and becomes a negative force in helping children change their behavior. When linked with guidance, discipline becomes a learning experience that relies on a child's interaction and involvement. Children should be disciplined, but in ways that foster thinking and problem solving. The challenging behavior should be seen from the perspective of "What should I do to help this child learn from this experience?" not "How can I punish this behavior?"

What Is Punishment?

Punishment is a harsh consequence for misbehavior. The degree of the punishment is a matter of the degree of the consequence, which may or may not be connected to the offense. Punishment is usually based on negative strategies such as threats, withdrawal of affection or privileges, spanking, isolation, and other punitive methods that promote shame and humiliation to eliminate unwanted behavior. Because it is often a split-second reaction, punishment is an adult release rather than part of a strategy to help a child learn self-control (Gordon & Browne, 2013). When punishment is used, there is an assumption that you can get rid of the behavior without understanding the cause. The behavior may stop, but the reason a child misbehaves is still unknown. The adult who insists on obedience alone does not give the child an opportunity to learn both cause and consequences.

How Discipline and Punishment Differ

Three-year-old Maxine runs over to Lilly, grabs a book from her hand, and shoves her away. Maxine laughs and runs away. Lilly looks startled.

Solving Problems with Guidance and Positive Discipline. The teacher sits down with Maxine while another teacher comforts Lilly.

Teacher: Pushing other children is not okay, Maxine. We can't let you hurt other children, just as we won't let them hurt you. Why did you push Lilly?

Maxine: I wanted her book. It's my favorite.

Teacher: I know how hard it is to wait for something you want, but I can't let you just grab it from her. She has stopped crying now. Let's go see if we can talk to her about giving you a turn with the book.

Together they walk toward Maxine and begin to negotiate a time when Lilly might be finished with the book.

The Point: Learning takes place for both Lilly and Maxine. The children learn from caring adults who acknowledge their feelings and guide them in problem-solving skills. Both children maintain some control over the situation: Lilly gets her book back, and Maxine gets to have a turn. Lilly learns that she and her possessions will be protected. Maxine learns how to ask someone for a turn. The focus is directly on the children's behavior, and there is a direct link between the action and the consequence. The adult models good communication skills to help the children verbalize their needs. The strategy is age-appropriate for 3-year-olds.

Using Punishment. The teacher grabs Maxine as she runs away.

> **Teacher:** "That's a bad thing to do. You can't hit other children. Go sit in the time-out chair and wait there until I come back to get you.

The teacher keeps a hold on Maxine's arm, leads her to an isolated corner, and sits her down in a chair. Maxine begins to cry.

> **Teacher:** Crying won't help. You were bad. Now sit here for a while and think about what you did to Lilly.

The teacher leaves and returns to the center of the classroom.

The Point: Because the teacher took control over Maxine's behavior, very little, if any, learning took place. The teacher made no connection between Maxine's hitting and the punishment she imposed. Rather than help Maxine gain some inner control, the teacher imposed external controls over her, diminishing her self-esteem, and shaming her by calling her "bad." The teacher made no attempt to understand Maxine's behavior, no feelings were discussed, and the punishment had no direct relation to the behavior. Maxine does not know what to do if she feels like pushing another child again, not even the language to use. She has not been given any strategies for managing her urges. An isolated period of time sitting in a chair does not help her separate her feelings, actions, and thoughts so that she learns any effective strategies for coping.

Why Children Misbehave

There are many reasons young children behave the way they do. For the most part, children's motives arise from frustration and anger that they do not know how to express any other way. Misbehaving is a normal part of growing up as children test their limits. One of the teacher's most important roles is to help children learn the cause of their misbehavior and then provide appropriate and equitable guidance.

Misbehavior and acting out are signs that a child is somehow troubled and needs help and may be due to any number of circumstances. At least five factors affect a child's behavior (Gordon & Browne, 2011):

- *Environmental.* Sometimes the setting creates opportunities for inappropriate behavior. Class size, teacher–child ratios, and trained teachers have great influence on a child's behavior in any setting. There also may be too much or too little stimulation, inappropriate and insufficient materials and equipment, furniture that doesn't fit children's bodies, materials that are inaccessible, not enough time for activities, overcrowded work and play space, or too much time sitting and listening. The effect of environment on behavior and the importance of curriculum in guidance will be discussed at greater length in Chapter 5.

- *Developmental.* Young children are just beginning to acquire greater language and social skills that will help them learn acceptable behavior. Teachers need a solid background in child development to guide children according to their individual developmental abilities. A teacher's awareness of the physical, social, emotional, and cognitive range of a child is necessary when planning guidance strategies. A schedule that requires 3-year-olds to sit for a 30-minute group time or an expectation to have toddlers share a single toy are both unreasonable and set the stage for misbehavior.

- *Individual.* When children are hungry, thirsty, tired, bored, restless, or ill, they may exhibit problem behavior. A child's basic temperament (i.e., easygoing, slow to warm up, difficult) may also account for the way he or she behaves. When teachers are aware of the individual temperament of each child in the class, they can choose guidance measures that are tailored to meet the specific needs of that child.

- *Social and Emotional Needs.* Some behavior problems occur when children are trying to express social and emotional needs. A child who wants attention, or is fearful, embarrassed, or lonely, may act out those feelings for lack of words. Family situations, such as divorce, new baby, illness, or death, may cause young children to act out in inappropriate ways. Challenging behavior may also occur when adults have expectations that are too high or too low and when they do not set appropriate limits. Guidance strategies should be chosen that help children with language for solving conflicts and recognition of their emotions and feelings.

- *Cultural Influences.* When the family and the school cultures differ, children may be caught in the middle. Guidance and discipline issues are embedded in the values of each family. Behavior issues often arise when there are different expectations between home and school settings that highlight cultural child-rearing practices. Respect for these differences, valuing each child's family without bias, and working together toward compatible solutions create a climate in which positive behavior will thrive. Figure 3.3 offers tips for teachers about how to choose effective guidance strategies.

Understanding and Guiding Behavior

Figure 3.3
Twelve Tips for Choosing Effective Guidance Strategies

By fostering cooperation and positive behavior in many ways, teachers encourage good behavior and problem solving.

Effective guidance and positive discipline happen when you:

- *Are aware of your body position.* Place yourself so you can see most or all of the room. Get down low to the children's level when you are talking to them.
- *Ask, don't tell.* Ask the children "What's going on?" "What happened here?" "What's not working?"
- *Acknowledge and express children's feelings.* You might say "You sound angry/hurt/sad, etc." "I know you want that truck now." "I know it is hard for you to wait for a turn."
- *Enlist children's cooperation to solve the problem.* Ask "What should we do next?" "How do you think we should handle this?" "What could everyone do to make this better?"
- *Use humor.* Say "Oops! I guess someone forgot that the puzzles don't put themselves together at cleanup time."
- *Check the space arrangements.* Are too many children trying to play in one area? How can you enlarge it?
- *Know the teacher–child ratio for the classroom.* If there are 18 children and 3 teachers, where are your 6 children? Am you devoting too much time to one child?
- *Think before you speak.* Make sure the words you use are what you mean. For example, "Danny, run and get me a sponge." Do you really want Danny to "run"?
- *Give children choices that are appropriate and acceptable.* "Do you want to go inside now?" is not a choice at certain times. A more effective approach is "Do you want to walk backward toward the door or on your tippy toes? "It's time to go home now. Do you want to put on your coat before or after the story?"
- *Recognize and acknowledge responsible behavior.* Tell the child "What a great job you did in cleaning the fish tank." "That was kind of you to let him have the first turn."
- *State the positive.* Instead of "Don't ride so fast down the hill," say "You're riding pretty fast. You might want to slow down." "Don't spill your juice" could be "Look at where you are pouring the juice. Find the edge of the glass and make sure it goes inside the rim."
- *Learn the group dynamics.* Which children are easily frustrated? Easygoing? Sensitive? Bossy? When do things start to fall apart for them?

Developmentally and Culturally Appropriate Guidance

The basic idea behind *developmentally appropriate practice* (DAP) is to start where children are and help them achieve their potential. In doing so, teachers make decisions about behavior and guidance based on what is *developmentally appropriate.*

Three Criteria

Three aspects of a program, activity, or teaching practice must be considered when planning guidance strategies and teaching methods: age appropriateness, individual appropriateness, and cultural and family responsiveness.

Age appropriateness is what we know about how children learn and grow at certain ages of their development. These age-related characteristics allow us to predict within an age range what activities, materials, interactions, and experiences will be challenging and achievable to children of that age.

Individual appropriateness is what we know about each individual child: the strengths, challenges, and interests. This information helps us create flexible, open-ended learning experiences that are adaptable and respond to individual differences within a group of children.

Cultural and family responsiveness is what we learn about the family that helps us understand the influences on

Use guidance techniques that are individually suited to the age, strengths, and interests of each child.

each child. We must be sensitive to a child's culture and background when planning guidance strategies. The ethics of the early childhood profession prohibit physical punishment, yet in some cultures, spanking and hitting children for their misbehavior are considered appropriate. To ensure that guidance techniques are compatible between the home and the school, teachers must work closely with families to understand their cultural needs and concerns. The NAEYC has criteria for making the connections between home and school. Chapter 9 will deal with these issues in greater depth.

How to Apply DAP to Guidance Challenges: A Case Study

How does DAP work in choosing guidance techniques? All three criteria are woven together to plan appropriate methods for each child, as with Garth, for example:

> *Seven-year-old Gracie is having difficulty getting along with her classmates. She has a good sense of humor, but she uses it to create unflattering drawings of many of the children in the class. Like any 7-year-old, she complains of not being liked and wants to have more friends, but many classmates won't play with her.*

What would a developmentally appropriate guidance plan look like for Gracie? Her teacher would first look at the overall *age characteristics* and find that 7-year-olds want to be "one of the gang" and, although charming, tend to show aggression through insults and name-calling. They are also seriously exploring art for the first time. These characteristics seem on target with Gracie's acting-out behaviors. We also know that 7-year-olds are willing to share and cooperate, understand the relationship between cause and effect, and like to be a teacher's helper.

Seven-year-olds are becoming proud of their accomplishments, have greater interest in the process of creativity than in the product, and like to work cooperatively on tasks and projects. At that age, they make their social connections through play and tend to have friends of the same sex.

With these characteristics in mind, the teacher would focus on Gracie as an *individual* and gain more insight into her behavior. Gracie is one of the few girls in the class who participates readily and enthusiastically in art activities, and seems to enjoy honing her techniques and skills in drawing. When other children ask Gracie about her drawings, she laughs, does not respond to their comments and questions, and then moves on to another activity.

As to the third criteria of *family and cultural context*, Gracie is the only girl of four children in a household that is boisterous and loud. Gracie is often teased by her brothers for liking to paint and draw. Her parents try to support her interest in art, but their time is taken up with an aging grandmother who lives with them.

Looking at all three criteria in relationship to one another gives us a more complete picture of Gracie and some insights into a guidance plan that might help her change her behavior and gain more friends. Since art seems to play an important but unappreciated role in Gracie's life, the teacher talks with Gracie about her drawings, showing sincere interest in her skills. She enlists Gracie's help in setting up a new art project that will be presented at Family Night. Gracie agrees to be on the team of four students who will determine the scope of the project and is given the responsibility for much of the drawing. She also agrees to help other students learn to create some of the figures that are needed, and she seems excited about being a "teacher" to her peers.

The teacher was counting on the fact that 7-year-olds do like to be "know-it-alls," and Gracie is no exception.

As the project proceeds over the next few months, Gracie's ability to work with her peers improves. Some of the children are able to recognize and enjoy the cartoon quality of her drawings of people. Gracie, in turn, begins to show them how to draw cartoons. At Family Night, Gracie's family seems genuinely stunned by her artistic ability, and her grandmother asks her to draw some pictures for her room. Gracie's parents make an appointment to see the teacher and discuss how to foster her talent in appropriate ways. Classmates now volunteer to work with Gracie on other projects.

Developmentally appropriate guidance means that teachers have age-appropriate expectations, know about the individual children who are in their class, and have a working knowledge of the families of those children.

With those criteria in mind, guidance strategies emerge as part of a well-thought-out approach to behaviors that are challenging.

Guidance Strategies That Work

Some guidance methods are subtle; others are more obvious. Each situation requires a strategy that best meets the needs of the child, the adult, and the group at that particular time. No one method applies to all situations—or children—at all times. The top 10 list of guidance techniques is shown in Figure 3.4. Guidance strategies run along a continuum, from the understated approach (ignoring the behavior) to the more obvious intervention (intervening physically), with a wide range of options in between. Just as the guidance triangle (Figure 3.2) helps you understand what is going on, the Guidance Continuum (Figure 3.5) helps you decide what to do to resolve the problem.

Indirect Guidance

Children's behavior is strongly influenced by the people and environment in which they live, work, and play. When children enter a classroom, indirect messages tell them what is expected of them. A room full of neatly lined-up desks says, "Sit and work here." A room with a long, open space leading from the entry to the outside says, "Run!" Daily time schedules that allow only a few minutes for transitions or cleanup create an anxious, tense climate. Too few teachers can lead to children who are undersupervised and out of control.

Indirect guidance is a teacher's way of establishing control and setting the stage for what they want to happen within the classroom. Teachers use their knowledge to ensure that their use of indirect guidance is based on their knowledge of the following:

- *Child development*, which helps teachers set appropriate expectations for children's behavior. For instance, group times for 4-year-olds

---

1. Set appropriate expectations for the age and individuals.
2. Model behavior and respect.
3. Observe and document behavior.
4. Have appropriate environments and curriculum.
5. Listen and reflect.
6. Reinforce positive behavior.
7. Redirect and give choices.
8. Set reasonable limits and follow through consistently.
9. Use problem solving for conflict resolution.
10. Intervene and set consequences.

Figure 3.4
Top 10 Guidance Techniques

are longer than for 2-year-olds who are not yet ready to sit and listen for 15 minutes.

- *The impact of the setting*, including space arrangements, schedule, materials, and resources. For each transition during the day, plenty of time is allotted for children to move from one activity to another without being hurried.

- *How to accomplish the goals of the program* by using the environment as a teaching tool. For instance, independence is fostered when materials such as puzzles, paper and crayons, glue, and scissors are situated on low, open shelves so that children can serve themselves and not have to wait for an adult to help them.

- *How to set the tone for positive interactions.* Teachers make sure that there is more than one truck, telephone, wagon, or easel so that children are not frustrated by a long wait, and to encourage social interactions.

- *How to create culturally responsive environments.* Throughout the classroom, books, photos, fabrics, arts and craft objects, multiracial boy and girl dolls, and multicultural dress-up clothing are used, especially those that reflect the heritage of the children in the class.

- *Curriculum that needs to engage children at all levels of their development.* Blocks and their accessories, books, puzzles, crayons, markers, and paper are the types of open-ended materials that children enjoy, no matter what their developmental age or ability is (see Chapter 6).

Indirect guidance, such as the examples just stated, involves some of the simplest guidance techniques that teachers build into the program. In Chapter 5 you will learn more about the environment and its influence on indirect guidance.

Direct Guidance

The indirect guidance elements create the conditions that promote optimal behavior. Direct guidance techniques are those that teachers use while interacting with children to help them solve problems, make friends, become self-confident, and learn new skills. Direct guidance methods cover a broad range of options. They may include:

- Giving a look of reassurance, approval, concern, or questioning
- Offering a smile of encouragement (paying attention to positive behavior)
- Providing a touch of support, awareness, caution, or praise
- Observing and moving close to the situation
- Listening and reflecting at eye level

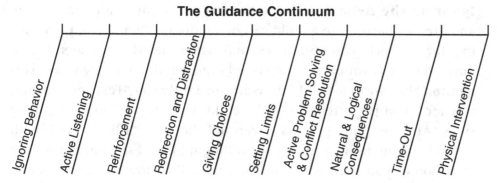

Figure 3.5 The Guidance Continuum

The Guidance Continuum identifies direct guidance techniques, from the least intrusive to more intervening strategies.

Source: From Ann Gordon & Kathryn Williams Browne, *Guiding Young Children in a Diverse Society.* Published by Allyn & Bacon, Boston, MA. Copyright © 1996 by Pearson Education. Reprinted by permission of the publisher.

- Modeling behavior and respect
- Giving directions that are clear, consistent, and supportive
- Comforting a crying or hurt child
- Physically restraining a child
- Verbalizing negotiating skills

The following techniques, outlined in the Guidance Continuum (see Figure 3.5), are all direct guidance methods. After analyzing what is going on, the teacher selects an appropriate technique to address the child's behavior. Teachers take into consideration the needs of each child, the adult, and the situation (refer back to Figure 3.2, the guidance triangle). Each of the techniques should be used in the context of the overall goals and the guidance philosophy of the program. Your choices will change as children learn new behaviors and you alter your expectations.

Start with the least intrusive strategy to allow children time to work out the problem themselves. At each step on the continuum, the expectation is greater for the child's involvement in problem solving. If teachers value helping children to master their world, they select strategies that are least intrusive yet still provide a level of intervention and support.

Effective Guidance Techniques

The strategies listed along the Guidance Continuum begin with those that require the least amount of teacher intervention to those that have the greatest teacher involvement. This way a teacher can choose the most appropriate method for a workable solution for the situation.

Ignoring the Behavior. Some behaviors that are mildly annoying and are not harmful to a child can be ignored. When a child is whining, for instance, you do not respond while the whining persists and may even focus your attention elsewhere until the whining stops. This method also works for children who constantly call "Teacher, teacher, teacher." You pay attention to the child when the whining or calling stops. At some time, you may even tell the child "I like to talk with you when you aren't whining (or calling me), and so I am not paying attention to you until you stop. That way, I'll know you are ready to talk and play again."

Active Listening and "I" Messages. In this method, you are looking for feelings as well as words by listening carefully to what the child says. You then reflect back in your own words what you think the child is saying. Knowing the child and the situation, you make an educated guess about why the child is upset.

- In *active listening*, your voice should convey interest, respect, and trust.

  Child: I hate school.

  Teacher: It sounds like you are really disappointed that Ruby and Danika wouldn't let you play with them.

  Child: I had some good ideas, and they still wouldn't let me play. They wouldn't listen.

  Teacher: You do have great ideas. It seems to me that you might not have heard some of their ideas.

  Child: Well, I wanted mine.

  Teacher: Because you have good ideas and Ruby and Danika have good ideas, let's go over and talk to them about how these ideas might work together. Do you think that would work?

  Child: Sure.

- With *"I" messages*, adults can reflect back to a child how his or her actions affect other people. They are nonjudgmental statements that make an observation, without blame, about what has happened. Each statement a teacher makes begins with an *I*.

  Teacher: I feel sad when you tell me you don't like me.

  Teacher: I get angry when I see you hitting other children again. Remember our talk earlier? Let's sit down and review our agreement about hitting.

  Teacher: I'm disappointed because no one cleaned up the art table today. What can we do to see that this doesn't happen again?

Reflective Incident "I Didn't See It"

Mimi is a 4-year-old who lies constantly. She is not just making up stories; she is telling lies that cause problems for other people. Yesterday, two other children saw Mimi take Ray's sandwich from his lunch bag, but she denied it when confronted by the teacher. Today, Mimi told the teacher that Marcy hit her with a book. Again, several children who had witnessed the incident said it was Mimi who did the hitting. Honestly, I don't know what to say or do! —Ani

Your Thoughts

1. How would I feel?

2. What would I do?

3. What might the results be?

Reinforcement. Reinforcement is a method of rewarding positive behavior based on the belief that children will repeat the same action in the future because it has been noticed: "Tomás, you were very patient while you were waiting for your turn. I saw you find a book to look at until Mason finished his work on the computer." Social reinforcers, such as smiling, talking, interest, and attention, are useful tools with young children at any time, but especially when you want to emphasize certain behaviors. To be most effective, the reinforcers should be focused on the action the child has taken, not on the child. The teacher specifically told Tomás that his patience was what she noticed so that he knows exactly what behavior she wants him to learn. Children will try harder to behave in appropriate ways when they are noticed for positive behavior. See if the following Reflective Incident might call for some teacher reinforcement.

Redirection and Distraction. There are times when children's behavior is not *mis*behavior but is taking place at the wrong time or in the wrong location.

- *Redirection* helps preschool and school-age children. For example, on a rainy day, Neela and Ramona had been reading together in the Book Nook. They began throwing small pillows at each other. As the behavior escalated, the teacher approached:

> **Teacher:** Looks like you two are having fun throwing. This isn't a good place to do that because it bothers the other children who are trying to work. Let's go find the beanbags and put some small baskets in that corner. You can continue your game by tossing them in the containers.

The teacher first had to assess what the girls really wanted to do. In this case, they seemed to enjoy tossing pillows back and forth. The teacher considered some alternatives that allowed for tossing and redirecting the form of the activity to something more suitable. The substitute activity must be a valid one. In this case, the girls were not being deliberately destructive. They were expressing their curiosity, imagination, and social skills. Positive redirection helped them accept an alternative activity, taught them how to solve a problem, and enhanced their self-concepts.

- *Distraction* is related to redirection, but with some fundamental differences. Distraction is usually used to help focus a child's attention to another activity that may or may not relate to the previous behavior. Younger children, especially infants and toddlers, can be distracted fairly easily, as seen in the following example.

  Bruno, a 2-year-old, was lining up trucks in the block corner. Tyrese toddled over and grabbed two of Bruno's trucks. Bruno yelled, "No!" Tyrese raised his arm as if to hit Bruno. The teacher approached the boys.

  > **Teacher:** Bruno is playing with those trucks, Tyrese. I see there's a place for you at the clay table. You can play there for a while and pound the clay. Let's go play with the clay.

  The teacher knows that Tyrese likes to pound the clay, and that makes this an appropriate distraction for him. This method calls for well-timed intervention so that the child will accept the alternative.

Giving Choices. Choices are one of the easiest and most successful methods for helping children who are being resistant. When you give children choices you allow them to maintain some control over the situation as well as practice self-direction and self-control.

> **Teacher:** Su Jin, do you want to work with Rosie on her project, or do you want to help Bonita with her story?

> **Teacher:** Armando, we're going to the library. Do you want to walk with Hector or Dale?

In each case, it is assumed that the child will make the decision and follow through. At the end of the day, when children are likely to be resistant,

Teachers help children make choices about what they might enjoy.

you might say, "It's time to go home now. Do you want to put on your coat now or wait until the story is over?"

Too many choices can be overwhelming. Suggesting two choices gives children the option and makes it easier to choose. Give simple choices that are legitimate and are given only when you mean for a child to make the decision work most effectively. Notice that either decision Su Jin or Armando might makes would be acceptable to the teacher.

Choices have consequences and children need to know what they are before they make the choice. "You may play outside a little longer, if you like, Darragh, but you will miss snack time if you do."

Setting Limits. Limits are the boundaries we set so that children will not harm themselves or others. At various stages in their early lives, children need boundaries to help them learn to monitor their own actions. As they learn greater self-control and responsibility, the boundaries expand. In the classroom, limits are set to protect children and to prevent the destruction of materials and equipment.

In setting limits, we are teaching children to respect themselves and others. We know that it is in children's nature to test, explore, wiggle, giggle, talk, and act out at times. Our job is to keep school safe for all the children and help them learn to accept limits that are reasonable and equitable. Children need to know that you care enough about them to set boundaries on behaviors that may be harmful to them and others.

To be effective in setting limits, you should:

- *Match the situation, the child's age, history, and emotional development.* "Hans, I know it is the first day back at school since you broke your arm, but it is time to listen to the story. You and Aisha may talk later."

- *Be consistent in reinforcing the same rules.* "Monica, we walk inside. Both of the teachers have had to remind you several times today."

- *State limits simply, clearly, and directly.* "Nick, no pushing on the slide. Make a space between you and the person in front of you."

- *Follow through.* "Okay, Nick. You'll need to find another place to play because you keep pushing other children down the slide. Jackie has started a kickball game. Let's go tell her you'd like to play."

- *Accept the consequences and be prepared for the next step.* "I know you want to continue playing on the slide, Nick, but you need to find another place to play right now. You were hurting other children, and I can't let you do that. If you don't want to play kickball, I can help you figure out something else to do."

- *Respect and acknowledge the child's feelings.* "I know you are angry, Franco. It hurts your feelings when they won't let you be on their team. Let's see if we can find another place to play with some other friends."

- *Act with confidence and authority.* "I won't let you throw things at other people, Mustafa, and I won't let them hurt you either. I want school to be a safe place for all the children. Put the book down."

- *Involve children in creating appropriate limits.* "We are going on our first field trip next week, and we'll need to have some rules to follow so that we can all enjoy the trip. Let's make a list. Meera, do you have an idea?"

Active Problem Solving and Conflict Resolution. As children learn more and more self-control and social skills, they can learn to confront their differences with one another and work together to solve their problems. Children need to understand how to take someone else's point of view and to recognize their own feelings as well as those of others, a valuable process that can begin in early childhood.

Active problem solving calls for teachers who guide the process and see that children have positive experiences in conflict resolution. It is a collaborative effort in decision making and problem solving where teachers intervene, yet let the children create the acceptable solution. Teachers ask open-ended questions to help children focus on the problem and begin to suggest possible solutions.

"What could you do?"

"Do you have any ideas?"

"Have you noticed that . . .?"

"How do you think he feels?"

"What might happen if . . .?

The teacher's involvement is aimed at helping the children clarify what happened and helping them explore the ideas that will lead to a resolution. Several other guidance techniques are integrated into this approach: active listening, reinforcement, making choices, and natural and logical consequences. As children suggest various alternatives to the problem, the teacher will need to help them think through the consequences of the actions they propose.

Figure 3.6 outlines a six-step process for active problem solving and conflict resolution. The children are full partners in creating a solution, giving them a greater commitment to making it work, a sense of power and control, and a sense of self-worth.

Natural and Logical Consequences. As a child, you probably heard someone tell you "Don't touch the oven. It is hot and will burn you." You touched it anyway and burned your hand. The cause and effect were clearly defined, and the outcome was a natural result of your behavior. There was no adult interference in your choice or judgments.

Natural consequences follow simple statements of what will happen if you choose a certain action. The following are other examples of natural consequences:

- "If you don't eat dinner, you will be hungry by bedtime."
- "When you don't learn your spelling words, you don't pass the test."
- "If you don't practice the piano, you will play poorly in the recital."

The outcome rests with the child and the choices he or she will make. For behavior that consistently causes problems, natural consequences can be an effective change agent.

Figure 3.6
Conflict Resolution:
A Plan That Works

Source: Based on Gordon &
Browne (2011).

1. *Approach and describe the scene.* Children need to see that you are aware of what is happening. Move in to stop any inappropriate or harmful behavior. Ask to hold the object that is the source of conflict, if there is one. Listen to what the children are saying to each other. "You both look unhappy, and I see the blocks are in piles all over the floor." "He made me do it," cries Jackson. "No, I did not! He did it by himself," answers Esme. Rephrase what the children say: "You both are blaming the other one for what happened." Refrain from assessing blame to anyone, and make no judgments or suggestions.

2. *Sit down with the children and ask them to take turns describing what happened.* Ask such open-ended questions as "How did the blocks get knocked down? "What were you both doing just before that?" "What did you say to Jackson?" "Jackson, how did you respond to what Esme said?" Let the children help define the problem. "He was using up all the triangle blocks, and I need them," said Esme. "I had to have them for my tower," replied Jackson. "Yeah, but you didn't need all ten of them," snapped Esme.

3. *Help children collaborate on exploring different solutions.* "How can we solve this? Do you have an idea?" Esme suggests that she could get a turn using all 10 triangles. Jackson thinks that isn't fair, so the teacher asks Jackson what he thinks would work. "I could build a tower with all the round blocks instead of the triangles. And then we could trade." Esme likes this idea and adds, "Or we could each use half the triangles and half the round ones." Give this step plenty of time, and encourage the children to look at how each solution may or may not work.

4. *When the children agree to a solution, rephrase and/or repeat it.* "You both want to use half of the round blocks and half of the triangles, right?" Modify their solution, as needed, for safety, time, or other factors.

5. *Help with follow-up.* Check to see if the children are playing and working on the solution they agreed upon. If taking turns is involved, be sure to let the children know that it is almost time to share the object that was in conflict. Reinforce the children's abilities to work together to solve a conflict. "You are good problem solvers, Esme and Jackson. It looks like you made the right decision, and your buildings are really looking great. Now let's take a snapshot!"

Logical consequences are similar. They are also the reasonable outcome for a specific behavior, but with adult intervention and guidance to ensure success.

- "Oops. You spilled the milk while you were pouring. Let's go get a sponge and you can clean it up."
- "Lenny, if you draw on another child's paper again, you will have to find another place to work."
- "Jessica, you interrupted me again. Please find a quiet place in the book corner and read until we finish this story."

The link is made with cause and effect and the consequences are immediate. Nelsen (2006) cites three criteria for using logical consequences successfully:

1. The consequence must be *related* to the action (cleaning the table after spilling milk).

2. The consequences must be *respectful* and without humiliation. ("Oh, oh. You spilled the milk," instead of "How could you be so sloppy and spill your milk?")

3. The consequence must be *reasonable* (finding another place to work rather than being punished, helping to clean up the milk).

It takes patience and creativity to ensure that logical consequences do not turn into punishment. These "three Rs" ensure that learning occurs in positive ways and that children's mistakes or misbehaviors are viewed as "teachable moments" rather than actions that require punitive measures.

Time Out. When children are removed from the group and placed in a chair or an isolated part of the room, it is referred to as a time-out. This strategy is often overused and, in many settings, has taken on the characteristics of punishment and humiliation of a child. Telling children to "sit here and watch other children play nicely" or to "sit in this chair and think about what you have done" is ineffective at best. There is no link made between the behavior and the consequence, and the strategy does not help a child learn the skills needed to behave appropriately.

There are times, in order to protect themselves and/or others, when young children need to be removed from the situation. Children whose intensity and emotions overwhelm them often need a place to bring themselves under control. With a teacher's care and guidance, the child can calm down, talk about the incident, and gain self-control. Used in a positive way, a time-out gives children the opportunity to monitor themselves, to assume some responsibility for themselves, and to choose when they wish to reenter play. In this way, a time-out is not a punitive action controlled only by the adult but is a supportive and caring way to help children learn about their behavior.

Time out is one of the more invasive strategies along the Guidance Continuum and should be used judiciously, if at all. A more effective approach would be to use active problem solving or logical consequences before the behavior becomes so disruptive.

Physical Intervention. At times you may need to step in and use physical restraint to prevent children from hurting themselves, others, or property. Jaxson jumps on Aaron and begins to punch him. The teacher moves quickly to protect Aaron, pulling Jaxson off of him while saying "Jaxson, stop!" He remains calm as he moves Jaxson away, holding Jaxson's flailing arms close to his body. "I can't let you hurt Aaron. Let's move over here so we can talk about this." They sit together for a few minutes until Jaxson becomes calm.

To keep one child from hurting another, you may need to use physical intervention and close proximity to stop the harmful behavior.

Physically restraining Jaxson and moving him away from Aaron is only the first step in the process. The teacher also needs to determine if Aaron is seriously hurt and to provide comfort to him. Sometimes another teacher will be able to comfort Aaron.

The teacher decides whether or not to talk with both children at the same time or if each needs to be spoken with separately. They all go to a quiet place after both boys have calmed down enough to respond to the teacher's questions. The teacher then proceeds with active problem-solving and conflict resolution techniques that engage the children in the problem-solving process. They learn to resolve their conflict in a positive manner. If either child has problems with aggression on a regular basis, a long-term strategy that includes observations and assessments should be considered.

The longer you teach, the more experience you will have in using the top 10 guidance strategies. Think of them as a tool kit for guiding young children. You have an assortment of choices for each situation. Choose the least intrusive first to allow children time to work out a situation themselves. As stated earlier, if we value helping children master their world, we will select strategies that are the least intrusive yet still provide a level of teacher interaction and support. Try the screwdriver before using the hammer!

Guiding the Infant and Toddler

The first 3 years of life are filled with dramatic changes in the physical, emotional, cognitive, language, social, and creative domains of the developing child. Guiding the young child's behavior begins in infancy. Some of the strategies along the Guidance Continuum are useful, but with these very young children, more subtle, indirect guidance is more effective:

- Make the environment safe for infants and toddlers to move around and explore. Keep it clutter free, and make sure the nap area is a quiet, nonstimulating place.
- Allow plenty of floor space and constant supervision with few but necessary limits.

When a Child Hurts a Teacher

Situation: Stephanie is student teaching in a lively preschool class. Jake, a 3.5-year-old boy who is large for his age, is often overly aggressive with other children. One day as Stephanie tried to intervene when Jake charged after a group of girls who were playing on the climber, Jake kicked Stephanie in the shins. Surprised, she let out a painful yell that stopped Jake in his tracks. "How could you do that?" she asked. "Don't you know how much that hurts?" Jake looked remorseful and made no comment. Stephanie immediately reported the incident to her supervising teacher, Kendra.

Code of Ethical Conduct References
Section 1: Ethical Responsibilities to Children:

I.1.2–To base program practices upon current knowledge . . . in the field . . . as well as on particular knowledge of each child.

I.1.5–To create and maintain safe and healthy settings that foster children's . . . development.

I-1.7–To use assessment information to understand and support children's development.

P-1.4–We shall involve all those with relevant knowledge (including families and staff) in decisions concerning a child.

P-1.7–We shall strive to build individual relationships with each child; make individualized adaptations in teaching strategies . . . and consult with the family so that each child benefits from the program.

Solution: Kendra called a staff meeting to talk about Jake. Since this was the first time he had been aggressive with a teacher, Padma, an assistant teacher, suggested they observe Jake to establish what triggered his aggressive impulses toward others. Kendra suggested that Stephanie talk with Jake the next day about the incident and how his outbursts affect other children and teachers. She gave Stephanie guidelines that helped her approach Jake with a gentle but firm attitude. Padma, who was one of Jake's teachers last year, said she would pay extra attention to Jake when he was not being aggressive. All agreed to try these strategies for a week. Stephanie reported that her talk with Jake led her to help him explore more strenuous games when outside and that seemed to be a good outlet for his high energy and size. Padma noted that Jake responded well when she praised him for helping others. Kendra and the staff compared their observation notes and found that the amount of time Jake spent in aggressive behavior was significantly lower than during the previous week. Kendra said that she would be bringing this updated information to the meeting she had with Jake's family next month, as they had discussed his aggressive behavior in previous conferences. Stephanie reported to her faculty instructor that she saw how a team effort could be successful and that what she learned in her observation class was really useful.

- Create a healthy environment where handwashing is essential and frequent.
- Small group size prevents young children from being overwhelmed.
- Model the behavior you want the children to adopt: gentle interactions; smiles; soft-spoken, soothing comments.
- Verbalizing is important in preventing conflicts and helps young children anticipate what is and will be happening. Talk to them about

what is happening: "Billy wants to touch the pretty bow in your hair. If that's okay, I'll help guide his hand so that he won't hurt you."

● Be responsive: Attend to crying and clinging rather than ignore it. Verbalize children's feelings and help them label what they are feeling: "I know it makes you sad when your daddy says good-bye." "You seem to want to be held so let me sit with you on my lap." "Yes, that loud noise frightens me, too."

● Pair words with action: Say "Put the book on the shelf, Tomás," while you guide his arm toward the cabinet.

● Teach self-help skills at appropriate developmental stages. "Here's a tissue. Let's see you blow your nose by yourself."

Direct guidance methods, noted earlier in this chapter, are useful with infants and toddlers and set the foundation for future guidance strategies.

Infants. Crying is the language of infants and is the only way they have to tell you something is wrong. Babies use their cries to have their needs met and communicate through cries that become differentiated to express hunger, discomfort, and pain. We help babies learn to develop trust—a key ingredient to guidance—by responding promptly to their needs, maintaining consistent routines, and providing positive affectionate caregiving. Infants learn through their senses, so that when they are upset, we cuddle, hold, rock, talk, and sing to them, assuring them that they have been heard and will be taken care of. Attachment, the emotional bond that needs to form between infants and their loved ones and caregivers, is built on these close and caring interactions.

Although they may appear to be helpless beings, babies are in fact persons with feelings, rights, and individual natures. Feeding, diapering, playing, and other daily routines are not only the curriculum of this age group but also the foundation of a positive guidance approach. Magda Gerber, a pioneer in infant care, coined the term *educaring* to describe the use of these reciprocal and responsive interactions between baby and caregiver. Observing, listening, smiling, talking, and reading babies' cues are key elements in guidance as well as educaring. (Gordon & Browne, 2011).

Toddlers. Toddlers are not only walking; they also are learning new words at a rapid rate. These developments offer greater challenges for guiding their behavior as well as more options for guidance strategies. The Guidance Continuum is more useful with this age group in conjunction with reinforcements, distractions, giving choices, and setting limits.

The need for autonomy and independence combined with perpetual motion describes toddlerhood. In their quest for autonomy, toddlers are often ambivalent: independent one minute and helpless the next. Their transition between being a baby and a child is often uneasy and frustrating. Power struggles arise with family and caretakers as toddlers move to establish their own identity. Three issues in particular pose challenges for guiding the toddler: temper tantrums, a contest of wills, and biting.

Temper tantrums help the toddler discharge pent-up energies, express conflicting emotions, and test their own control. They also indicate a struggle within the child as they tip up and down the emotional seesaw of anxiety/fear and control/frustration. Too young to control themselves, toddlers explode in a tantrum that may include screaming, running around, throwing whatever is in reach, and holding their breath. In other words, they are overwhelmed, terrified, and may refuse to be comforted. Prevent them from hurting themselves and others, stay nearby, and be ready to offer gentle comfort when they are ready. Do not try to argue, scream back, or shake them to stop the tantrum for that will only add to their distress. Temper tantrums are a normal part of the toddler's development and taper off over time as their language skills improve.

A *contest of wills* usually begins somewhere between the child's second year of life and 2.5 years of age. Having a strong sense of self has long-term benefits in knowing who you are and feeling confident to grow and try new things. Toddlers push out the boundaries and push anyone— including adults—who get in their way as they run away, squirm out of your grasp, refuse to stay in their crib, refuse to take a nap, and delight in shouting "No!" to everyone. You have a number of choices from the Guidance Continuum to help your reign in the toddler without getting into a power play. Some behavior can be ignored and some redirected. Giving a toddler a choice of two alternatives ("Which truck do you want to put on the shelf? The green one or the black one?") and setting appropriate limits ("You don't have to sleep, but you do need to have some quiet time in your crib.") are effective strategies.

Biting is one way a toddler has to express negative feelings, frustration, and anger. A biting incident requires immediate attention to the child who is bitten and to let the biter know why it is not acceptable behavior. Show your concern in a firm but caring voice: "You may not bite people. It hurts them. If you feeling like biting use this (a carrot, a rubber or plastic teething ring)." Report the incident immediately to your supervisor, who will follow through by contacting the parents of both children. The staff will want to observe the biter for several days to help determine what caused the biting, especially if it is repeated, and to strategize various approaches.

Temper tantrums, a clash of wills, and biting are common behaviors in toddler classrooms. If the behavior escalates and the child does not respond to positive guidance strategies, parent involvement and possible professional consultations may be needed to determine the origins of the behavior and the best possible approach.

Figure 3.7
A Variety of Disabilities Teachers May Encounter

These disabilities may range from mild to severe. Some children may have more than one exceptionality, and each child will specific limitations and safety needs.

Source: Data from Gordon & Browne (2012).

Speech and Language: hearing impairment, stuttering, articulation difficulties, cleft palate, chronic voice disorders, learning disabilities

Physical–Motor: visual impairment, blindness, perceptual motor deficits, orthopedic difficulties such as cerebral palsy, spina bifida, loss of limbs, muscular dystrophy

Social–Emotional: self-destructive behavior, severe withdrawal, dangerous aggression toward self and others, depression, phobias, psychosis, autism spectrum disorders such as Asperger's syndrome and Rett syndrome

Health Impairments: severe asthma, epilepsy, hemophilia, congenital heart defects, severe anemia, malnutrition, diabetes, tuberculosis, cystic fibrosis, Down syndrome, fetal alcohol syndrome, sickle-cell anemia, Tay-Sachs disease, AIDS

Specific Learning Disabilities: difficulties with language use and acquisition, spoken and written language problems, perceptual dysfunctions, brain injury, minimal brain dysfunction, dyslexia, and developmental aphasia

Guiding Children with Special Needs

Children with special needs exhibit a wide range of atypical conditions ranging from short-term to long-term physical, emotional, cognitive, language, and social problems. The children with some sort of exceptionality and those who are gifted comprise the "special needs" category. Figure 3.7 lists some of the exceptionalities that occur in young children.

Indirect guidance is important when dealing with children with special needs. The room arrangement should be safe and accommodate specific disabilities: clear pathways for children with vision impairment and wheelchairs, accessible materials on low shelves, tables and sinks at wheelchair level, and teachers who are trained in special education practices. It is important that the teaching staff establish a supportive and inclusive attitude and model appropriate skills and behavior for all children. Figure 3.8 suggests strategies that are successful with children with attention-deficit hyperactivity disorder (ADHD).

Figure 3.8
Effective Guidance Strategies for Children with ADHD

Guidance strategies foster children's social and learning skills in positive ways.

Source: Data from Gordon & Browne (2011).

1. Maintain regular and consistent routines and rules: "Remember, Charlene, we always wash hands before snacks."

2. Have realistic expectations: "I know it is hard for you to wait. Why don't you go over to the other cabinet to see if there are more markers in there."

3. Make eye contact when giving directions, using clear and simple explanations: "Look at me, Toby, so I know you are listening. Good. Now let's go over the assignment together."

4. Allow time for transitions by giving a plan for the next step: "In three minutes it will be time to get ready to go home. When the other children begin to leave, I want you to get your coat and come back here to sit with us."

5. Select jobs in which the child can be successful: "Connie, please collect the milk money today."

6. Recognize accomplishments: "Good job, Marco. You gave everyone two pieces of paper, just like you were asked."

Since all children are more alike than they are different, most techniques found on the Guidance Continuum are appropriate with children with special needs, but some are used more frequently than others. Reinforcement, natural consequences, and time out can be appropriate as well. When the child's behavior is more aggressive, physical intervention would be necessary. Adaptations of guidance strategies include breaking down tasks into small sequential steps so that a child may feel less frustrated and more successful. Help Jordan learn to make his bed by first pulling up the covers yourself, and have him place the pillow on top before asking him to do the tasks completely on his own.

Children who are gifted may exhibit behavior problems because they are bored and feel unchallenged by the program. Adapting for children who are gifted and who have special needs enhances the opportunities for all of the children in the classroom. Letting children do things their own way will challenge the gifted student as well as lessen the frustration of children who are resistant. Support the gifted child's exceptional abilities as you would any other child's accomplishments. Keep the praise specific ("You worked really hard on that!") rather than encourage perfectionism ("You are so smart and do everything so well!"). Remember that there are many ways to be gifted and encourage the strengths you find in all individuals. Help gifted children appreciate that some children have difficulty learning because they learn in different ways.

Although all strategies on the Guidance Continuum will work with children who are gifted, there are other ways to prevent problems with indirect guidance techniques:

- The Project Approach (see Chapter 6) is particularly exciting since children are encouraged to stretch their limits;
- Provide leadership opportunities to engage their social skills.
- Invite them to make suggestions and offer alternatives for solving problems and changing tasks and activities.
- Create a challenging and stimulating environment with open-ended materials and enough time to pursue individual interests.

Children with exceptionalities and children who are gifted require attention; their unique abilities must be included, challenged, and stimulated within all early childhood programs.

Good guidance practices help teachers create the kind of atmosphere that promotes healthy social relationships, respect for self and others, and the ability to accept responsibility for your own actions. In "Lessons from the Field," mentor Mary Jennings shows how to help children to trust you.

"Help Children to Trust You"

by Mary Jennings

Head Teacher, United Methodist Co-op

Reflecting on our first childhood experience, many of us remember our preschool teacher as a substitute for the warmth and caring of a parent. Having a caring and responsive relationship with their first teachers provides children a safe and nurturing environment, allowing them to grow socially and emotionally. A teacher who understands young children will help guide them to develop skills that will last a lifetime.

As children enter a facility, a teacher positions herself to greet each child. Olivia likes to hear "I've been waiting for you," while Will smiles when you tell him "How nice to see you this morning." A warm and accepting teacher will build a trusting relationship.

When Darlene came to student teach here, she did not know how to get the children to trust her. She began by observing but seemed reluctant to talk much to them. By worrying about saying the wrong thing, she did not talk much to them—and they ignored her. Then we had a Valentine exchange, and she helped the children read each other's cards. They flocked to her to get her help. The next week, I noticed how she got acquainted with Tommy in the book corner, learning that he was ready to sound out a few words in a favorite story. Once she tried to enter the sand-digging activity and was discouraged when they told her they didn't need her help, so that backfired. But then she tried to bring them some special shovels, and it worked!

A teacher will have numerous opportunities to strengthen the relationship with children by providing a program that understands children's needs. Student teachers become part of the routine that gives the children reassurance that each school day they are part of a group and together they will participate in activities, like having a snack and playing outside. Children feel comfortable with teachers who realize the importance of developmental needs such as time for large movement as well as activities to practice fine motor control like painting or working with play dough.

Student teacher Vikki discovered that in these classes, the children are given a lot of room for exploration, meaning that the teachers have limited "no's" and encourage the children to explore, question, and experience. I was pleased to see that she saw how children begin to trust teachers who want the children to experience and question activities, because that is how they learn, not because they are difficult or spoiled.

The child–teacher relationship will be further reinforced when the teacher shows respect for the child by using words that encourage and offer support. "I noticed you used a pattern with the colors" signals your interest in a child. "You were really concentrating while you cut the paper" ensures a child that you were paying attention and care about accomplishments.

A trusting relationship between teacher and child will provide a firm foundation for guiding behavior. Giving children choices will allow the child to have control over his environment. "Would you like to pick up the blocks or put away the dishes in the playhouse?" gives the child a choice and you authority.

Teaching expected behavior also helps guide children. Modeling appropriate manners—"Please pass the crackers"—and setting limits provide boundaries to ensure accepting responsibility—"You need to put these books on the shelves." Using action statements will provide clarity and communicate a task. "Sarah is picking up the puppets," I overheard student teacher Ena tell the children, and James immediately joined in. Both Ena and James learned the value of encouragement as they built a trusting relationship together.

Practicum Activity

Interview another student in your class and ask the following questions:

1. What is your approach to discipline?
2. What do you think influences children's behavior?
3. What are the "rules" at your school? How are they explained to children?
4. What happens when rules are not followed?
5. What guidance strategies do you find most successful?
6. Is there such a thing as developmentally appropriate discipline?

Journaling Assignment

Interview your supervising teacher on his or her approach to guidance and discipline.

References

Bronfenbrenner, U. (1979). *The ecology of human development*. Cambridge, MA: Harvard University Press.

Gordon, A. M., & Browne, K. W. (1996). *Guiding young children in a diverse society*. Boston: Allyn & Bacon.

Gordon, A. M., & Browne, K. W. (2011). *Beginnings and beyond: Foundations in early childhood education* (8th ed.). Belmont, CA: Wadsworth Cengage Learning.

Gordon, A. M., & Browne, K. W. (2013). *Beginning essentials* (2nd ed.) Belmont, CA: Wadsworth Cengage Learning.

Nelsen, J. (2006). *Positive discipline*. New York: Ballantine Books.

Web Sites

Empowering People/Positive Discipline
www.positivediscipline.com

ERIC Clearinghouse on Early Childhood and Parenting
http://ceep.crc.uiuc.edu/eecearchive/index.html

chapter 4

Observing and Assessing Children

LEARNING OUTCOME

Identify methods of observation, interpretation, documentation, and assessment to positively influence children's development and learning.

Observation

Look outside the window. There is Nicholas, poised at the climbing pole. Feet aligned, he grasps the top of the side poles and climbs into the structure, a sliding tube, on his hands and knees. At the top, left arm grasping a rail, he pulls himself up with bent knees. He shouts at a peer in the distance and slides down the tube and looks back and forth as he stands up. Immediately he sprints, pumping with bent arms, across the yard of 150 feet! In the distance, he sits criss-cross style in a circle with two other boys and a teacher. Suddenly, he shoots up with both hands pushing on either side of his body, then runs away 20 feet and comes back, bending down on his knees. He has a stick and hits it against the ground. The other three people throw their arms over their heads, and he hands the stick to another boy.

Children are fascinating! Whatever Nicholas was doing, student teacher Theo tried to capture it. From this snippet of behavior, Theo could see that Nicholas had refined gross motor skills and was adept at climbing and running. He was able to observe some of his social skills, such as initiating contact with peers and entering a game. Moreover, Theo gained insight into Nicholas's thinking, noticing his facial expressions and gestures and how he involved himself in this child-made game with rules.

How did this student teacher assess the child's development so quickly? In reality, Theo did not understand the significance of his observation until later. After making this observation, Theo tucked away his notes when he was called by a group of children to join them. Later, with his mentor teacher, he went over his observation. The two of them could make sense of what he saw and verify it by rereading his documentation. They were able to use this observation in Nicholas's portfolio and in their curriculum planning for group games, as well as in determining how to develop a relationship with the child based on his interests and behavior.

Why Observe?

Observational skills are very important to being a good teacher. When you watch children, you see what they need, then provide the environment and tools they need to learn. You build relationships with them to understand better how they operate and why. Children notice that you value what they say and do when you are attentive and focused on them. Observational skills, comments student teacher Di,

What are children telling us about themselves as they play? We learn by observing what they do and say.

> are as important to being a good teacher as they are to scientists. I have been working in cancer genetic research, where our focus was to find a new cancer gene. The results we got from the DNA and RNA samples looked very similar, and the previous researcher gave up. But when my group did very careful observations and repeated the experiment several times we found differences. We made a novel discovery and found a new gene, which is very important for cancer development. Our observations with children are no less important!

Scanning Versus Observing

Seeing children in a physical sense is different from seeing them in an observational sense. For instance, you can "see" children when you scan a room or yard: You can see who is there, how many children are in an area, and even can supervise the activity in a broad way. Observing, however, requires closer inspection. You need to look carefully, focusing your attention instead of scanning. You have to narrow your view, and at the same time stay a little apart from the activity. Theo would never have been able to capture the details of Nicholas's activity if he had been just watching the yard. He may have missed the small but significant detail of Nicholas's shouting to the group. Again, student teacher Di comments: "Without observation, we would treat children the same, and the result of teaching would be unsatisfactory. Only by doing very careful observations can we find the best way to teach children."

The Tools of Recording

In the 21st century, teachers have a number of methods for recording children's behavior. Teachers use digital and video cameras to capture children's behavior on tape, and they can collect samples of the children's work. At the same time, much of children's growth in a playful setting such as a center will be best documented by a teacher's written notes. Thus, student teachers should make time during their practicum to learn to observe and record children's behavior as it occurs.

Through careful listening, teachers can truly be "in the moment" with children. Through listening, teachers can spontaneously support and challenge children. Documenting what happens is a kind of visible listening, as it records on paper or as a moving image what is going on. Your attention sends a message to children that what they do has value and meaning.

This means that you must practice watching and listening to children at play, and try to write down what they are doing and saying in the moment. This isn't easy, and takes practice, as you will note in the following Reflective Incident. Start by equipping yourself with these tools:

- Small notepad and pencil (can be on a necklace; may include a camera or video recorder)
- Clothes with a pocket (to stash your notes when duty calls)

Next, select a time and place to take notes. Place yourself in an area where children are interacting with materials and/or other children independently. This is usually during free play (sometimes called choice time, interest area, or work time) rather than a transition or teacher-directed activity, which requires more adult intervention.

Student teachers often find themselves overwhelmed with how fast children move, talk, and change direction. Over time, they become more proficient at getting the important parts of behavior when they work at the skill.

Start by writing everything you see and hear; you are trying to capture in as much detail as you can the children's behavior, language, and interactions. Teachers often find it easier to write in their home language, scribbling what they see in shortened form and rewriting the key segment later.

Carmine grabs a scarf and begins to dance, twirling and whirling, hopping and bending in time to the music. It is Greg and Steve, and he really likes the high rhythm of this stuff! Following the teacher's lead. Carmine balances on his toes and waves his scarf high over his head. Sarah and Juanita join him, ~~but he doesn't care about them.~~ He can keep time with the music! ~~I didn't know 3-year-olds could do that.~~ He keeps swinging his scarf after the music stops. It doesn't matter to him that the tape is over—ha! ☺

Reflective Incident "How Can I Do It All at the Same Time?"

Tanya is doing her first observation. The teacher assigns her to observe Jerome. She takes a chair behind the puzzle table where Jerome is working and begins to record what she sees. A few moments later, Chandra comes up and plops herself on Tanya's lap. Alan walks up to them and asks Chandra what she is doing. Meanwhile, Jerome leaves the table and heads outside. As she breaks away from Chandra and Alan, Tanya wonders, "How can I do this? How do I keep up with Jerome and concentrate just on him?"

Your Thoughts

1. How would I feel?

2. What would I do?

3. What might the results be?

4. How can I teach and record at the same time?

5. Where do I go from here?

Note the lines that are crossed out later, as the teacher selects those items that will describe the child's activity with *objectivity* and *accuracy*. Only with practice and reflection can we document in writing what we see in children's daily activities.

Observational Methods

Good records should reveal authentic child behavior and provide a detailed portrait of a child. Observing a child in multiple situations and over time should document individual progress. A teaching team with competent observation and documentation skills allows for evaluations from more than one person, validating both teacher observations and program accountability to families, communities, and colleagues. Check with your fieldwork

Eyes and ears are the best recording tools a teacher has.

Figure 4.1
Building Authentic
Pictures of Children
Through Observation

Authentic assessments must
serve specific purposes to be
useful to professional
teachers.

Source: Information compiled
from Beaty (2009).

Observational records should...	To discover ...
• Document children's experiences • Document children's relationships and achievements • Determine the child's abilities and strengths • Determine the child's present abilities in relation to program goals • Serve as an effective tool in parent–child communication • Serve as a basis for identification of special needs and from this, referral • Be useful in determining program changes and staffing needs	• How the child learns • How the child interacts and builds relationships • What each child is interested in learning • Where the child's development is and should be going next • What will enhance the family–child relationships • Where further evaluation is needed, as well as intervention or accommodation • How development can be promoted

site for its developmental record plan, and compare it to Figure 4.1. How many of these purposes does your plan fulfill?

Types of Observations

There are several types of observations. Some are more useful in clinical settings or for experimental purposes, and others work best for observing children in more natural settings. Three types that teachers use most often are narratives, checklists, and behavior samplings.

Narratives are observations in the form of anecdotal records. They are the most common method of recording child growth and behavior. They are known as "running record" or "anecdotal narrative" and are used in diary descriptions and journals. Narratives offer rich detail but require a command of descriptive language. The running record makes a written sketch of a child, a kind of snapshot in time. It should be accompanied by a teacher's insights about what it means and what to do with the findings. Do not try to add your conclusions while you are engaged in documenting children's behavior; rather, you can make these interpretations either immediately afterward or at the end of the day while the situation is still fresh. Figure 4.2 shows a sample narrative recording form.

Checklists, at first glance, appear easier to compile than the narrative because a teacher can simply make a mark (Yes/No, rating scale of 1–5, etc.) instead of writing longhand. However, the richness of an anecdote is lost. Further, a checkmark allows no verification for either objectivity or accuracy. Figure 4.3 illustrates a sample checklist.

Figure 4.2 Sample Narrative Recording Sheet

- Child-initiated activity
- Teacher-initiated activity
- New task for this child
- Familiar task for this child
- Done independently
- Context (where, when, etc.)

- Done with adult guidance
- Done with peer(s)
- Time spent (1–5 min.)
- Time spent (5–15 min.)
- Time spent (15+ min.)

Child observed: _____
Date/Time: _____
Observer: _____
Desired results: _____
Developmental domain: _____

Observation:

_____
_____
_____
_____
_____
_____
_____
_____
_____
_____
_____
_____
_____

Interpretation:

What developmental theme did he or she engage in? What experiences, knowledge, and skills did he or she build on?

_____
_____

What did he or she find meaningful? Frustrating? Challenging? List questions, problems and solutions, and unique attributes demonstrated.

_____
_____

What question comes to mind about the child or your next step?

_____
_____

Source: From Mary Meta Lazarus Child Development Center, College of San Mateo, San Mateo, CA. Used with permission.

Figure 4.3 Sample Developmental Checklist

Note that checklists offer a quick assessment but lack the rich detail of a narrative.

Prekindergarten Checklist: Self-Help Skills	Yes	Needs Practice	No
Puts shoes on correct feet			
Can dress self independently			
Able to use buttons and snaps correctly			
Puts away personal belongings			
Pours liquid from small pitcher into cup			
Spreads soft food with blunt knife			
Uses spoon, fork, or chopsticks skillfully			
Washes hands correctly			
Toilets independently			
Blows and wipes nose independently			

Behavior sampling condenses the narrative record into small segments for easier recording. There are two major kinds of behavior sampling: one that focuses on time and the other on events. A *time sampling*, for instance, can help teachers see what kinds of play occur in their group. By breaking the record into timed segments and common play categories, they can efficiently capture what is happening.

Using Figure 4.4, a teacher can scan the room every 15 minutes and make note of how many children were engaged in each type of play. At

Figure 4.4 Time Sampling of Children's Play

Time sampling is one kind of observational behavior sampling. Teachers usually include an "interpretation" segment to add their conclusions and expertise to the record.

Time	Onlooker	Solitary	Parallel	Associative	Cooperative
9:00 a.m.	IIII	III	II	I	
9:15 a.m.	II	III	III	I	I
9:30 a.m.	I	II	III	II	II
9:45 a.m.		II	II	III	III
10:00 a.m.	I	II	II	II	III

Interpretation: *Children seem to "warm up" over the hour of play, engaging in more interactive play as time goes on. Should we invite children to join activities more, or is this pattern developmentally "on target" for this group at this time of the year? Let's observe where these activities take place, and consider rearrangements.*

the end of the play period, the team would then have a record of what happened in each time period. Further, they could look for patterns that may emerge to give them direction on what they might change or adapt. What patterns do you see in Figure 4.4, and what might this tell you about the effect of time during a free play period?

Event sampling is similar to behavior sampling: recording data on a sheet that is used for a predetermined event, as in Figure 4.5. Teachers can go about their ordinary work, picking up their sheets to record important data only when the event occurs. This technique is often used when teachers want to find out what is really happening in a problem situation. For instance, student teacher Michelle's team wondered why there seemed to be fighting in the classroom before circle time. They asked Michelle to observe this transition every day for a week. She made an event sampling sheet that noted the time the fight started, who was involved, what was said during the quarrel, how it was resolved, and the duration of the entire

Figure 4.5 Event Sampling of Children's Fighting

To look for a pattern or understand children's behavior better, teachers may choose an event sampling observation method.

Observer: *Michelle*
Children observed: *Kid's Club After-School Care*
Children's ages: *5–7 years; Kinders; Grades 1 & 2*
Observation context: *After snack & before circle time*
Date of observation: *February 8*
Time begun and ended: *3:15–4:00 p.m.*

Time	Children	Place/Material	Cause	Outcome
3:15 p.m.	Sam, Hiro	Computer	Both want a turn	Teacher makes waiting list
3:25 p.m.	Jamie, Chris	Homework table	Pencil fight	Teacher brings pencil box
3:50 p.m.	Jamie, Sam	Jigsaw puzzle	Fight over pieces	Teacher holds pieces until they decide what to do
3:55 p.m.	Jamie, Sam	Same place	Flinging pieces	Teacher sends them to block area
3:58 p.m.	Jamie, Sam	Block area	Grabbing blocks	Teacher hands them each a block to put away

Interpretation: *The same four children were involved in nearly every outbreak. Let's choose two to shadow next week and listen closer. They may need modeling or prompts with conflict resolution.*

---

sequence. What do you think they discovered when they analyzed the results on Friday?

Interpreting What You See

Children do more than we observe, and much more than we can ever record. However, to really see children, we must practice observing them carefully and be planful about documenting what we see. As you focus your attention, you will discover the complexity of children's development, their personalities, and what influences them. To observe and record well, these three guides are helpful:

1. *Begin to recognize your own biases.* Ming discovered that loud and destructive behavior distressed her, and she had begun to feel negative about the group of older boys that reveled in building and crashing block towers indoors and played active superhero games in the yard. By recording their behavior and talking over her interpretations with her mentor teacher, Ming began to address her attitude regarding what was typical 4-year-old behavior but which she had been taught was unacceptable in her culture (although more for girls than boys, she noted).

2. *Get familiar with the tools of observation and documentation.* Yuri had worked in a private center that engaged only in informal notes. His student teaching site was a publicly funded program that required annual child portfolios to be developed in the fall and updated in the spring. By learning to observe and record children's behavior—including taking photos and video clips—Yuri added to his teaching skills and his own professional development.

3. *Decide what to do with the information gathered.* Notice the questions at the bottom of the observation form in Figure 4.2. Once a teacher has made an objective and accurate observation, the next step is to consider its significance and implications. Think carefully about what children "teach" us with their behavior. Their strengths and interests can be used to build curriculum. What is challenging to them can also be woven into classroom experiences. And the unique flavors of each child are ready to permeate the environment, if only we notice and use them well.

What is the next step? Observing and recording children's behavior takes a lot of effort. Interpretation needs to be part of the learning process for teachers, too. Make the process meaningful by tying it into your ongoing work with children, rather than recording behavior and then saving it for a conference or formal assessment later. By reflecting on what you see, you gain insights that will help you work with them.

- Look for behavior that is repeated.
- Look for circumstances under which repeated behavior occurs.
- Ask yourself how the observed behavior is affecting the child's learning and relationships with others.
- Look for specific efforts the child is making to satisfy needs and accomplish developmental tasks. Are the efforts appropriate? Are they getting results?
- Listen carefully to the conversations of the child. Try to pick out the questions children ask. This will help determine what they want to know about the world around them.

Figure 4.6
Guidelines for Interpretation

By following professional guidelines for interpretation, teachers use what they observe to promote quality education and accurate information about children.

Interpretation puts the observation into perspective, making sense of what has been recorded. It helps teachers decide if they need to observe further to see the cause of a child's behavior, or if they need to make environmental and curricular changes for the child. It can serve as a springboard into action about the schedule or strategies for working with a group of children. Perhaps most important, interpretive notes add the teacher's expertise and make meaning of the observation itself. Look back on Figures 4.4 and 4.5; following the observation section you will find space for interpretation that includes analysis, evaluation, inference, and conclusions. Figure 4.6 provides guidelines for interpretation.

Figure 4.7 provides an example with both narrative observation and interpretation. Student teacher May is observing 2-year-old Frankie as he arrives at the toddler class with his mother, who is participating that day.

Narrative Observation	My Interpretation
F. sits at art table, points to pen & looks at mom. He takes it and begins to color on the table. Mom gives him another pen, and paper; he colors on that. The pen then drops to the floor, he says "Uh-oh" and looks under the table, then sits back up. He picks up another pen and tries to color on the table again. Mom asks if he is all done; he shakes his head no. He looks at the other children at the table, continues to color on the table. He leans over and colors on 2 children's papers. He puts the cap on, then takes it off again. Repeats twice, struggling with getting it on securely. He looks to his mom and grunts as if to ask her.	Is he trying to get her attention? Does he know how to use the pens on paper already? His grasp of the pen makes me wonder about his level of experience with this media. What is his relationship with his mother and their usual level or kind of communication? What is his level of language development? I don't hear any words to know his articulation or speech level. He appears to find this activity appealing but frustrating. He seems intrigued and not sure why the cap is not going on. I need to ask my mentor teacher about Frankie's level of development in ALL domains!

Figure 4.7
Narrative Observation and Interpretation: 2-Year-Old Frankie and His Mother

Observing and Assessing Children

Assessment

In the last two decades, education in the United States has undergone a shift toward standards-based teaching at nearly all levels. With learning standards for children come processes for checking the progress toward those goals.

> Policymakers, the early childhood profession, and other stakeholders in young children's lives have a shared responsibility to . . . make ethical, appropriate, valid and reliable assessment a central part of all early childhood programs. To assess young children's strengths, progress, and needs, use assessment methods that are developmentally appropriate, culturally and linguistically responsive, tied to children's daily activities, supported by professional development, inclusive of families and connected to specific, beneficial purposes: (1) making sound decisions about teaching and learning; (2) identifying significant concerns that may require focused intervention for individual children; and (3) helping programs improve their educational and developmental interventions. (Hyson, 2003, p. 9)

Check with your program for its goals and assessment plan to define and then monitor what children are to know and be able to do.

Assessing Early Development

Assessment is "the process of gathering information about children from several forms of evidence, then organizing and interpreting that information" (McAfee, Leong, & Bodrova, 2010). Figure 4.8 offers the top 10 characteristics of good child assessment.

Older children may be able to demonstrate their knowledge in structured, test-like conditions, whereas younger children, who have a limited repertoire of behaviors that can be assessed, are best studied through observation. Young children express themselves in actions more than in words, so a test situation may not reveal much of what they know. Unlike older children and adults, young children do not set aside or hide their feelings, or substitute for emotions with other socially approved behaviors, so observing them in action will likely yield more accurate information.

Assessment of children's skills must include regular observation and recording of their behavior in their natural setting.

1. It is an ongoing process.
2. It cannot be based on what is wrong with a child.
3. It must be authentic and cannot be based on tests in artificial situations.
4. It must be based on what you see, not what you think you should observe or the child should be doing, and it must have meaningful artifacts and work samples.
5. It must be diversified with multiple measures—that is, it cannot be based on a single observation or situation.
6. It must state the facts, not interpretations, judgments, or conclusions.
7. It must be confidential, with note-taking materials kept handy but easily set aside.
8. It must have an interpretive piece based on your expertise to put it in perspective.
9. It must be based on your center or program learning standards.
10. It needs to raise relevant issues that require action.

Figure 4.8
Top 10 Characteristics of Quality Child Assessment
Incorporating these characteristics into your child observation and assessment plans will ensure accuracy without unnecessary interference.

Early development is subject to a wide range of individual variation. For example, while the onset of walking averages at 12 months, the range is 9 to 18 months. Many children try to walk holding a hand, while others prefer to crawl without assistance. Since muscle strength, maturation of the brain's motor cortex, and practice must combine to enable toddlers to walk, it is no wonder there is great variation. Children who are carried or pushed in strollers may get less practice than those who log in hours on the floor. They will all walk, but at different rates of development. Variation in timing is normal.

Child Assessment Systems

Because using systematic observation has become an important part of a classroom staff's daily responsibilities, student teachers will need to become acquainted with the many child assessment systems used in contemporary programs. One practicum class was polled about how the centers assessed children. Responses included the following:

- An initial assessment within 45 days of enrollment
- A home visit, family conference, and individual learning plan within the first semester
- Biannual anecdotal assessment done in fall and spring
- Narrative assessment by parent request only
- Spring prekindergarten motor and language checklist

Gabriela found that her center's assessment process was at first overwhelming; see her reaction over time in the My Reaction feature that follows.

Good assessment tools will define the behaviors to be observed and provide space for teachers to write what they see that describes the specific

> ## *My Reaction*
>
> ### "From Observing and Documenting to Portfolios and Curriculum to Me!"
>
> I talked with my supervising teacher today about child observation and assessment. I was quite overwhelmed with all the information that I received about the process. I assumed it to be a complex process, but—oh man—I didn't think it would be this much work!
>
> In summary, each teacher observes a designated group of children in four basic areas of development (physical-motor, cognitive and language, socioemotional, and creative). The three of them can use their preferred method of observation, but they have to create a portfolio for each child. Along with their notes, they include children's work and photographs to capture a thorough picture.
>
> But this is not the end! The head teacher writes a final summary of findings and completes group summaries that show how the class is doing as a group. They use this to plan curriculum. Whew! Just explaining the process was exhausting!
>
> So how do I take my skills to the next level? When my teacher observes me, she documents the children's responses to my directions and interaction. Since I'm working on small-group activities, she records what happens there, and then debriefs me by going over together what she saw. It inspires me to try to get some of this down on paper myself. You sure can use these skills everywhere.
>
> —GABRIELA

learning goal. For example, the state of California has identified four goals, or desired results, for children in publicly funded programs:

- Children are personally and socially competent.
- Children are effective learners.
- Children have physical and motor competence.
- Children are healthy and safe.

The assessment tool, called the Desired Results Developmental Profile (DRDP-R), further articulates the behaviors for each desired result, described in terms of the various age groups (infant/toddler, preschool, kindergarten, primary). Both public and private centers have adopted this tool or have adapted their own assessments to parallel these results. One program used the tool to develop a method of documenting levels of competence within each category, leaving room for the observer to note the date it was observed and requiring anecdotal notes to be attached that validate the rating. A few of the areas can be seen in Figure 4.9.

Figure 4.9 Sample Child Assessment Competencies Form

One example of a child assessment is an adaptation of California's Preschool Desired Results Developmental Profile (Revised) for Personal & Social Competencies.

Personal and Social Competencies			
Exploring	**Developing**	**Building**	**Integrating**
Self-Concept: Identity of Self			
Shows recognition of self as individual, recognizing own name and names of familiar people	Describes self or others in terms of basic physical characteristics	Describes self and others in terms of preferences	Accurately compares self to others
Date:			
Self-Concept: Recognition of Own Skills and Accomplishments			
Shows interest and/or pleasure when someone reacts to something he or she has done	Characterizes self positively in terms of specific activity that he or she is doing or has just finished	Characterizes positively own skills involved in doing a task	Characterizes self positively in terms of generalized ability or skills
Date:			
Social Interpersonal Skills: Expressions of Empathy			
Shows awareness when others are unhappy or upset	Offers simple assistance when he or she thinks it is needed—even if not really needed	Accurately labels own and others' feelings	Uses words or actions to demonstrate concern for what others are feeling
Date:			
Social Interpersonal Skills: Building Cooperative Relationships with Adults			
Seeks interaction with familiar adult for company, help, or comfort	Attempts to establish a relationship with an adult by cooperating and interacting	Seeks to share experience or get information from adults	Works cooperatively with an adult to plan and organize activities and to solve problems
Date:			
Social Interpersonal Skills: Developing Friendships			
Interacts with another child side by side as they play with similar materials	Names another child as a friend or seeks out a particular child with whom to play	Engages in social games and pretend play with a particular child	Prefers to play with a particular child who also expresses preference for him or her
Date:			

Source: From Mary Meta Lazarus Child Development Center, San Mateo, CA. Used with permission.

As we conclude this section, we wish to emphasize again that observations are the backbone of assessment. Whether you are a preservice or a paid intern, you are involved in discovering the development, strengths, and challenges of a group of children in your care. So much can be done with accurate observations: You will be more effective in guidance, more able to create environments and schedules to suit the group, better prepared to plan curriculum, and far better suited to assess their skills if you hone your observation skills now during your student teaching.

Cautions About Evaluations

Authentic assessment can capture who the child is. To do this, it must occur in a variety of settings, over time, drawing on many sources of information. As the teacher, you observe and then record what you decide is significant. You are making a choice about what to record, and this is based on what you value. Anyone involved in evaluating children should appreciate the challenge and try to avoid the following pitfalls (adapted from Gordon & Browne, 2011):

- *Unfair comparisons*. Do not use assessments to compare children with one another in a competitive manner.
- *Bias*. Evaluations can label unfairly or prematurely the very people for whom they are intended.

To be authentic, information is gathered over a period of time through multiple observations.

- *Overemphasis on norms.* Remember to individualize the process rather than try to fit a child into the mold created by the assessment tool.

- *Interpretation.* There is sometimes a tendency to overinterpret or misinterpret results.

- *Too narrow a perspective.* Sampling only children's skills as the single measure would lead to conclusions that are neither reliable nor valid.

- *Too wide a range.* It is appropriate to measure a child's ability to print at age 6 but not at age 2.

- *Too little or too much time.* The evaluation that is too lengthy loses its effectiveness in the time it takes.

Think about these issues as you read about the standards movement in the following section.

A Pressure Cooker

In the United States, federal funding for education comes primarily from the Elementary and Secondary Education Act (originally passed in 1965, with regular reauthorization from Congress). In the last decade, there has been a systematic focus on closing the achievement gap between disadvantaged and minority students and their more privileged peers through legislation titled No Child Left Behind (NCLB). Major provisions of the act pertaining to early childhood include the following:

1. Adequate annual progress must be monitored, as evidenced by testing of reading and math (with a third area left to states' choice) at third grade.
2. All teachers must have a B.A. degree and be state certified in their assigned teaching level.
3. Reading and literacy are highly funded with the goal of all children achieving grade-level reading proficiency by third grade.

Many educators worry that these provisions are creating an unbalanced curriculum and too much time and focus on testing. Such pressure can trickle down to earlier grades in elementary school and even into programs for preschoolers. Early learning standards could result in any of the following:

- Lead to teaching to the standards only in a cookie-cutter-style curriculum. Then, the uniqueness of early childhood education is lost.
- Bring a pressure of accountability with the risk of a push-down in curriculum and inappropriate expectations for younger children. (Gronlund, p. 23)

Developmentally appropriate practices indicate a broader curriculum emphasis on the whole child and play; moreover, developmentally appropriate practice (DAP) and child development knowledge imply that our assessment practices avoid inappropriate testing.

Assessing Children with Disabilities

Although in many ways children are more alike than different, watching and working with them exposes the many ways in which children are diverse. Developmental theory tells us that, although development is predictable and follows a sequence, individual children will grow at different rates and will display a range of temperaments and learning styles. In addition, genetic and environmental differences can be seen. Student teachers often wonder if the differences are evidence of special needs.

Public educational policy since 1975 entitles everyone from 3 to 21 years of age to a free and appropriate public education and states that every child with a disability be educated in the least restrictive environment (Allen & Cowdery, 2011). In addition, parents may bring concerns about a child's development to the teacher's attention. Equally likely is the possibility that teachers will observe unusual behavior within the context of school. Therefore, student teachers will probably see a range of both typical and atypical behaviors in their practicum sites (DEC & NAEYC, 2009). This can pose a challenge, as seen in the Ethical Dilemma that follows.

Early Diagnosis and Intervention. When a child's behavior or skills are different from those of other children of their age, it may be an indication of undiagnosed special needs. Observation and documentation are the first steps in the assessment process. Student teachers are not diagnosticians; however, as in the Ethical Dilemma feature, they provide a critical first step in recognizing that a problem might exist. Sharing observations and insights with the family, and then a physician or therapist, plays an important role in the child's program. Parental consent must be obtained for teachers to consult directly with a professional or outside agency, and sensitivity and confidentiality are essential.

Whereas most teaching staff are not trained in special education testing, many programs may use some kind of tool to determine if and how a child has mastered developmental milestones. Figure 4.10 is a sample child questionnaire that might be used to describe atypical development.

"What's Wrong with Him?"

Valeria has joined the ongoing preschool class midyear for her semester of student teaching. After getting settled and working there the first month, she notices one child who is at or above developmental levels in all domains except language. "What's wrong with him?" she asks. Head teacher Tobias works one on one with child and in small group work and agrees that the child is at least 1 year developmentally delayed in language. It is time to call the parents in for a conference, and Tobias wants Valeria there. What should she do?

Code References: *Section I: Ideal-1.7* To use assessment information to understand and support children's development and learning, to support instruction, and to identify children who may need additional services.

Principle 1.4 We shall involve all those with relevant knowledge (including families and staff)

in decisions concerning a child, as appropriate, ensuring confidentiality of sensitive information.

Resolution: Valeria's observations are part of the assessment process in documenting the child's language level, as are the notes and informal assessments Tobias has made. At first, Dad is devastated to hear his child isn't perfect. Mom says that she remembers the child swallowing meconium during childbirth, and wonders about any long-term effects. Tobias has come to the meeting with a list of resources for having the child assessed for speech and language, but everybody agrees to begin with the pediatrician. The physician diagnoses a significant hearing loss, fits the child with hearing aids, and prescribes a speech therapist. Valeria is lauded for her observational skills and understanding of typical development as well as markers of possible problems that she learned during her college work.

A Child's Portfolio

Many early childhood educators have embraced the idea that a portfolio of children's work samples and teacher assessments is an excellent way to document individual learning and faithfully capture the child's development. If your practicum site creates child portfolios, ask to see one. Look for a collection plan, and check how the work samples are stored and organized. Make a note of how teacher commentary is incorporated into the portfolio, and how it is shared with families or other professionals.

During the past few years in my teaching career, I find myself adjusting my assessment system to work optimally with my work load. I use a portfolio assessment system whose categories are based on the state standards. I rely on my teaching team to help collect and analyze the data for the portfolios. Novice teachers or teachers who are instituting an assessment system for the first time, tend to provide short, simple observations and sometimes have difficulty interpreting the data while more seasoned teachers tend to have more detailed documentation with reflective evaluations. (Wiggins-Dowler, unpublished personal correspondence, 2009)

Figure 4.10
Sensory Regulation
and Social Interaction:
A Rating Scale

Source: From *Floortime: DVD Training Series: Sensory Regulation and Social Interaction*, by S. Greenspan and S. Wieder, 2006, Bethesda, MD: Interdisciplinary Council on Developmental and Learning Disorders. Used with permission.

Use the following questionnaire to determine which milestones your child has mastered and which still need work. Use the rating scale to rate your child in each one, as he or she is now. If the skill is always present, record at what age it was mastered.

Rating scale: N = ability never present; S = ability sometimes present; A = ability always present; L = child loses ability under stress (hunger, anger, fatigue, etc.)

Milestone: Purposeful Emotional Interactions (4–9 months)		
Ability	**Current Rating**	**Age Mastered**
1. Responds to your gestures with intentional gestures (e.g., reaches out in response to your outstretched arms, returns your vocalizing or look)		
2. Initiates interactions with you (e.g., reaches for your nose or hair or for a toy; raises arms to be picked up)		
3. Demonstrates the following emotions: • Closeness (e.g., hugs back when hugged, reaches out to be picked up) • Pleasure and excitement (e.g., smiles joyfully while putting a finger in your mouth or while taking a toy from your mouth and putting it in own) • Assertive curiosity (e.g., touches and explores your hair) • Protest or anger (e.g., pushes food off the table or screams when desired toy not brought) • Fear (e.g., turns away, looks scared, or cries when a stranger approaches too quickly)		
4. Recovers from distress within 10 minutes by being involved in social interactions		

Student teachers often find documenting children's learning overwhelming. Student teacher Gordon found that "my biggest challenge in engaging in the assessment process was learning the assessment terminology and also learning the sequential process of how to get from point A to B to C and that the process builds on itself. It reminds me of, 'Now that I have my driver's license, how do I drive?'"

Portfolios present an image of each child as a competent learner who actively constructs knowledge within a social and cultural context. What is visible is the child's classroom history and learning, complete with a window into temperaments, styles, strengths, interests, and disposition. Molly and Luisa's mother offers this note:

> The portfolios that Karen created for my two children remain among my very most treasured possessions. This record of all the different parts of their emotional and cognitive growth gave me such a clear picture of how they were developing, and let me into their inner world. The contents of the portfolios were so helpful during our parent–teacher conferences in expanding the connection between what was happening at school and what I could be doing at home to provide reinforcement. At the time, I never thought I'd forget any of "those moments," but now that my children are in grade school, I regularly pull out their portfolios to show other parents "what they were like when they were little." I love them! (Wiggins-Dowler, unpublished correspondence, 2009)

Check with your supervising teacher about the learning standards and assessment tools in your site. Ask yourself these questions:

1. *What is their purpose?* Legitimate needs are to support learning, identify special needs, and monitor program quality.

2. *What methods are used?* Appropriate methods include observation, samples of children's work, teachers' anecdotes, and documentation.

3. *What resources are available?* These include materials for parents and for you to learn about how to deal with concerns and also to work with children who have identified special needs in your program.

Remember, just as it takes practice to improve observation skills, it takes time and reflection to identify, define, and understand a variety of assessment techniques and to analyze how they can be used to measure specific child and program goals. Still, it is essential to assess children. To help children grow and learn, we need to know exactly who they are and where they are in their development. Frequent observations, accurate recording, and clear documentation help us get up close and personal with the children. "Observing and assessing is not just about being a good teacher, it's about serving the children—our observations and assessments should be used to benefit them, not just so we can call ourselves good teachers, [but also] it helps us help the children" (Yuen, 2009, personal correspondence).

We end the chapter as we began: Children are fascinating. Learning to observe and assess their growth and development is a fundamental part of becoming a competent teacher, and this takes time to master, as described in the "Lessons from the Field" that follows. Practice makes better, so incorporate regular observation and documentation into your daily student teaching.

"My Personal Journey into the Land of Child Assessment"

by Kären Wiggins-Dowler

Mentor Teacher, Mary Meta Lazarus Child Development Center

My journey as an early childhood educator has kept me constantly revisiting the concept of assessment and documentation and how to best facilitate an appropriate assessment system. As a new teacher, I viewed assessment as a necessary requirement to fulfill my duties and responsibilities as a teacher. During my first year of teaching, I was given a checklist to fill out on each child. I relished the fact that checklists are easy to comprehend and quick to fill out without much mental debate. Get the children to perform certain tasks, record their responses, and then, at a future date, inform the parents as to the progress of their child.

Without much formal training, I successfully replicated my own "report card" experiences and used the checklist as a framework for my parent–teacher conferences. The assessment tool exuded power in the simple declarations of can she/he do or not do, know or not know. As a new teacher, this brought me a sense of security and relief, especially as it related to talking with parents. One of my mentors, Jennifer, a seasoned teacher of several years, remembered her parent–teacher conferences at the beginning of her career: "I wasn't so honest about negative behavior due to fear of parental actions. I didn't have the ability to internalize; everything was so external. After years of experience I now know how to approach parents when talking about child concerns in a non-blaming manner. I also now do a disclaimer for the paperwork. The assessment list that I use is just a theoretical benchmark of growth that doesn't take into account the individualism of your child."

After several years of gaining confidence in my abilities as a teacher, I began to feel that the assessment tools that I had been using were inadequate in revealing who each child was. I also hated the feelings associated with an assessment system based on a *deficit model* . . . is the child able or not able to perform, know, or do? Growing up, I myself never performed well on tests, and I spent much of my energy trying to make the grade instead of engaging more deeply in the learning experience. Life would be so much better without the stress of tests! I found myself starting to read articles and books about assessment, testing, and different ways to document children's growth. I laugh at myself now when I think back to the beginning of my teaching career—I would have never guessed that I would be interested in testing and assessments.

So, how was I going to adequately represent the child? The more I stood back and observed the children under my care, the more I realized that my role as a teacher included being an anthropologist and a historian. What the children were learning and how they were learning it needed to be documented more fully with the due respect that the children's efforts deserved. Finishing his practicum experience, Gordon remarked that "it was a joy getting inside a *child's* world. Through the observations I noticed the little subtleties and nuances that I just would not see without taking the time to observe. I now understand the significance of this information for them as individuals and for the program. Now my eyes are open all the time. My problem now is to develop the knowledge of what to record and what not to record."

Another student teacher, Lisa, said, "I had the absolute luxury of only observing one child without any other responsibilities." Honing in on your observational skills is one thing; try the observational challenge of a classroom of 24 children.

Scores do not reflect the uniqueness, knowledge, skills, and dispositions of each child. What

I needed to do was to collect more data and work samples in order to develop a more complete picture of each child. Making close observations of children had to become a part of my regular classroom behavior because trying to recall details at the end of the day was next to impossible due to mental exhaustion. Tiana, a new teacher, reflects that she finds "it difficult to pull back and write observations because it interrupts my relationship with the child." This comment reminds me of my own concern with the development of optimal teacher–child interrelationships during my initial teaching years.

Many years later, I now perform a balancing act of interacting with the children and then stepping back to make written observations. With the intense daily coordination of two dozen children, families, and a team of teachers, I find that these written observations, pictures, and work samples provide me with the necessary details to reveal and to understand the development of each child. A well-planned and ongoing system of observations and work samplings informs us how a child learns, what stage of development that he/she is at, how the child develops relationships with peers and adults, what are the child's interests, strengths, and dispositions, what will be our next steps with the child, and are we, as teachers, actually accomplishing our program goals and objectives.

When this system is incorporated into the classroom culture, even the children feel its importance. I once had a 4-year-old child approach me and insist, "Support me!" I asked, "Support you? What does that mean?" He replied, "Write down what I'm doing. It's important!"

So where does my journey go from here? I am working on refining my techniques to include data from the beginning, middle, and end of the learning experiences that the children are involved in so that I can focus more on the learning process of each child. I also want to develop more analytical systems in order to help others use the portfolio system more efficiently. As Lillian Katz said, "No one was ever born an expert." This is a lifelong journey of learning, and it still intrigues me. Also, if you have any suggestions about how to get more hours out of every day, please let me know! I am up to the test!

Practicum Activity

Bring to the practicum the assessment tools that your center uses for assessment. Compare them with those from other centers. Which ones do you like (and why)? Which ones have problems, and what are they? Make a chart together, compiling the forms, their purpose, and a joint list of their assets and liabilities.

Journaling Assignment

Write about how your center assesses children. Be sure to ask your supervising teacher about the goals, strengths, and challenges the team sees in this effort.

References

Allen, K. E., & Cowdery, G. E. (2011). *The exceptional child: Inclusion in early childhood education* (7th ed.). Belmont, CA: Wadsworth/Cengage.

Beaty, J. J. (2009). *Observing development of the young child* (7th ed.). Upper Saddle River, NJ: Merrill/Pearson.

DEC & NAEYC. (2009). *Early childhood inclusion: A joint statement of the Division of Early Childhood (DEC) and the National Association for the Education of Young Children (NAEYC).* Washington, DC: Authors.

Gordon, A. M., & Browne, K. W. (2011). *Beginnings and beyond: Foundations in early childhood education* (8th ed.). Belmont, CA: Wadsworth Cengage Learning.

Greenspan, S., & Wieder, S. (2006). *Floortime: DVD Training Series: Sensory Regulation and Social Interaction.* Bethesda, MD: Interdisciplinary Council on Developmental and Learning Disorders.

Gronlund, G. (2006). *Make early learning standards come alive.* St. Paul, MN: Redleaf Press.

Hyson, M. (Ed.). (2003). *Preparing early childhood professionals: NAEYC's standards for programs.* Washington, DC: National Association for the Education of Young Children.

McAfee, O., Leong, D., & Bodrova, E. (2010). *Assessing and guiding children's development and learning* (5th ed.). Upper Saddle River, NJ: Pearson.

Wiggins-Dowler, Karen (2009). Unpublished personal correspondence.

Yuen, Kim (2009). Personal correspondence.

Web Sites

Council for Exceptional Children
www.cec.sped.org

National Association for the Education of Young Children
www.naeyc.org

National Center for Research on Evaluation, Standards, and Student Testing (CRESST)
www.cresst.org

National Institute for Early Education Research
www.nieer.org

chapter 5

Environments and Schedules

LEARNING OUTCOME

Identify the components of effective environments and schedules to create positive learning experiences for children.

Two fundamental aspects of developmentally appropriate programs for children are the environment and daily schedule. When creating environments and schedules for young children, teachers must take a realistic look at what they have to work with—and with whom they need to collaborate—to make the best of what is at hand. The first part of this chapter introduces you to the basic elements of environments, and the second offers key points for schedules.

Environments for Early Childhood Programs

Early education teachers think about the physical environment as a key ingredient when planning program and curriculum for young children. The environment is a powerful teaching tool, for children in the early years are sensitive to the world around them and take cues and lessons from what is offered to them both indoors and outdoors, all day long, and while they are with you and everyone else.

Considerations

Ask your supervising teacher what to consider when creating the indoor and outdoor space. Chances are, teachers are very aware of the limitations: Your program may be in a church basement, a portable trailer, or space intended for other uses. Resources are usually limited, and the environment is often not optimal for young children. Still, early childhood teachers can be creative, flexible, and innovative in how they use the space they have.

Using the space they have, quality school programs strive to become models of effective and joyful places of learning for children and adults.

Physical Plant. How can you make the setting beautiful and inviting? The environment may be a powerful teaching tool, but it is also a place where children experience their childhoods and where teachers live their professional lives. We give meaning to the spaces in our lives, and in turn we are deeply influenced by them.

One influential program model in environmental and schedule design is that of Reggio Emilia. Developed in Italy in the mid-20th century, the Reggio approach builds on Italian community values of esthetics and creativity, and its philosophy grows out of attention to beauty and the creative process. The environment reflects these priorities in several ways: Visual appeal to both children and adults is a primary consideration in how space is arranged. Often an area or room is set aside specifically for artwork (see the Lessons from the Field feature about an atelier). Time periods and experiences are arranged so that children can deeply study objects and space and make creations that reflect their thinking.

Environments for various types of programs have unique spaces, resources, and program goals. At the same time, every physical plant must be created with children in mind. First, you must rescale the space to fit their size. A good way to do this is to get on your knees at the door and look around at what the children will see. For infants and toddlers, the floor is where their primary activity takes place; preschoolers are able to reach low shelves and tables; school-age children can make use of higher cupboards and counters.

In the United States, each state sets its own standards for the licensing of educational centers; often this responsibility is given to smaller regions or counties. The National Academy of Early Childhood Programs (a division of the National Association for the Education of Young Children) recommends a minimum of 35 square feet of usable playroom floor space indoors per child and 75 square feet of play space outdoors per child (Ritchie & Willer, 2008). Check with your local area for its requirements for physical space. At the same time, look at how the space functions when in use, not only square footage. Spaces that are insufficient or in poor repair can lead to conflicts among children, materials becoming disorganized, and tensions among staff (Cryer, Harms, & Riley, 2003). A safe, clean, attractive, and spacious environment is the goal.

Program Goals. Before placing furniture or stocking shelves, teachers must think about their goals for children. Social interaction is a likely goal; therefore, the environment will need to be arranged so that children can play together. Small tables near shelves of toys and spaces that are protected from constant intrusion will suit this purpose better than rows of desks or wide-open areas that invite running more than focused connections. See if you can infer the goals of your program from the room and yard arrangement.

An educational focus is an important part of a program's goals. One such goal is a *self-help* focus. A community supermarket is a good example

Good environments for children promote cultural diversity and anti-bias sensitivity by providing a variety of clothing, dishes, and other materials for children to experience.

of a self-help, or self-reliant, environment because the shelves are set so customers can reach and select for themselves. Some stores now have self-help checkout areas as well. An early childhood self-help environment will have toys on reachable shelves marked with pictures or names of the items, and tables or floor space nearby. Easels are set up for children to put on an apron, paint jars are already in a tray, and a drying rack is nearby with pins that children can use to hang their paintings.

Another example of an educational goal is the *anti-bias* approach in which the focus is for children to learn tolerance and acceptance of diversity. These environments reflect a variety of styles in family life; for instance, the house corner is likely to have woks, tortilla presses, and pasta rollers as well as soup pots and frying pans. Dress-up clothes will go beyond a business suit or party dress to include dashikis, sarongs, and other items worn by diverse families.

Health, Safety, and Connectedness. "Our designs shape children's beliefs about themselves and life. In a well-designed area, children are engaged and feel secure. A well-designed area can facilitate predictable, consistent and intimate care for each child" (Olds, 2000). These basic considerations hold for every early childhood environment. Regardless of program philosophy or physical plant, the teaching staff keeps in mind these four areas as fundamental priorities. Providing for children's health and safety is essential:

- Keeping children healthy involves sanitation, temperature, ventilation, lighting, and proper nutrition.
- Keeping communicable disease at a minimum includes strong practices and good health assessment of children and adults.
- Guarding children's safety involves creating a hazard-free environment that still offers challenges and risks, and monitoring for potential problems as well as being prepared to administer first aid and deal with natural disasters.
- Handling vehicle safety includes attention to arrival and departure places and routines as well as transportation on field trips.

Finally, maintaining children's well-being involves setting the emotional tone, preserving children's play (see Chapter 6), and addressing threats to children both in the program and beyond, such as at home or in their community. In particular, infants and toddlers should be in programs that practice "continuity of care" (WestEd, 2009); that is, that each teacher is a primary caregiver of a few individuals and continues with those children throughout their care until preschool age.

Children who are emotionally connected to the "important others" in their lives—including you as their student teacher—will be better able to take advantage of what an early childhood environment has to offer.

Planning Space

The Prepared Environment. A phrase Maria Montessori coined over a century ago, the *prepared environment* describes a wealth of ideas about the physical space and materials as the key to children's educational experiences. Child-size furniture, a sense of order, a place for everything, and materials accessible to children are all hallmarks of the Montessori influence (Montessori, 1967).

Although you will encounter a variety of places and spaces in early childhood programs, there are some key elements that all good early educational environments will share. Activity areas should be located for predictability and flow, with boundaries that include ways to move within and between them, with freedom to explore and privacy (Community Playthings, 2012). Organizing a room and yard can be facilitated by referring to the figures in this chapter as well as the well-known and researched environmental rating scales (Harms, Clifford, & Cryer, 2005) that outline the kinds of arrangements that work well for play, privacy, and routines.

In addition, the following key dimensions, outlined decades ago, are still basic considerations when planning indoor and outdoor space (Prescott, Jones, & Kritschevsky, 1972):

- Soft (pillows, grass) and hard (tile floors, cement)
- Open (dress-up clothes, sand) and closed (puzzles, slide)
- Simple (climber) and complex (with slides and ropes)
- Intrusion (blocks area) and seclusion (loft)
- High mobility (trike lanes) and low mobility (board games table)

Look at your environment with an eye for these environmental components and key dimensions. Chances are, the better they match up, the more functional and productive the children's play and learning become.

Positive Behavior. Children's positive behavior can be enhanced by attending to the physical environment. It is said that the environment is the children's third teacher (Dodge & Colker, 2010). The physical space communicates to children about where they can go, what they can and cannot do, even how they are to behave. For instance, leaving a large open space in the center of the room may invite preschool wrestling; reconfiguring it into several areas for small groups encourages children to choose and stay in an area. The 2-year-olds who pull all the lids off marking pens are also the young children who enjoy pushing the pens back into the lids that are affixed to the bottom of a pen tray (Gonzalez-Mena & Eyer, 2008). School-age children who see sign-up sheets near the computers and the ball room are more likely to engage in an orderly process than if there are no environmental cues about how to get a turn.

Adapt and Accommodate. This best describes what early childhood professionals do to provide productive environments for children. Few programs have a perfect environment. Moreover, as soon as children enter a space, their teachers find themselves making changes so that the group and each individual can succeed (see the "My Reaction" feature). Other circumstances, such as weather, scheduling problems, staffing changes, even unexpected guests, mean that teachers need to add adapting and accommodating to their outlook. Young children are new to the world and easily overwhelmed; when changes occur, it is easier for the adult to adapt. When Mike comes to school announcing his displeasure about his new sister, you may need to adapt the dramatic play area by adding some dolls and baby bottles, and accommodate this "big feeling" by locating books about becoming a big brother for the library area.

Adapting the environment is one of the first components for including children with special needs. For instance, the condition of cerebral palsy is usually caused by a lack of oxygen to the brain that results in permanent but nonprogressive damage to the motor center of the brain. If the child is in a wheelchair, doorways and floor space between areas need to be broad enough, and the outdoors must be accessible, including a special harness and adapted trike if possible. As for what happens in the space, Paasche et al. (2004) recommend the following:

- Give the child as many life experiences as possible, such as handling animals and taking trips.
- Work with all different media (play dough, clay, sand, water, finger paint).
- Develop activities that foster playing together and will support learning to share and take turns such as doll center opportunities, using and interacting with puppets, dress-up clothes.
- Encourage use of hands: grasping, balancing, and manipulating small toy materials such as small blocks, large pegboards, plastic fitting-together types of large toys.

The physical environment will need to be adapted as the circumstances of a day unfold. For example, the finger painting activity you had planned may need to be postponed when you are told to host a group of prospective parents and explain your program while in class; or the surprise thunderstorm cancels the planned walking field trip, and means you need to get the parachute and soft balls out onto the patio instead of simply doing a clay project.

Space is often used in many ways, so teachers find themselves adapting the environment frequently. Look at your practicum site: What is the primary use for each area of the environment? What else happens there in the course of a day or week? A countertop may start the day as a staging area for preparing materials, then for drying art projects, then for setting up snack trays—all before 10:00 a.m. The block area transforms into the area for circle time and then gets several nap cots on it for naptime. The same asphalt driveway that is the trike lane gets used for relay races and for parachute play.

Sample Environments. Looking at room and yard plans helps student teachers examine space carefully so they become more proficient in teaching young children. It is said that there are as many ways to make a school space as there are teachers to plan them. Indeed, NAEYC deliberately avoided dictating specific arrangements or yard items in its work on developmentally appropriate practices in recognition of the diversity of environments, and space challenges, in early childhood programs. Figures 5.1 to 5.4 offer a few ways to organize space for three different age groups. Compare them with your space to see what elements you have in common, and how the environments differ.

My Reaction

"Is This a Good Environment for Young Children?"

When I first walked into the classroom, I immediately focused on the small desks and chairs in a "U-shaped" formation. I was caught off-guard: Why would a structured setup be of value with 3- to 5-year-olds? Then I reconsidered with the thought that maybe the more structured setting is developmentally appropriate for these children with special needs, to keep them connected from one activity to the next. Don't get me wrong—they have tremendous activity centers for children to play together and personal cubbies to mark individual spaces for privacy. While the desks surprised me, now that I am working here I can see each child is receiving and meeting his or her personal needs and education plan.

—RACHYL

Figure 5.1
Infant and Toddler Environment

A toddler environment has safety and accessibility in mind, while helping children work in small groups so they can be maximally involved with a minimum of distraction from others.

Source: Data from Gordon & Browne (2011).

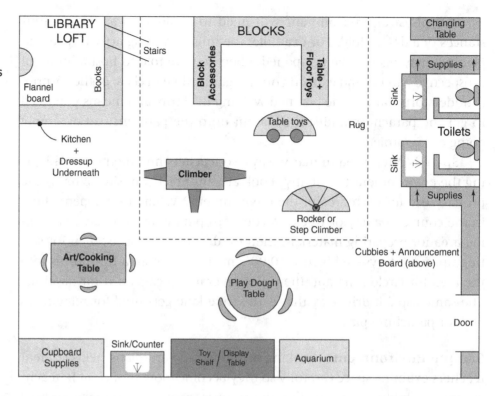

Figure 5.2
Preschool Environment

A preschool child care center needs clearly defined boundaries and obvious pathways to make it easy for children to use this space independently.

Source: Data from Gordon & Browne (2011).

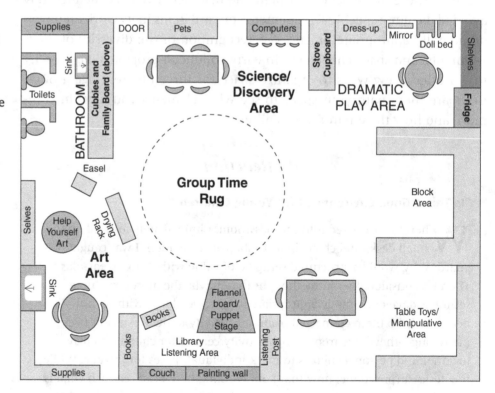

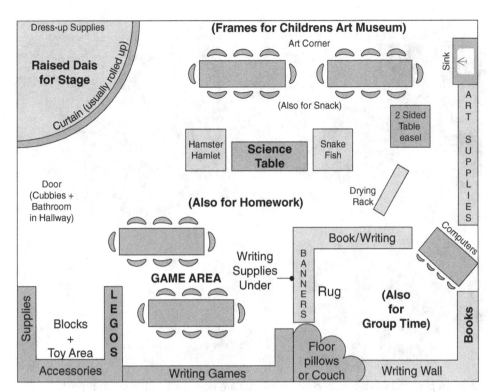

Figure 5.3
School-Age Environment

A school-age environment has learning centers to allow children to make clear choices and engage in active learning through play.

Source: Data from Gordon & Browne (2011).

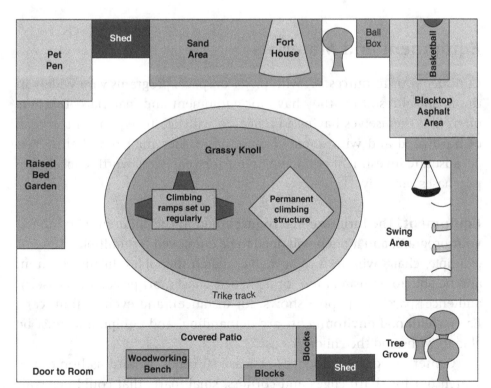

Figure 5.4
ECE Playground

A playground/yard, suitable for ages 4 and older, will give children a sense of security and adventure.

Source: Data from Gordon & Browne (2011).

Children play and work best in classrooms that are equipped with age-appropriate materials and equipment.

Equipment and Materials

Consider your resources. As with physical space, programs vary widely in the financial resources they have for equipment and materials. Teachers often find themselves having to make do with plastic equipment instead of hardwood and with donated materials rather than new items. Yet, because the investment will have to last for years, it is worth considering purchases carefully.

Equipment. The furniture in a room should fit the children who inhabit your program, and it often will need to be employed for multiple uses. For example, chairs will need to be stable, match the tables, fit the children, and be able to withstand use for activities, snacks, art projects (as easels), audience space (for puppet shows, for instance), and even as train cars. Early childhood environments are demanding, and equipment must be able to withstand the children's use.

Center use of equipment is at least 10 times as hard as home use. Watch out for sharp edges and corners, small parts that could be swallowed, and toxic finishes. Will the item be pulled or tipped over? Will it wear or break in a manner that then makes it dangerous? Does it allow for cleaning and disinfectant? Things need to be the right size and scale for all children, including those with special needs (Greenman & Stonehouse, 2007). Ample storage shelves and tote box units help staff display what is available and set aside items for rotation.

Stocking the Room or Yard. Outfitting a space happens once the furnishings are in place. It is time to put materials into the interest areas. Adequate, reachable, and labeled (with a picture) materials are vital for orderliness in every age group. All children learn through their senses and with concrete, hands-on materials. In addition, the inclusion of children with disabilities in a regular classroom has benefits for all when teachers have materials that are universal in design and that work for many levels of age and ability. Look at the activity areas in your room and yard, and think about the group of children you teach as you compare your materials list with Figure 5.5

Finally, just as the overall environment should be responsive, materials and equipment should be flexible. Offering a variety of materials to children provides them with many options for learning in their environment. For example, materials such as puzzles and self-correcting graduated cylinders can be used in only one way, so it is important to have some materials that can be used in various ways, such as blocks, construction sets, and dramatic-play items. Teachers can make equipment super-complex by providing water for dry sand, rollers and garlic presses for play dough, or different kinds of brushes for the paint jars.

Environments for the very young, as well that those in family child care, are likely to be less structured and divided into interest areas, as noted in Figure 5.1. Crawling infants and waddling toddlers need space to move and be seen, with special care to provide safe, interesting, clean materials and somewhat less concern about curriculum materials as they are described for older children. Bring interesting items to children to touch, such as a basket of scarves or your sturdy old guitar, and be ready to bring them to interesting places, such as lifting an infant to touch a mobile or bringing toddlers to watch the road being repaired outside the fence.

Reuse and Recycle. *Reuse* and *recycle* are catchwords that describe most early childhood programs. Along with the overarching goal of being mindful of the environment as a whole, and of the heavy footprint most Western habits make on the planet, early childhood educators find it necessary to stretch their budgets by being resourceful in reusing and recycling materials. One student teacher made recycling her curriculum focus, sending a letter to families with items to save and send with their children, and having them ask their children how

Figure 5.5 Basic Materials in an Early Childhood Classroom and Outdoor Playground/Yard

Although not comprehensive, this list starts to organize the environment for a variety of play, both indoors and outdoors. Note the adjustments that must be made to accommodate different ages.

Teachers organize the environment for a variety of activities, adjusting for different ages and abilities, both indoors and outside.

Art

Easels with a variety of paint types (tempera, watercolor) and colors

Brushes in a variety of head sizes & shapes (¼- to 3-inch, foam)

Marking pens, pencils with a variety of colors and sizes

Scissors, hole punches

Glue, paste, glue sticks

Tape in a variety of styles (masking, clear adhesive, colored)

Collage materials (cloth, corrugated and plain cardboard, small boxes or plastic, buttons)

Assorted paper (plain, colored, lined, graph)

Play dough, clay

Infants/toddlers: Use open shelves and offer one or two choices.

School age: Have both a self-help table and a teacher-directed project; consider stapler and graphing tools.

Blocks

Unit blocks, alphabet, small colored, and/or hollow blocks

Accessories (road signs and gas pumps, figures of people and animals, cloth scraps)

Support props (doll house and furniture, garage and transportation toys)

Infants/toddlers: Substitute soft or cardboard blocks for unit blocks; limit props and accessories to one or two types, include push–pull toys.

School age: Increase number and types of unit blocks; add castle or farm blocks, pattern blocks; add paper and pencils for children to make signage; make homemade blocks from milk cartons, shoeboxes, other assorted containers.

Discovery and Science

Nature materials (pinecones, leaves, smooth pebbles, moss, sticks)

Textured materials (cloth, buttons and snaps, extruded foam pieces, bubble wrap)

Sensory/water table materials (funnel, water wheel, plastic tubing, cups, sieve, measuring cups and spoons)

Magnifying glasses, mirrors

Scales (both food and floor)

Small pets (fish, hamster/guinea pig, turtle/snake, songbird)

Infants/toddlers: Simplify for safety (aquarium).

School age: Elaborate for research (computer).

Dramatic Play

Safety mirrors

Furniture: Child-size table/chairs, stove/refrigerator, cupboards, doll beds/highchair

Clothing: variety, non-stereotyped

Dolls: both male/female, diverse ethnicities and accessories

Cooking tools: chopsticks/wok; tortilla press; pots/pans; utensils

Food items: variety of plastic foods, produce.

Carrying cases: purses, suitcases, briefcases, backpacks, stroller

Infants/toddlers: Keep simple; add hats or dolls that can get wet.

School age: Vary materials according to themes such as prehistoric cave, space station, campground.

Language and Books

Books: a variety of types and styles, with bookshelves to display

Flannel board, accessories

Photos: basket of photos of children and their families

Lotto games

Records, tapes

Writing center: typewriter, pads, and pencils

Infants/toddlers: Cardboard books; other items available with adult only.

School age: Basal readers, listening post, homework table/corner

Table Toys/Manipulatives

Puzzles

Construction toys: Legos, Tinkertoys, etc.

Math toys: Unfix cubes, Cuisenaire blocks, attribute blocks, colored cubes, lacing, stringing toys, pegboards

Dressing frames

(continued)

Figure 5.5 (*continued*)

Montessori materials: pink tower, graduated cylinders, golden cube, etc.; collectibles: buttons, keys, shells, etc.; cooperative games: lotto, dominoes, matching games

Infants/toddlers: Puzzles with knobs, or soft ones; replace math toys with large plastic beads, nesting boxes, stacking toys, easy dressing frames for toddlers.

School age: Add board and card games; emphasize Lego-like construction and math toys

Outdoor Playground/Yard

Ground: Offer a variety of surfaces (grass, asphalt, gravel/sand, tanbark), and have available natural habitat

Equipment: Climbers with ramps, slide, pole, ladder; swings (various types); house/quiet area; "loose parts" such as tires or boards for ramps, etc.

Sand/water area and toys

Riding area and various wheel toys (tricycle, low-riding 3- and 4-wheelers, carts)

Balls (rubber, soccer, waffle ball/bat/tee, Nerf ball)

Blocks (often hollow blocks)

Dancing/parachute/tumbling mat materials

Dramatic-play props

Easel and drying rack

Garden (raised bed, hose, compost)

Pet area (rabbit, chickens)

Workbench and woodworking/clay materials

Infants/toddlers: Simple riding toys, no woodworking, low and simple apparatus and/or foam wedges.

School age: Increase game area, such as adding basketball; may eliminate or reduce wheel toys; add stage or boat; increase material for child-created forts.

Source: Based on Gordon/Browne (2011).

they could reuse items at home. Note the items requested and the uses the student teacher offered to families:

Cereal boxes	Make a puzzle, create a matching game, cover with paper to create building blocks
Water-bottle tops	Put in beans for shakers, use them for Bingo counters, make a ring-toss game
Plastic coffee and frosting lids	Use lids as a base for a bird's nest, punch holes for a lacing card, or make a stepping-stone game.
Bubble wrap	Tape to floor with duct tape and let kids stomp on it, tape to table and use toy hammers to pop, let children cut it out for collage work

Selecting materials for young children is as varied as the environments for children. Consider using the lists in Figures 5.5 and 5.6 to evaluate what you find in your practicum site.

Appropriate Schedules for Young Children

The daily schedule defines the structure and flow of each program. If the environment defines where things happen, the schedule determines *when* they occur. The format tells children and adults in what order things will happen and for what length of time.

Figure 5.6 What Makes Good Playthings?

Appropriate materials for young children must have certain characteristics to be useful and educational.

Source: Excerpt from *Children Come First,* used with permission from Community Playthings, www. communityplaythings.com.

- Simplicity of detail
- Versatile in use
- Easily comprehended design
- Easily manipulated
- Involve the child in play, including large muscles
- Encourage cooperative play
- Warm and pleasant to touch
- Durable
- Work as intended
- Safe
- Generous in proportions and quantity
- Price based on durability and design
- Sized to fit children
- Work for children with disabilities

Schedules and Program Goals

Daily schedules reflect children's ages and their needs while meeting the program goals. The time of day and timing of activities show what is valued in the program. Programs that focus on children's self-care skills will allow the time needed for children's dressing, eating, and toileting. An academic program would likely schedule substantial time for teaching subject matter such as math and literacy.

Priorities in Scheduling. Look at the schedule at your center and calculate the minutes for children's-choice and teacher-directed activities, for transitions and routines, for small-group and whole-group times—the more minutes given, the higher the priority. Then ask your supervising teacher to rank those activities and see if the stated priorities match the time given to each.

For instance, student teacher Candice discovered that "the daily schedule does provide enough time for unhurried play, because the first hour is for free play. The periods that create tension are the transitions because they are hurried and very rushed. At the beginning of the day the pace is more leisurely; even for cleanup, the Barney song is put on and all the children participate in the process. But as the end of the day nears it often seems more rushed and the children back off and teachers are nagging everyone. We should build in cleanup time at both ends of the day."

Children's behavior is a good indicator of how a schedule works. As seen in the "Ethical Dilemma" below, teachers need to think carefully when they see something that is uncomfortable. These feelings may indicate the need for a change.

"Is This Schedule Right for These Children?"

Student teacher Briana is working in the "Terrific Twos" class of 2- and young 3-year-olds. It is a lot of fun, but she has a concern about the schedule. Once everyone arrives, it seems that the children are rushed through the play period and clean up in order to get to group "on time." These whole-group circle times tend to last up to a half hour, with many reminders and moving of wiggling children. She will be doing a group time soon and dreads it. What should she do?

Code References: *Standard I, Ideal -1.2*—To base program practices upon current knowledge and research in the field of early childhood education, child development, and related disciplines, as well as on particular knowledge of each child.

Standard III, Principle-3B.5—When we have a concern about circumstances or conditions that impact the quality of care and education within the program, we shall inform the program's administration or, when necessary, other appropriate authorities.

Resolution: Briana talks to her college faculty instructor who recommends that she talk with her head teacher about her concerns, and helps her write up a list, both what she sees daily and what she has learned about developmentally appropriate practices. Though nervous, Briana brings two articles about DAP circle times and talks with her supervisor, who allows her try a group that is shorter and more active than usual. It is a success! The head teacher suggests that all teachers might try these shorter, more active circles in the future, but everyone will have to be ready to move.

Components of Schedules. As a schedule is created, teachers should keep in mind variety, choice, pace, and balance.

> Our homes are where we feel secure and competent and *it* reflects us when *it* is familiar and predictable. Children's places need ordered time and space that furthers the program goals while making the program a pleasant place to live and work for all those (large and small) who inhabit the program. . . . The order provides a comforting framework that does not harshly interrupt the activities of children; instead, the order allows for more experiences and for children to anticipate their day. (Greenman, 2006, p. 53)

For example, Michelle found at her center an "open-door policy" where the children have the choice to go inside or outside from 10:30 a.m. until lunch. Her supervising teacher Nataliya pointed out that children choose to play inside when there are new or interesting things on tables, or when they are pursuing a theme or activity with certain friends. Some children head outside as soon as the door opens, and return after vigorous play; others will play outside even in wet or chilly weather. The choice seems to be encouraging to children; Michelle observed over the course of the semester that participation levels increased for *all* children during the semester for that time slot.

A common element in all early childhood program schedules is a time to eat.

General Guidelines

What is important for children is the security of knowing a sequence, rather than a certain number of minutes.

Common Elements. There are common elements in all developmentally appropriate schedules, regardless of the age or time period. Figure 5.7 outlines these elements.

Flexibility. Even while following these guidelines, teachers should adjust their schedules to fit the needs of the group as well as be flexible

Figure 5.7
Top 10 Tips for Building Developmentally Appropriate Schedules

1. Include time for routines, transitions, and groups.
2. Alternate quiet, sedentary activity with loud, active play.
3. Offer time indoors and outdoors.
4. Allow both structured and unstructured time.
5. Include teacher-directed and child-choice experiences.
6. Make time for children to be alone, in small groups, and with the whole group together.
7. Set the schedule with the group age range and developmental level in mind.
8. Allow for flexibility to change because of weather, emergencies, children's moods and interests, and spontaneous surprises.
9. Have a beginning and an end, so each child or family is greeted and dismissed warmly.
10. Turn the unexpected into "teachable moments."

for individuals. See the "Reflective Incident" about flexibility in response to the unexpected. In addition, keep these four ideas in mind:

1. *Offer more choices as children grow.* Two-year-olds need fewer toys on the shelf than do 4-year-olds. Toddlers can be either indoors or out, but preschoolers may be able to handle making a choice, and certainly school-age children can.

2. *Transitions are handled differently with age.* Older children may be able to move as a group from the classroom to the library, but preschoolers will do better in small groups and certainly with more adult help. Kindergartners can walk along with partners, but 2-year-olds will need an adult's hand or a rope to hold.

3. *The daily structure changes over time.* Free-play and teacher-directed activities must be balanced for the age of the group. The shift is from relatively few directed activities for younger children to more of them for the nursery school and child care ages. A kindergarten and primary schedule provides more structure, individual work projects, and teacher-focused time.

4. *The content and duration of circle time expands with age.* Toddler group time is short and simple, perhaps a song and a story. In preschool this increases to include acting out a familiar story or fingerplay, brainstorming how to solve a problem. By kindergarten the circle time has expanded to include concept introductions and more elaborate discussions.

Think about what changes you might make to accommodate children's developmental stages and skills at your fieldwork site.

Sample Schedules

Because early childhood practicum courses involve teaching in settings for children from infancy to school age, the schedules you encounter will be varied. These sample schedules outline programs for children ages 2 to 8. Charlotte, doing fieldwork at her work site, notes that "creating a schedule is a difficult task, and it is hard to plan it when you haven't yet met the children. We make it up so that the children are, hopefully, intrigued by what they will be doing throughout the day. The schedule may not always be followed, but it is important to have some sort of map for all of us to know."

Look at the schedules in Figures 5.8 to 5.11. They offer ways to plan a day for children in each of the major age groups. Compare them with the schedule at your placement site. Remember, daily schedules provide structure so that children have time to learn and thrive.

Figure 5.8
Toddler Half-Day Schedule

A sample daily schedule for toddlers includes options for flexibility, a consistent routine, and responsiveness to individual children as they learn self-regulating skills such as toileting.

8:00 a.m. Welcome children and families
Free play indoors: Easels, play dough, books, blocks, ramp
8:45 a.m. Optional music/dancing group
8:50 a.m. Cleanup song
9:00 a.m. Door opens to outdoors
Free play outdoors: Slides, bridge, climber, sand
9:45 a.m. Optional organized game
9:50 a.m. Cleanup song
10:00 a.m. Handwashing and toileting/diapering
10:15 a.m. Snack at small groups
10:25 a.m. Optional stories at small groups
Indoor or outdoor free play
11:20 a.m. Cleanup song
11:25 a.m. Circle time (optional: families join group for story)
11:30 a.m. Good-bye to children and families

Figure 5.9
Preschool Full-Day Schedule

A program for preschoolers involves a comfortable pace with time for play, routines, and transitions.

7:30 a.m. Arrival: welcome and breakfast
8:00 a.m. Indoor free play
9:00 a.m. Cleanup song
9:15 a.m. Circle time: songs, games, today's events
9:30 a.m. Focus choices: art, cooking, science
10:30 a.m. Cleanup and handwashing for snack
10:45 a.m. Snack at small groups
11:00 a.m. Outdoor free play
11:00 a.m. Field trip or walk, swim lessons, music or art teacher
Noon: Cleanup and handwashing for lunch
12:15 p.m. Lunch
12:30 p.m. Put away lunch, toilet, prepare for nap
1:00 p.m. Nap time, individual stories or story tape
2:00 p.m. Nonnappers do quiet activities and snack prep
3:00 p.m. Snack time
3:15 p.m. Circle time: music, special options
3:30 p.m. Indoor or outdoor free play
4:00 p.m. Walk to park, play group game, or movie
5:30 p.m. Departure: Check in with families

Figure 5.10
Preschool Half-Day Schedule

The traditional preschool program is half-day with an emphasis on play and social interactions.

9:00 a.m. Arrival and greeting
9:00–9:45 a.m. Free play indoors: art, blocks, dramatic play, table toys, water table
9:45 a.m. Cleanup and handwashing
10:00 a.m. Circle time
10:15 a.m. Snack at small groups
10:45 a.m. Outdoor free play: climbers, swings, sandbox, woodworking, wheel toys, group games
11:45 a.m. Cleanup
Noon: Story time and dismissal

Noon Kindergarten arrival: welcome, handwashing, lunch

    12:30 p.m. Kindergarten circle time: news, choices

    12:45 p.m. Choice time: indoor free play and cooking

    1:45 p.m. Outdoor playground available and games

    2:45 p.m. Cleanup and all indoors

    3:00 p.m. Grades 1–3 arrival: welcome, put away belongings

    3:10 p.m. Circle time for all: news, choices

    3:20 p.m. Snack time

    3:30 p.m. Grades 1–3 homework; kindergarten art project

    4:00 p.m. Grades 1–3 outdoor teams, indoor clubs; kindergartens free play indoors

5-6:00 p.m. Indoor or outdoor free play, bus, departure

Figure 5.11
School-Age and Kindergarten Through Grade 3 Schedule

With older children, schedules include plenty of group opportunities as well as support for homework.

Reflective Incident "The Fire Drill During Circle Time"

I finally did large group time. I've been dreading it for weeks now, as I watched Bushra and Theo do it so effortlessly. It seems that Bushra just lights up when she is in front of the whole group, and the kids love whatever Theo tries. I've become a trusted teacher to these children over time, and have a small group of my own now—well, it's really my mentor teacher's group, but she has given it over to me by now.

So, I got the children settled with a good song ("If You're Happy and You Know It"), then we read a story (*The Very Hungry Caterpillar*), and they were practicing on their carpet squares how to wiggle like caterpillars . . . when there was a fire drill!

It was almost funny; the kids kind of froze but were still wiggling. Then we all lined up at the door to go outside. But one child was very upset because she wanted to stay standing on her piece of rug. Preschoolers really make you look at how something you are doing affects them emotionally, as well as physically!

—Monica

Your Thoughts

1. How would I feel?

2. What would I do?

3. What might the results be?

Environments and Schedules

Planning environments and setting schedules are critical aspects of teaching, and each includes a complex array of tasks to master. At the same time, it is these elements that set the stage for the curriculum to come alive. Although student teachers can feel overwhelmed at first, early childhood professionals—indeed, all teachers—find tremendous satisfaction when their plans can be realized, as in the "Lessons from the Field" feature.

lessons from the field

"Creating the Atelier, One Box of Recyclables at a Time"

by Patricia Dilko

Co-Coordinator, San Mateo, CA Regional ECE Mentor Teacher Program

In August 1998, a small child care program opened its doors for the very first time to a community of children and families who had eagerly anticipated its arrival. I must admit this was not the first "startup" that I had facilitated, but it was special: it was a child development laboratory for a small community college in the San Francisco Bay Area. Not only did we have 50 children and their families to think about, but we were also responsible for students stopping in to do child observations or administrative interviews, and semester-length student practicum placements. While I had run larger programs before, I had never had such responsibility to the community; our college housed the ECE department, and we were the child development laboratory. You can imagine how nervous I became knowing that students and faculty from many classes would be observing us and talking about the program in ECE classes!

Opening a state-of-the-art early learning environment in a 2,000-square-foot, one-room, relocatable building can be tricky. The plan was to become NAEYC accredited after we had been open for a few years, so for everything we did we kept an eye on those requirements. The building sat on the crest of a hill overlooking a beautiful valley with the coast mountain range beyond, so we wanted to mirror the natural beauty that surrounded us. We decided that the classroom environment should tend toward natural materials and neutral colors; the furniture

was light maple, with baskets on the shelves holding manipulatives, and the textiles and furnishings blended into the background. We wanted the brightness and joy of the children to be the focal point of the environment.

At the beginning we chose a traditional classroom design with the usual interest areas, including a pretty basic art area that was easy to close off during other activities. At the end of the first year the staff met to talk about our plans for the next year, and I brought up the concepts that I had been hearing from the preschools in Reggio Emilia, Italy: Projects, Documentation, Transparency, Planning Time, Parent Involvement, and the Atelier. After lengthy discussion, we decided to open up the art area into a mini-atelier!

The concept that captured our imaginations was "transparency." We began to look at our space as if to make it borderless—without walls. We installed deep, metal kitchen shelving so that children could see all of the wonderful materials that we had gathered. We transitioned to all clear boxes or low baskets for materials to accomplish the same visual effect. And we went to two local recycled materials centers to gather interesting, open-ended supplies.

When we reopened the center for fall semester the children were fascinated, the parents were curious, and the teachers were overwhelmed! At first it seemed like we could not establish any boundaries, and the children did not understand the freedom that they had with materials. Frankly the place was a mess, and we weren't seeing anything positive from our experiment. But as the semester rolled by, and we developed a language of expectation for the children, the mess subsided, and the creativity exploded! We found it to be true that even very young children can manipulate colored pencils and pastels if they are given repeated opportunities. And we found that the more precious the materials we used, the more gentle and respectful the children became. They learned, as we modeled for them, the importance of caring for the environment.

Slowly we began to see ourselves as a Reggio-inspired program, and yet we were uniquely ourselves. Much of our culture came from being part of the college community. The ebb and flow of the semester cycle became a part of our project planning, and the materials in the atelier reflected the seasons and needs of the projects. Parents became involved with gathering and displaying materials as well as photographing children and assembling documentation panels. We learned not to be afraid of taking big risks because the children will guide the way. We learned to trust the team of teachers that we worked with because our collective wisdom was far greater than anything one person could develop on their own. And we learned to honor and respect the competencies of young children.

Practicum Activity

Make a sketch of the indoor and outdoor environments where you teach. Note the problem areas: too many children, not enough space, an area ignored, and so on. Now design your own environment for the age level in which you teach. Show how your environment improves on your placement.

Journaling Assignment

What "trouble spots" do you see in the daily schedule where you teach? Are there times where children are hurried? Parts of the day where children chronically have behavior problems? Identify these in the schedule, and make recommendations for changes that would remedy the problems.

References

Community Playthings. (2012). *Spaces: Room layout for 0–5 year olds.* Retrieved June 2, 2012, from www.communityplaythings.co.uk/resources/downloads/spaces.pdf

Cryer, D., Harms, T., & Riley, C. (2003). *All about the Early Childhood Environmental Rating Scale.* Raleigh-Durham, NC: Pact House.

Dodge, D. T., & Colker, L. J. (2010). *The creative curriculum for preschool* (5th ed.). Washington, DC: Teaching Strategies, Inc.

Gonzalez-Mena, J., & Eyer, D. W. (2008) *Infants, toddlers, and caregivers: A curriculum of respectful, responsive care and education* (8th ed.). New York: McGraw-Hill.

Gordon, A. M., & Browne, K.W. (2011). *Beginnings and beyond: Foundations in early childhood education* (8th ed.). Clifton Park, NY: Thomson Delmar Learning.

Greenman, J. (2006, July/August). The importance of order. *Exchange Magazine*, 53–55.

Greenman, J., & Stonehouse, A. (2007) *Prime times: A handbook for excellence in infant and toddler care* (2nd ed.). Redmond, WA: Exchange Press.

Harms, T., Clifford, R., & Cryer, D. (2005). *Early Childhood Environmental Rating Scales* [FACERS, ECERS-R, ITERS-R, SACERS]. New York: Teachers College Press.

Montessori, M. (1967). *The Montessori method*. Cambridge, MA: Frederick A. Stokes Company.

Olds, A. (2000). *Child care design guide*. New York: McGraw-Hill.

Paasche, C. L., Gorrill, L., & Strom, B. (2004) *Children with special needs in early childhood settings: Identification, intervention, inclusion.* Clifton Park, NY: Delmar Learning.

Prescott, E., Jones, E., & Kritschevsky, S. (1972). *Group care as a child-rearing environment.* Washington, DC: National Association for the Education of Young Children.

Ritchie, S., & Willer, B. (2008). *Physical environment: A guide to the NAEYC Early Childhood Program Standard and Related Accreditation Criteria.* Washington, DC: NAEYC.

WestEd. (2009). *California Infant/Toddler Learning and Development Guidelines.* Sacramento, CA: CDE Press.

Web Sites

Community Playthings
www.communityplaythings.com

FPG Child Development Institute
www.fpg.unc.edu

HighScope Educational Research Foundation
www.highscope.org

Teaching Strategies
www.TeachingStrategies.com

The Program for Infant/Toddler Care
www.pitc.org

chapter 6

Curriculum

LEARNING OUTCOME

Design, implement, and evaluate meaningful curriculum that is play based, integrated, and grounded in active learning.

Start at the Very Beginning

Long before a room is designed and arranged, the daily schedule set, and the curriculum created, the early childhood professional reflects on the "how," "what," "when," and "why" of young children and the learning process. Experienced teachers will almost unconsciously run through the underlying factors that affect their thinking before they plan the curriculum. Beginning teachers can benefit from reviewing the process of creating sound learning environments and curriculum for young children.

How Young Children Learn

A group of kindergarten and first-grade children are kneeling on the floor of the after-school center, making a large map of the neighborhood where they live. They have markers, scissors, magazines, glue, and colored paper. The conversation is lively:

Corey:	My house is around the corner from Luke's. Where is yours, Nedi?
Nedi:	On Second Street; that's two blocks away. I'll get some string and we can measure from each house to the school. I wonder which one is closer.
Luke:	We should go past the fire station today and see what's in the lot next to it since Nedi says the drugstore is there and Rosalie says it isn't.
Merleen:	This doesn't look right. How do you draw a fence?

Rosalie:	We have to do street signs. I'll print their names. My street is easy, but yours is hard. Mrs. Garcia, how do you spell "Montgomery Street"?
Mrs. Garcia:	Let's sound it out together, Rosalie, and I'll print it on the board for you.
Corey:	Oops! There's no road to get cars through. Let's make the road go all around the town. Luke, you start at that end, and I'll start over here.
Joey:	I'll cut out some real neat cars and glue them on the streets.

Watching children interact, you notice they are active, curious, eager to learn, and creative. They question, explore, and experiment with ideas, language, and imagination. The children collaborate, negotiate, and learn from one another as they construct their own knowledge in making the map.

Hands-On Learning. *Hands-on learning* is the most effective way young children make sense of their environment and form their own understanding of how the world works. As active learners, children have to explore and manipulate materials in a variety of ways. Pushing, pulling, stacking, building up, taking down, sorting, measuring, digging, taking apart, putting together, pouring, and climbing are some of the ways children learn. The value of discovery cannot be underestimated as children find out for themselves how things work. The concept of *balance* is meaningless until children have built block structures, watched them fall, and learned how to make them stable. This is a tangible, physical experience necessary for learning the concept of balancing. Much of the map making is physical and takes place on the floor, as children move around the space, working on different parts of the map with different materials and responding to each other's comments and suggestions.

Children are eager to learn and need materials they can manipulate to help them create their own knowledge of the world.

Firsthand Learning. *Firsthand experiences* are the beginning of learning. Young children construct knowledge by expanding on their own experiences. In the block area for the last few weeks, the children in the map-making story have been building complex structures and have created a town. To extend their interest and learning, Mrs. Garcia suggested they create the town on butcher paper. Daily activities in the community provided the firsthand understanding the children needed to begin their map, starting with their own home and street. The children's own experience in the park, at the drugstore, or at the fire station fueled their interest and excitement. As the children created a visual representation of their neighborhood, their concepts of spatial relationships, area, volume, and measurement were more clearly defined. The knowledge and skills the children acquired through this project began with block building and will expand in the future as the children make more sophisticated maps with three-dimensional objects, create dioramas of buildings, and use graphs to build their structures to scale.

Meaningful Learning. *Meaningful learning* makes for optimum results. Involvement is guaranteed when the learning experience touches on children's own interests, needs, and concerns. For the young child, this means activities that include children and their families, friends, pets, community, and the environment in which they live, work, and play. Making the map was exciting because the project related to the children's own neighborhood and called on them to think about things that are important in their daily life, such as how far they walk to school and who else lives and works in the neighborhood. As they play, these children will build on what they have learned and apply that to how they understand and define the meaning of neighborhood. Later, that knowledge expands to other maps of the city, state, country, and world.

Cooperative Learning. *Cooperative learning* takes place when children work and play together. Children can be resources for one another and expand one another's awareness and knowledge as they play together. Cooperation and shared learning are important lifelong skills that young children learn by being actively engaged with others in the learning process. Throughout the mapping activity, children and adults discussed and solved problems together, stimulated creativity, expanded social skills, and fostered new concepts. Children gain social skills as they find the need to share both materials and space with others and strengthen their communications skills as well. Working and playing together enhance their enjoyment as well as their learning, as seen in the "My Reaction" feature from a student teacher.

Learning Through Play

Play is the way children learn how to learn. Children have a natural curiosity that motivates them to stop and watch a bug make its way across the sidewalk or to pour water over and over into different-size cups. The

> ## My Reaction
>
> ### "Cleaning Pennies"
>
> Today's activity was to clean pennies. The first group of children was enthralled with the solutions used to clean the pennies (vinegar, salt, and/or baking soda). The objective was for the children to dip their brush into the vinegar and then choose either the salt or the baking soda to scrub the penny. They started doing it this way, but it became more of a science experiment to see what happens when you combine the solutions together. So they started adding the salt to the vinegar, and it would fizz and bubble a little. Their expressions were priceless. They were in awe. I asked the questions "Which do you think would have the most reaction when you add it to the vinegar: the salt or the baking soda?" Half said the salt, the other half said the baking soda, so they tried them both and came to the conclusion that the reactions were about the same. The next group of children that came to the table was not interested in the solution, but in the cleaning of the pennies. I explained what they were supposed to do. They showed me their pennies and were so proud that you could see the copper shining through. The question I asked this group was "Which do you think cleans the pennies better: the salt or the baking soda?" Again, some said salt, a few said baking soda, and a couple said both. So they tried them both and even mixed the salt with the baking soda. Their consensus: They both worked! I really, really liked this activity.
>
> —Vikki

intensity, persistence, and creativity of their play are the tools children use to learn about learning.

Play is a natural way for children around the world to express themselves and is a basic need of children throughout their school years. Piaget's seminal work on cognitive development (1962) defined three basic forms of play: practice play, symbolic play, and games with rules.

Practice or Functional Play

This type of activity is a child's earliest form of play and forms a basis for the types of play that follow. Practice play, sometimes referred to as functional play, occurs primarily in the first 2 years as the infant and toddler learn their physical capabilities and the cause and effect of acting on their environment.

Symbolic Play

This kind of activity includes both constructive play and dramatic play and begins around age 2. In symbolic play, children use an object or toy to stand for or represent something else, such as gathering twigs and pine-cones to make pretend food.

Constructive Play. This type of play is more intentional than practice play as children plan and construct, using a variety of materials. A long, rolled-out piece of clay becomes a snake or an arrangement of blocks becomes a skyscraper. Concrete materials are used to make a representation of objects and experiences in children's lives.

Dramatic Play. Dramatic play is a highly developed form of symbolic play and is based more on reality. Children imitate real-life people and situations and incorporate make-believe elements as needed. In the dress-up area of the classroom, Cora, pretending to be the doctor, tells Bahraim, "You need a shot. Don't cry—it won't hurt." She reaches for a crayon, saying, "This is the needle." Bahraim pretends to cry. Cora reaches for a pretend tissue and hands it to him. "Here. Wipe your nose and I'll give you a balloon." Dramatic play allows children to "think" out loud as their learning comes together, strengthening their knowledge and understanding of the world.

Games with Rules

Games with rules increase around age 6 or 7 when children are mature enough to accept and adjust to preset rules. Children acquire the ability to play games with rules gradually as they grow in cooperative social behavior and cognitive abilities.

In planning for play, teachers must consider how each of these three forms of play relates to the child's maturity and level of social development.

Kinds of Play

Children need opportunities for all levels of play and to incorporate materials and activities that allow for a variety of social interactions. Two chairs at a table of construction blocks will encourage social interactions with one another; an isolated area with soft pillows will give a child the chance to be alone for quiet time, and a stack of firefighter hats and hoses will encourage group and cooperative play. Parten (1932), in her classic study, defined six kinds of play and types of social interactions that occurred (see Figure 6.1).

The value of play as a means of social growth and development is one important aspect of play in early childhood environments.

Figure 6.1
Kinds of Play

Typical play behaviors of
young children.

Source: Based on Parten
(1931).

Unoccupied Behavior: Stuart stands by the cubbies watching the general activity in the room. A few minutes later he sits down and spends the next 5 minutes glancing around the room, getting on and off the chair, and standing again.

Onlooker Behavior: Seth sits near the easels and watches children paint. He continues to watch the children, speaking infrequently to them as they work. He makes no effort to join in painting.

Solitary Play: Lois is sitting alone at the puzzle table, working and reworking the same two puzzles, oblivious to what is going on elsewhere. She interacts with no one.

Parallel Play: Francesca and Mary Jane sit near each other at the clay table. Mary Jane is molding the clay into various shapes while Francesca is slapping and rolling the clay around the table. The girls play independently, in close proximity of one another, but with no interaction.

Associative Play: Corita, Terry, and Danna are playing in the block area. Corita has placed a series of cars along a strip of building blocks. Terry is building a tower, and Danna is making an enclosure for farm animals. They pass blocks to one another but do not play together. The three children are aware of and associate with one another at this beginning stage of group play.

Cooperative Play: Joel and Sammy are digging in the sand pit and are joined by Kurt, Kerry, and Liza. Joel and Sammy tell the other children where to dig and how to enlarge the hole they are making. All five children work toward the common goal. The digging effort becomes more complex as bridges are added and a water hose fills the "river." Each child takes on a specific role as the play continues. Kerry is in charge of the hose, Liza is finding wood for boats, Kurt and Sammy are building the bridges, and Joel continues digging. Creating a goal, negotiating roles, and building activity around cooperative interactions are all components of this stage of group play.

Play is an important way for children to learn.

The Value of Play

Play is often referred to as the child's "work," or as a window into the child's world. Play is all of that and more. Through play, children learn to:

- Use their imagination and be spontaneous.

- Invent new uses for materials and equipment.

- Be adventurous.

- Practice their physical skills and learn new ones.

- Negotiate and cooperate with others.

- Use an important avenue for self-expression and express their emotions.

- Make choices for themselves.

- Problem solve with words, ideas, people, and materials.

- Develop greater social and cultural understanding of others.

- Have fun.

Some parents and teachers do not easily recognize the value of play. It is the job of the childhood professional to help families understand what is happening when children engage in play. Look around the classroom where you teach and notice where children are playing, how they are playing, and what they are saying as they play. Learning is taking place in every interaction. Share these examples with families as illustrations of their child's imagination, abilities, competence, and creativity.

Developmentally Appropriate Play

When planning for developmentally appropriate play, early childhood teachers bring to bear all of their knowledge about how children grow and learn, as well as an understanding of the cultural context in which the children live. From that base, play experiences are woven into the curriculum to meet the developmental needs of the children in the class. Two key concepts in developmentally appropriate planning are to set reasonable but challenging goals for each child and to meet children where they are (Copple & Bredekamp, 2006). In an inclusive classroom the curriculum is developmentally geared to the abilities of children with various exceptionalities.

Joyce, a 3½-year-old, lives on a hilly street and has never ridden a tricycle. Her teachers plan the curriculum with Joyce in mind. Indoors, music activities call for children to create bicycle motions with their legs. Outdoors, pumping on swings and running games help Joyce develop some of the large motor skills she needs as she learns to ride a trike. Although this activity is focused on Joyce, the teachers are also aware of how this part of the curriculum will help Richie to find ways to handle his excessive energy and Gina to participate in more group activities. The teachers intentionally build on the children's known abilities but at the same time provide challenges for them to meet.

The significance of play in the development process cannot be underestimated. All the developmental domains are enhanced through play. The children in the mapping activity, described at the beginning of this chapter, for instance, are building social (cooperation, sharing), cognitive (problem solving), emotional (self-identity, competency), physical (gross and fine motor), intellectual (measuring distance), and creative (drawing) skills as they play. Play challenges children to use all of their abilities, and in doing so the *whole* child is affected when play is developmentally appropriate.

Through unstructured play, children take a part of their world and rehearse, restructure, and refine it in order to understand how it works. Practicing for life is an important job for young children, and they need teachers who appreciate and value the role of play in the early childhood setting. Figure 6.2 highlights the teacher's role in facilitating play.

Figure 6.2
The Teacher
Facilitates Play

The teacher should be a facilitator and use "teachable moments" as they arise in the natural environment.

Source: Based on Gordon & Browne (2011).

- Start with the children's thoughts and ideas; do not enforce your viewpoint on the play.
- Guide the play; do not direct or dominate.
- Model and participate in the play when needed by showing how a character might act, or how to ask for a turn.
- Give children verbal cues to help them follow through on an idea.
- Extend play potential by helping children start, end, and move onto a new place or idea.
- Clarify what is happening by asking questions.
- Focus children's attention on each other to encourage peer interactions.
- Help children name and express feelings as they work through conflict.
- Interpret children's behavior aloud to help them learn to verbalize their thoughts and ideas.

Curriculum in the Early Years

Curriculum does not just happen. A great deal of planning is needed to create a high-quality early childhood setting with an appropriate curriculum. Long before children enter the classroom, teachers make decisions on what is developmentally appropriate for the age group, the strengths and interests of each child, and the cultural context of the children in the classroom. The goals of the program, the school's underlying philosophy, and the needs of the families are also woven into the planning.

Setting the Stage

To set the stage for learning, the environment, schedule, and curriculum merge to create a program that children will enter into with enthusiasm and interest. No matter the age group, teachers use the space, room arrangement, outdoor play area, materials, and daily schedule as a scaffold on which to build learning experiences to meet the varied interests, abilities, and needs of each child. How well the curriculum and environment are blended is reflected in the children's independent use of materials, how free they are to explore and satisfy their curiosity, and how they practice and master skills as they develop competencies. The role of the environment and schedule were previously explored in Chapter 5.

Teachers also set the tone: the emotional framework in which children work and play. The classroom atmosphere is influenced by a teacher's body language, facial expressions, tone of voice, and nonverbal and verbal gestures (Gordon & Browne, 2011). The interpersonal climate within the classroom is as important as the arrangement of furniture and the quality of the curriculum. Young children are very sensitive to an adult's manner and attitude, as well as how children treat each other. A positive atmosphere supports a child's need for a safe and nurturing place to learn. (Chapter 3 discussed strategies for guiding children's behavior.)

What Exactly Is Curriculum?

Curriculum for young children addresses all aspects of a child's growth, including social, emotional, physical, cognitive, and language development. The whole child is challenged when planning includes each of the developmental areas.

Curriculum is not just a lesson plan, field trip, or project. Curriculum is fluid: It moves with the children's interests and needs. Flexibility can be challenging for teachers, yet provides them with the raw materials for a fascinating conversation about worms, or a detour from a planned activity to a surprise earthquake drill response. Figure 6.3 illustrates the broad scope of curriculum.

Bredekamp and Rosegrant (1995) define curriculum as an "organized framework" with four areas of focus:

- The *content* consists of *what* children should learn and how it reflects their interests, needs, and experiences.

- The *process* includes *how* and *when* learning takes place, the choice of activities, how they are integrated with one another, and the time frame within the daily schedule.

- The *teachers* are the people who *use* their knowledge of child development theory to individualize the activities to meet the needs of all the children in the class.

Curriculum happens everywhere and includes:

- What needs to be taught and how to teach it.
- Everything that happens in a school day, planned and unplanned.
- Formal, written lesson plans and spontaneous on-the-spot change of plans.
- Small- and large-group-time experience, story times, transitions, free play.
- Interactions children have with others: what they say, how they reflect their understanding of the world, what questions they ask.
- Exploration and creativity that happens when children manipulate materials and equipment.
- Learning through play to make friends, be creative, follow rules, make mistakes, solve problems, make choices.
- Challenging children to master appropriate developmental tasks by building on their current strengths and knowledge.

Figure 6.3
Scope of Curriculum
Curriculum is fluid and flexible and happens throughout the day.

● The *context* is *why* certain projects and activities are chosen and is based on the program's philosophy and goals in conjunction with families and the community

These factors work together during the planning process to help teachers develop curriculum. The goal of the process is to translate theories of education and development into practice, based on the children's interests and the adult's awareness of children's needs.

Curriculum models that promote good practices in developmentally appropriate learning for young children and that have their own philosophical thrust include High/Scope, Bank Street, the schools of Reggio Emilia, Montessori, and the Creative Curriculum, among others. Many schools adopt one particular model or integrate elements from several into their planning. By now you may have taken a course in curriculum that describes these approaches in greater depth. During your student teaching experience you may be placed in schools that partially or fully implement these philosophies.

Developing curriculum is a decision-making process. You make decisions about what materials children will use, what activities will bring balance to the day, how to adapt the curriculum to meet the needs of children with special needs, what small group a child may be assigned to, what teacher will be responsible for science this week, and how the room arrangement is set up for learning. These decisions are based on your knowledge and insight about young children.

Essentials for Creating Curriculum

The most effective curriculum happens when teachers consider the essential elements, as noted in Figure 6.4, when creating meaningful and appropriate curriculum.

Figure 6.4
Top 10 Questions When Creating Curriculum
Ask yourself these 10 essential questions whenever you plan a lesson or activity.

Is the curriculum:

1. age appropriate?
2. individualized?
3. culturally responsive?
4. inclusive?
5. integrated?
6. emergent?
7. balanced?
8. related to learning standards?
9. written?
10. evaluated?

Essential Elements for Planning Curriculum

There are 10 essential elements that are used to develop curriculum. Lessons and activities are created along the following guidelines.

The Curriculum Is Age Appropriate. What do you know about how 2-year-olds learn? 5-year-olds? 7-year-olds? What do you know about their social skills, physical dexterity, language capacity, and intellectual abilities? You need an understanding of each age group in order to plan for children's growth and

Knowing the age level and interests of the children in the class helps the student teacher plan appropriate and appealing curriculum.

development. Teacher Maya is aware that 2-year-olds are beginning to share, like to watch each other, and often play parallel to one another. With this knowledge, Maya can plan appropriate activities that encourage more social interaction throughout the day. She also knows that as they turn 3, the children will enjoy simple poems and humor. Maya includes this information in her planning. Knowing the characteristics of the age levels above and below the ages she teaches, Maya will make sure that the curriculum for her class of 2-year-olds will include appropriate challenges for developing new skills.

The Curriculum Is Individualized. Children have different learning styles and intellectual strengths that help them process information. Both are important considerations when planning and implementing curriculum for all children, including those with special needs.

Young children use three basic sensory styles to learn: visual, auditory, and tactile-kinesthetic. Each child has a preferred mode, although it is not the only way a child integrates knowledge.

- The *visual* learner likes to represent learning by reading, writing, and drawing. After a field trip to the aquarium, Inez writes and illustrates a story about sharks.

- The *auditory* learner listens to others to learn and talks to others about what he or she learns. On the way home from the field trip, Darius makes up a song about a starfish. The teacher asks him to teach it to the rest of the group.

- The *tactile-kinesthetic* learner is a physically active learner who learns by doing rather than by listening. Back in the classroom, Miranda and Noemi head straight to the water table filled with plastic fish and begin to sort them into the groups they saw at the aquarium.

The teaching staff assesses children's skills, behavior, and play patterns and the effectiveness of the curriculum by observing and documenting what each child does during the school day. A teacher's notation may look like this:

Luz and Dario spent over 30 minutes going through the rocks and minerals display, sorting by color, size, and texture. We could expand their interest by taking a "rock walk" around the school yard later today. Let's ask them for suggestions about what else they might like to do with the rocks and minerals. This might become a project.

To individualize the curriculum further, the teachers must also know how each child is "intelligent." Gardner holds that children have multiple intelligences, which give them eight "different ways of knowing" (Gardner, 1993). Gardner's eight intelligences are listed in Figure 6.5.

We all have these eight intelligences to some extent, but we differ in the degree and combinations. Each person, including you, has sets of abilities and talents that reflect your experience, culture, and motivation. What do you think is your primary way of being smart?

The Curriculum Is Culturally Responsive. Teachers are challenged to present a curriculum that reflects contemporary U.S. society and to adapt the curriculum to the diversity represented in each class. All children learn best when the school environment is welcoming and says we care about and support you and your family. This is especially true for children and families whose culture and background differ from those of the teaching staff. Families need to see that their culture is woven into the curriculum in the books and literature, songs and dances, activities and field trips. Positive relationships with children's home and community begin with honoring the family's cultural values and creating avenues for working together in the child's best interests.

Figure 6.5
Gardner's Multiple Intelligences

Planning curriculum with Gardner's nine intelligences in mind is one way to plan children's experiences.

Source: Data compiled from Gardner (1993).

1. *Body-kinesthetic:* Uses one's body to solve problems and communicate; wants to be a participant, not a spectator.
2. *Intrapersonal:* Is sensitive to one's inner feelings and knows one's strength and weaknesses.
3. *Interpersonal:* Is sensitive to and understanding of others; is often a leader.
4. *Linguistic:* Uses words and language in many forms; reading and writing come easily.
5. *Logical-mathematical:* Can discern patterns and is precise and methodical.
6. *Musical:* Is sensitive to nonverbal sounds and connects with rhythms and melodies.
7. *Spatial:* Can visualize and think in images and pictures; excels at representational drawing.
8. *Naturalist:* Can discriminate among living things (plants, animals); is sensitive to features of the natural world.
9. *Existential:* Is sensitive to issues of meaning and spiritual matters, such as life & death, or life's greater purposes.

The Curriculum Is Inclusive. An inclusive curriculum is a step beyond creating curriculum that meets the needs of the individual child. An inclusive curriculum is broader in scope and challenges the teacher to provide opportunities for *all* children, regardless of gender, abilities or disabilities, language, culture, ethnicity, and religion. The activities and materials in an inclusive classroom are chosen to enhance the growth potential of each child and are sensitive to the diversity of abilities within the classroom.

All children need the same things from their learning environment. The question becomes how you accommodate this wide range of differences in children while planning curriculum. The true test of an appropriate activity is whether or not it will adjust to children with a wide range of skills and abilities. Quality curriculum is flexible enough to accommodate the needs of each child, where children can participate at their developmental and ability level, yet be challenged in their learning. Figure 6.6 shows how an art activity can be changed to support children who have disabilities.

The Curriculum Is Integrated. In a child development class you learned about the concept of "the whole child" and how it affects planning for children's growth and development. The whole-child approach stresses

---

Physical Modifications:

Ensure there is a clear path to the area and table(s).

Provide children with their own materials and space (avoid crowding).

Attach hook-and-loop fasteners to marking instruments or paintbrushes.

Provide adaptive art tools (chunky crayons, double ambidextrous scissors, cutting wheel).

Use contact paper or glue sticks (not white glue bottles).

Offer a few choices (rather than too many that may overwhelm).

Include play dough/clay regularly.

Visual Adaptations:

Provide a tray to mark the visual boundaries.

Offer bright paint to contrast with paper.

Go slowly and encourage children to manipulate the items as you talk.

Describe aloud the materials and how they can be used.

Auditory Modifications:

Use sign language as needed.

Face children and use gestures for emphasis.

Model the process in small steps.

Figure 6.6
Art Adaptations for Special Needs

Many accommodations in creative arts can be made for children with a variety of special needs.

Source: Based on Gordon & Browne (2011).

the interaction and relationship among the physical, social, intellectual, language, and cognitive areas of the developing child. So it is with integrated curriculum. Rather than teach subject matter (such as science, math, geography, or art) as separate topics, early childhood teachers teach them "across the curriculum." The subject matter becomes planned components of the total curriculum. To some, cooking in the preschool may simply be a fun activity. To the teacher, it is a coordinated learning experience in science, reading, math, social skills, small motor development, and multiculturalism. Any number of developmental areas can be woven into any aspect of the curriculum to reinforce concepts in the broadest possible way. This approach reflects Dewey's philosophy of education as meaningful, active learning and is used extensively in the schools of Reggio Emilia. Integrated curriculum is often used with a theme or project approach to developing curriculum. Figure 6.7 shows how sensory skills are enhanced through an integrated curriculum.

Figure 6.7
Exploring Sensory Skills: An Integrated Approach

Integrating the curriculum enhances the ability to learn on many levels.

Week Of: *April 10*   Teacher: *Mariko*   Group: *3-Year-Olds*

Focus: *Sensory stimulation*

Objective: *To explore the world through the five senses*

Day of Week	Activity and Learning Focus	Small-Group Activity and Learning Focus
Monday	*Soap painting: Encourages use of fine and gross motor skills; and creativity*	*Guessing game of textures: Cognitive exercise to identify soft and hard*
Tuesday	*Water table: Promotes social interaction, motor skills, and cognitive learning*	*Guessing game of smells: Memory exercise (cognitive) to identify familiar scents*
Wednesday	*Finger painting: Encourages use of fine motor skills and creativity*	*Guessing game of weights: Cognitive exercise to distinguish heavy and light*
Thursday	*Make a collage of materials collected on walk: Enhances social and physical skills*	*Identify and sort familiar objects: Exercise to develop memory and cognitive skills*
Friday	*Play dough: Promotes social and physical motor skills*	*Sample finger foods: Exercise to identify size, shape, texture, and taste; extends language and cognitive development*

The Curriculum Is Emergent. Emergent curriculum begins with assessing children's needs and interests. Through observations and awareness of children's play, teachers find out what children are attracted to and what captures their attention and their eagerness to learn. This information is blended with the teacher's knowledge of what the group and the individual children need to learn and what activities, materials, and equipment will enhance those specific skills. Together, teachers and children will cocreate the curriculum.

Each class or group of children is unique, so through continuous examination and dialogue, topics of interest emerge. The teacher who took notice of Luz and Dario's avid interest in the rocks and minerals display also noted that this activity might become a project. Mrs. Garcia helped the children extend their learning about maps for an activity that could emerge into a longer-term project. Emergent curriculum begins with an idea or activity that can be expanded for greater learning potential and that will reinforce children's interest and excitement about learning. Often, a project continues for days or even weeks. The project approach is an in-depth study of a theme and is especially appropriate in the older end of the early childhood years. Through projects, children learn to work cooperatively, do research, collaborate with adults, and evaluate their work (Chard, 2000). Emergent curriculum embodies the characteristics of integrated and inclusive curriculum as well.

Topics are chosen in many ways for different reasons: children's interests, teacher's interests, developmental tasks, resources available, the value of the topic, and curriculum requirements or standards. Emergent curriculum is a planning process in which teachers question children about what they know, what they might like to know, and how they might find out what they need to know. Emergent curriculum is an interactive and collaborative experience in which "children are our models and coplayers," which Jones and Nimmo (1994) expressed in one of the first publications devoted to emergent curriculum.

Figure 6.8 is an example of a project created and conducted by a student teacher. Called "Project Blueprint," it emerged from the children's interest in seeing a construction site near their school.

The Curriculum Is Balanced. Balance is key to an effective curriculum. Quiet times alternate with more active play. A story time follows outdoor play periods. Active play is scheduled after nap time or rest time. Look again at the scheduling section of Chapter 5 to see how this balance is achieved throughout the day.

Balance, too, is needed in the type of themes or activities. Those that focus on only one aspect of development, such as intellectual growth, ignore the social-emotional and physical growth aspects so necessary to learning. Some

Figure 6.8
Project Blueprint
The months-long curriculum that emerged from interest in a nearby construction project demonstrates how children's interests can be used to build skills.

Source: From Lam & Wiggins-Dowler (2005).

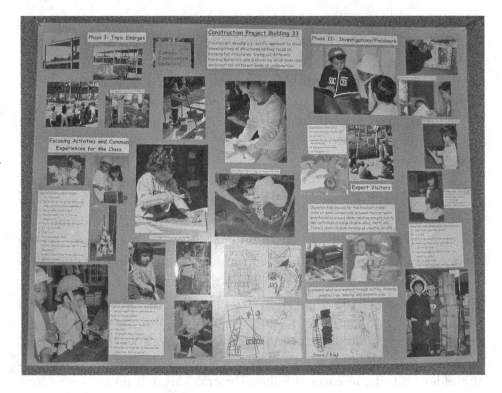

activities may stress social-emotional concerns, creativity, or literacy. The focus of themes should be diverse and balanced as you plan throughout the year.

A third way to provide good balance in the curriculum is to allow children the experience of playing alone, with one or two other children, or in a larger group. A balance of child-directed activities and teacher-guided activities provides opportunities for children to be self-directed at times and learn to make choices and decisions for themselves. Take a look at the classroom in which you teach and assess how balanced its curriculum might be in terms of small and large groupings.

The Curriculum Meets Learning Standards. Across the country early learning standards are being developed to create a set of expectations for preschool children. The terms *child outcomes*, *benchmarks*, and *performance standards* are used to measure the kinds of development and learning that are taking place.

Most of the individual states have adopted some form of standards or expectations of children aged 3 to 5 years and in school-age settings. You are more than likely teaching in a state that requires you to meet its standards (see Chapter 4). As an early childhood educator you will want to know whether your state has mandated early learning standards and, if so, what they encompass.

Early childhood standards can benefit children in numerous ways: by being linked to primary-grade standards they ensure school readiness; they

Balancing the Curriculum

Situation: Matt is student teaching in an after-school program where the children do homework first and then choose an activity. Matt notices that three boys always head for the computers and spend the rest of the afternoon playing games. In his curriculum course, Matt learned how to plan a balanced curriculum, and he feels the boys are not benefiting from the diversity the program has to offer. He takes his concerns to the head teacher, who seems indifferent and whose rationale is that the children have been cooped up in academic settings all day so they should be allowed to do what they want in the afternoon. "But," she says, "if you want to try something, go ahead."

Code of Ethical Conduct Resources:

Section I: Ethical Responsibilities to Children:

I-1.3–To recognizes and respect the unique qualities, abilities, and potential of each child.

P-1.2–We shall care for and educate children in positive, emotional and social environments that are cognitively stimulating.

Section III: B. Responsibilities to Employers:

I 3B.1–To assist the program in providing the highest quality of service.

Solution: Matt has been working with and observing the class for 4 weeks and has a good sense of the group's dynamics. Nathan and James love to play the various "battle" games" that dominate their afternoons on the computer. Matt remembers his own interest in games when he was their age, so he introduces the boys to a series of games and projects to recreate the Spanish Armada. Nathan and James are intrigued and begin to construct boats and dress up in clothes they called "uniforms." By capturing the interest of the dominant players, other children joined the activity, including a group of girls who made pirate costumes. Through his interest, ability, and ingenuity, student teacher Matt changed the afternoon learning environment.

can define the foundational skills for learning; they help teachers identify the next steps and have appropriately higher expectations for children; and they professionalize the field of early childhood (Gronlund, 2006).

Early learning standards pose potential risks as well as benefits. Too often, the standards do not address all the developmental domains necessary and are not adaptable for children with disabilities or those who are culturally and linguistically diverse. Many early childhood professionals are concerned that the current standards push direct instruction, inappropriate expectations and assessment of preschoolers, and lead to "teaching to the test" mentality (see Chapter 4, which dealt with the topic of standards.) Table 6.1 provides an example of how one state's preschool learning standards are linked to developmentally appropriate curriculum.

Written Lesson Plans Are Created. A *lesson plan* is a written outline that helps teachers articulate and implement the goals they have set, yet

Table 6.1 Linking Standards to Curriculum

By developing appropriate curriculum to meet learning standards, teachers ensure that children are engaged in meaningful activities while also progressing in their skill development.

Standard	Activity	Demonstrates Mastery
Personal and social competence: Identifies self by categories of gender, age, or social group.	1. Graph children's ages. 2. Make an "All About Me" book. 3. Create self-portraits with dictation.	1. Says correct age and shows correct number of fingers. 2–3. Says "I'm a girl," "I'm 4 years old," or "I'm Vietnamese."
Effective learner: Completes increasingly complex puzzles.	Play with knob puzzles, puzzles with and without frames, and floor puzzles.	Uses puzzles with interlocking pieces without the help of frames.
Physical and motor competence: Manipulates two or more objects at the same time.	String beads; play with Legos or Duplos; practice buttoning, zipping, lacing cards, and cutting paper.	Two hands manipulate object at the same time to complete task successfully.

Source: Data based on and adapted from Kim Yuen, San Mateo County Office of Education, San Mateo, CA. Used with permission.

such a plan is flexible enough to adapt to changes. Goals may be short or long range and may focus on skill development, themes, or projects. Written lesson plans stimulate teamwork and in-depth planning, and also provide a concrete format from which evaluation and assessment can be made (Gordon & Browne, 2011).

Student teachers often struggle with making lesson plans. With practice and a few simple guidelines, your planning skills will improve.

- Observe children in your program to find out what interests them. In Sam's class the children were interested in bugs.

- Decide on a topic and check it out with your supervising teacher. Sam asked his lead teacher if bugs were an appropriate topic for 3½-year-olds.

- Look at children's assessments to see where they are developmentally and what skills you wish to enhance. Looking at the children's portfolios, Sam found that most had unrefined fine motor skills, so he chose that as the focus.

- Plan the activity to promote the development of those skills. "The collection and investigation of bugs" became Sam's activity.

- Create a list of materials needed. Sam's list included small bags for collection. Then at the table he had small trays, flashlights, magnifying glasses, plastic tweezers, and, for himself, a clipboard.

- Outline the steps children will take and what they will do in the activity, including cleanup. Sam took his small group outdoors to collect bugs, then came back to the classroom and investigated them by putting them on a tray, looking at them with the tools provided and making a list together of what they discovered.

- Write a list of open-ended questions you will ask while they play: "What do you see? What does your bug look like? What are the differences between yours and someone else's? What will happen if you turn over the bug?"

A written lesson plan provides a map that may outline a single activity, an entire daily plan, or the focus for a longer period of time or project. A good lesson plan will also have a space for review and/or evaluation. Figure 6.9 is a sample of an individual activity lesson plan.

Figure 6.9
Planning an Activity
Good planning takes time and thought, and these questions can help a teacher focus on the important aspects of curriculum planning.

Activity name: _____

Purpose/goal: _____

Context: _____

     Location (indoor/outdoor, in what section of yard or room): _____

     Time of day: _____

     Type of and size of group: _____

Materials needed and how you will have children use them:

_____

_____

How you will introduce the activity, and what antecedents are necessary for this group?

_____

_____

What adaptations do you need to make for children with special needs?

_____

_____

Cleanup provisions (Will children be involved? How?):

_____

_____

Results:

     What were the children's responses? _____

     Did you achieve what you wanted? _____

     Problems? _____

     Solutions for next time? _____

     Implications for other activities? _____

Next steps/other activities: _____

Another way that teachers create written plans is the process known as *webbing*. Webbing is done in a variety of ways: alone, with other teachers, and often with children. Webbing involves identifying a key theme or topic that becomes the center of the web. Radiating from the center are other aspects of the theme, such as concepts and activities. This type of planning is fluid and continues to change with the participants' ideas. Figure 6.10 illustrates a curriculum web on the topic "Summertime." Starting with what children already know about the theme, or with what the teachers want the children to learn, the web grows with new ideas. Often, the activities, experiences, and materials that may be needed are included in the web.

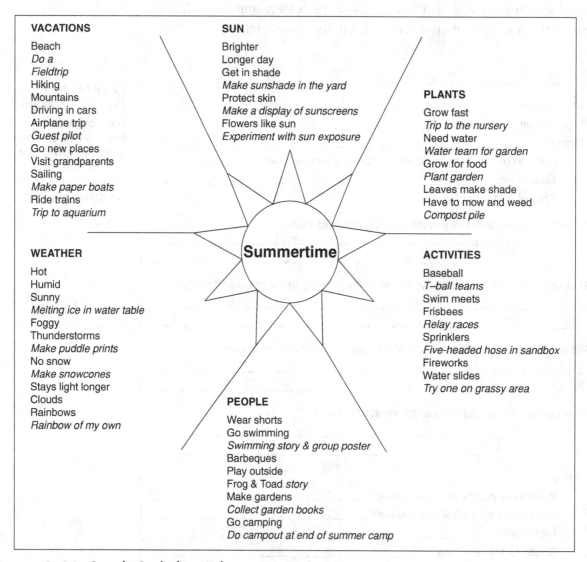

Figure 6.10 Sample Curriculum Web

When the kinder-camp staff members planned their curriculum, they began with a webbing activity for the children.

Note: The children's ideas are shown in regular type, with the staff members' planned activities in italics.

Curriculum Is Evaluated. Developmentally appropriate curriculum doesn't just happen. To keep meeting the needs, interests, experiences, and abilities of each child, curricula needs to be evaluated and refined frequently. Each day informal evaluations occur among the teachers.

- "No one spent much time at the woodworking table today. Should we put it away for a while?"
- "I noticed that three or four of the children are having difficulty cutting with the scissors. We'd better plan some activities that will help them learn that skill."

Evaluating the curriculum is an ongoing process as children change, grow, and develop new interests and abilities, and their teachers implement appropriate changes.

In more formal evaluations, children's responses to the curriculum are documented through a variety of assessment and observation methods, such as those discussed in Chapter 4. Evaluation points out the relevancy the curriculum has in the children's lives. A theme unit on subways was not particularly popular with a group of 4-year-olds in rural Indiana, but it may have great appeal for children living in the Bronx. Because both programs require that the children learn about principles of motion in their science curriculum, the teachers in the Midwest focus instead on the trailer trucks that ply their highways. Taking their cues from the children, early childhood professionals adapt the curriculum to activities that are more culturally meaningful to the class.

An effective curriculum is based on the goals and objectives of the program's philosophy, indicating what children are to learn and experience at each age level. The goals are intentionally broad because the developmental levels of the children in a classroom are so diverse. Ongoing evaluations inform the staff as to how well the goals are being met.

Mastering the art of curriculum planning is a challenge for teachers, yet it is one of the most satisfying aspects of working with young children. The plans come alive as you observe how children respond to learning and give you clues to the next challenges they need as noted in "Lessons from the Field" at this chapter's end.

Infant /Toddler Curriculum

The principles of developmentally appropriate curricula and the essentials for creating curricula apply to developing curricula for the very young child. For infants and toddlers, play is again the primary medium. Play integrates education and care (*educare*, defined in Chapter 3) into a cohesive curriculum. The point to remember is that infant care and education are not either/or; they are inseparable.

Curriculum for Infants. Infants learn through all of their senses so a curriculum for them includes activities and materials that stimulate their senses of sound, sight, hearing, and touch. Throughout the routines of the day, caregivers interact with and teach infants when they:

- Give the mobile a push as you walk by a crib.
- Respond to coos and babbling by imitating their sounds.
- Talk to babies as you diaper, dress, and feed them; tell them what you are doing.
- Play peekaboo as you change their diapers or sit them on your lap.
- Play quiet music as they nap.
- Place mirrors and pictures on the wall at an infant's eye level.
- Put infants on soft rugs.
- Put toys just out of reach when infants are on a rug.

These activities encourage infants to connect and focus on objects, enhance their physical development, and build relationships with their caregivers. As infants become more mobile, they need to play with grasping toys, cuddling toys, balls, puzzles, push and pull toys, trucks and cars that roll, balls, and simple blocks.

Curriculum for Toddlers. Toddlers are using toys and materials with greater purpose and skill so they need more open space to move, build, run, and climb. Toys should be on low shelves to allow for easy exploration. Provide at least two of each toy to avoid sharing conflicts. Everyday experiences should encourage sensory exploration and hands-on manipulation such as these:

- Simple art activities: sponge painting, finger and toe painting, water painting
- Water play table: with fish/boats; cups/pitchers/sieves; babies/sponges/soap
- Fill water table with sand, rice, cotton balls, and other textures
- Block play
- Looking at books: naming objects, shapes
- Puzzles and matching games
- Dramatic play equipment: dress-up clothes, telephones, dolls/doll beds, dishes
- Singing: using fingerplays

- Learning self-help skills such as dressing, brushing teeth, eating
- Music: moving, dancing, swaying, shaking, and/or using simple musical instruments

As toddlers grow and gain greater control over their environment, materials and equipment should keep pace with their increasing abilities. When adding or changing materials, remember that toddlers love to repeat and practice tasks they have mastered. For the most part, a toddler's play is solitary or parallel, with some associative play emerging. Caregivers and teachers still have a primary role to play in guiding toddlers' social interactions, physical challenges, and manipulation of materials.

Adapting Curriculum for Children with Special Needs

Curriculum is planned to meet the needs and challenges of the whole group. Children are more alike than they are different so that in an inclusive classroom children with exceptionalities will participate in the same routines and activities as do other children. The changes and additions will depend upon the type of disability and the skills and developmental level of the child. Look again at Figure 3.7 to refresh your memory about the variety of exceptionalities you may find in any classroom. Figure 6.11 suggests a number of strategies for adapting the curriculum.

Provide activities that allow children to respond in a variety of ways and according to their abilities.

Figure 6.11
Program Planning for Developmental Differences

No matter what the child's exceptionality or challenge, curriculum can be adapted to meet their unique needs.

1. **Modify activities to make them more accessible.** Tables can be made higher or lower for wheelchair access, or a teacher may spend extra time in the dramatic play area with individual children who need help interacting with their peers.

2. **Plan individual and group activities according to the age level of the class, considering the behavior patterns and learning styles that exist.** An age-level- appropriate gardening project for 4-year-olds will provide many opportunities for differences in learning styles. Some children will want to do the digging, others will want to plan out the flower bed with their friends, still others will want to draw pictures to label the various plants growing in the garden.

3. **Make sure the materials are in a variety of formats so that children can choose the ones that express their style of learning,** such as puzzles and manipulatives, writing and drawing materials, dance and movement accessories, building blocks, and storytelling.

4. **Know the individual children, their strengths, and their challenges.** Families bring further knowledge of each individual child, and that information must be added to the mix when planning activities that appeal to and motivate interactions with curriculum materials.

5. **Include the interests, abilities, and unique characteristics of *all* the children in the class, whether or not they have disabilities.** Movement and dance appeal to many children and are a staple of an early childhood curriculum. Yet Margie gets upset when the music is too loud, Aaron gets too overstimulated, and Carlo, who is in a wheelchair, cannot dance. Each of these children's needs must be accommodated in the planning. Dancing with scarves to softer music might help Margie and Aaron. Asking the children to dance with their hands and arms brings a new experience in movement and accommodates Carlo's disability without making a point about it.

6. **Throughout the year, assess each child's capacity for sitting and listening and plan strategies to help them expand their capacity.** Joaquin needs more time to develop these skills, so the team adds a small-group time midmorning to create a daily experience to develop task persistence.

7. **Select activities that allow for a variety of responses from children at different stages of development.** A pasting activity encourages creativity in the most adept 3-year-old and still allows the less skilled 3-year-old to explore the feel of the paste on fingers and hands.

Many children with special needs have an Individualized Education Program (IEP) created by specialists and an IFSP (Individualized Family Student Plan) that parents and teachers follow which will suggest adaptations and modifications to activities that will be useful to the individual child. The teaching staff, in collaboration with parents, will guide you to fully include children with special needs in your classroom.

Planning for Groups

At various times of the day, teachers often gather children together in small and large groups. The purpose of each group differs according to the needs of the children, the program, and the number of staff members.

Large Groups. A gathering of the whole class for group time (or circle time or class meeting time) creates a sense of community and belonging, and gives children experience in listening and participating in a large group. Whereas the teacher has an agenda, children often want to share something important with everyone. Early morning group times include a discussion about the day's activities and plans. Group times at the end of the day help bring about closure as the children reflect on the day's activities and plan for tomorrow. Depending on the age of the children, group times may last as little as 5 to 10 minutes with a class of 3-year-olds to 30 minutes in a primary classroom. Group times usually include a combination of songs, fingerplays, stories, and movement activities. Reading one of the children's (or teacher's) favorite books is also a popular group-time activity.

When you lead a large-group-time activity, keep in mind the following guidelines:

- Position yourself in a chair in front of the group and make sure there is an appropriate space for the children so that they can see you and be free of other distractions: "I'm going to sit right here so I can see everybody and you can see me."

- Open with the familiar: a song, chant, or fingerplay that captures the group's attention and invites everybody's participation: "You will know the words to this song, so sing them with me—'If You're Happy and You Know It, Clap Your Hands.'"

- Be prepared with several songs or fingerplays until the whole group gathers: "Let's sing about the Eeensy Weensy Spider, and then we'll sing it in Spanish."

- Maintain eye contact with all the children in the group to ensure their continued interest: "I see Juanita's eyes and Damion's eyes. Where are yours, Carla?"

- Be enthusiastic and keep the pace moving because children are influenced by your tone and actions: "This was one of my favorite books when I was little!"

- If you have a story or activity planned, move into it as soon as all the children are settled: "Good, you are all here. Look at the person next to you, and sit facing them for 'Row, Row, Row Your Boat.'"

- While reading a story or explaining the activity, ask the children questions, as this helps maintain their involvement, but don't get lost in them: "What do you think happens next to Curious George? I want three ideas. If you have one, put your hand in the air."

- Keep your focus and stay in charge, so that one or two children do not dominate the interactions and the group doesn't fall apart from lack of leadership: "I can hear two more ideas, and then we will finish the story and find out what really happens."

- Use phrases that demonstrate what is to occur and how to proceed to maintain control and give directions: "I am walking around with a box of scarves; please take one when I get to you."

- Conclude group time with a clear message of what children are to do next: "Will all the children with blue socks get their jackets on to go outside?"

A minimum of two teachers is needed for a large-group gathering. One teacher usually takes the responsibility for planning and conducting group time, and a second teacher acts as support, helps keep the children focused, and deals with any disruptions. With some groups, more adults may be needed to keep children's attention on the group leader, or to help individual children find a seat, learn to take turns, or raise their hand to speak, along with other large-group skills. As you can see in the "Reflective Incident," things do not always go well.

Age Group Activities

Planning for group time is different for each age group and its size, and should reflect the unique needs and developmental levels of each age level.

Infant/Toddler Groups. Kayla sits down on the floor with 6-month-old Rodney and places him next to 9-month-old Ernesto, who is sitting in Whitney's lap. "Hi, Ernesto!" says Kayla. "What do you have in your hand?" The two teachers talk back and forth with the boys, commenting on what each one notices. "You seem to like Rodney's red shoes, Ernesto. Do you want to touch them?" These interactions become the verbal curriculum as the caregivers help the two boys observe and explore their world.

Group activities for toddlers are loosely constructed times where teachers might sit on the floor with several 4- or 5-piece puzzles (the kind with large knobs). The curriculum is derived from the teacher's interactions with the children and her observations of their thinking skills, eye-hand coordination, language development, and fine motor skills. Matching games are also an effective way to have an age-appropriate group time. These activities are kept as short as the toddler's attention spans. Singing songs, patty-cake, and taking a small group outside for a walk or in a toddler cart encourages group interactions and learning.

Preschool Groups. Groups for 3- to 5-year-olds are often arranged in both small and whole group fashion, as in these two examples:

- Student teacher Janet meets with five 4-year-olds for small group time. Janet brings in a tray covered with a cloth and puts it on the table. She explains that this is a memory game where she will show them the six objects on the tray, then will cover it again and remove one object. The children are to guess what object she removed. This game helps Janet assess the memory and thinking skills of the group of children. Janet makes sure that each child has a turn and encourages the group to guess and discuss the objects taken off the tray.

- Casey, a student teacher in a 3-year-old group, is conducting large-group time. She uses music from a new CD that has a variety of rhythms and tempos. A box of scarves is on a nearby shelf. "First, let's listen to some of the music," she tells the children. "See if you can tell the difference between the fast and the slow, the loud and the soft music." Casey plays a very short sample of the CD and the children listen. "Loud?" "Soft?" "Fast? " asks Casey. They shake their head and/or say yes/no in response. "Now let's move our bodies to the music! Stand up, everybody!" As the children stand and the music plays, Casey sways and moves her body in time to the music. The children imitate her at first, then as their interest grows, they create their own movements. Very heavy, dark music plays, and Casey stomps her feet. The children also stomp and move around. To keep them from getting out of bounds, Casey then plays soft music and passes out the scarves. She had planned for this activity to last 10 minutes, but the children became so engrossed in matching their bodies to the tempo, she continued for another 5 minutes.

Primary Classroom Groups. Meetings for older children are held to build a sense of community where everyone contributes ideas, solutions, and to the group discussions. Children learn to listen to each other, become aware of different points of view, make choices, and solve their own problems through group time discussions. Notice the differences in these two primary class group times:

- Each morning in Mrs. Watanabi's first-grade class, all of the children gather together. She sings a song that welcomes each child by name, and the children join in. On the message board is the date and a list of today's activities. Mrs. Watanabi asks the children to volunteer to read the message. Irina raises her hand quickly and reads, "Today we will have a math lesson." Jonah raises his hand, stands up, and reads," Today we will go to the library." Mrs. Watanabi calls on Rachel to read the last message: "Today we will plan our garden." Then Mrs. Watanabi explains that Jordy's dad and Lacey's mom will come in and help the group talk about their plans for the garden. Right after lunch they will break into small groups for their discussions. Mrs. Watanabi asks if anybody has any questions, and after answering them she dismisses the children to write or draw in their journals.

● Mrs. Watanabi meets with seven children in a quiet corner of the classroom while Jody's dad and Lacey's mom do the same in other sections of the room. She begins by asking what the children already know about gardens, building on the experience they had the previous year. She then poses the question "What do we need to know in order to start our garden?" and listens to each child's response. "Barney, do you have another idea?" she asks a shy child. The children have now compiled a list of what they need, and next to it a list of where they will get the materials and equipment. Tomás's question, "How long will this take?" prompts another list, a time line for getting the work done. The children's enthusiasm prolonged the group time for 30 minutes. As group time comes to an end, Mrs. Watanabi explains that tomorrow all of the groups will share their information and create one plan out of everyone's contributions.

Reflective Incident "Leading Circle Time"

At circle time, I led the activity. I was really nervous. I pulled out the surprise bag filled with five frogs, one blue sheet, and one log. I introduced the song "Five Little Speckled Frogs," which we all sang together. I asked three children to come and stand next to me. Teacher Jeannie was in tune with my apprehensiveness and assisted when needed. We all sang the song again, and the three children jumped and "swam" back to their seats (well, sometimes they did this). In all honesty, it went okay, but I wasn't happy with it, and I'm not sure the kids really enjoyed it that much.

—Isabella

Your Thoughts

1. How would I feel?

2. What would I do?

3. What might the result be?

Small Groups. Many learning experiences are more successful with a small group of children. A smaller group encourages greater interaction between the teacher and each child, offers time for individual contributions, and allows teachers to observe more closely each child's growth and development.

Small groups are an important part of the daily schedule for many reasons. Teachers can focus on certain skills, such as listening and taking turns; encourage children in their social interactions; explore a topic in greater depth; or introduce a new concept, game, or activity.

One teacher can manage a small number of children for this type of group. The groups can be created informally ("All children with red shirts can go with Mr. Chang"), or the teachers may preselect the group in order to promote certain interactions, or to work on a specific task with children who need more assistance. In multiage settings, small-group times are scheduled for the individual age groups to offer appropriate-level activities.

The Teacher's Role. Successful group times come about through careful planning. One important rule to remember is that group times are for and about children. Sometimes inexperienced teachers have the impression that they have to carry all of the discussion and conversation. All group

lessons from the field

"The Value of Less"

by Stacey James

Mentor Teacher, Geo-Kids Menlo Park, CA

The curriculum that excites me the most is when I provide interesting, new, open-ended material and then stand back and watch. When working with open-ended materials, children are able to formulate for themselves the problems that most challenge them, and then they set about solving those problems. I have seen this occur with every age group with which I have worked, from infants to 4-year-olds. The idea that children create appropriate challenges for themselves and construct their own knowledge is basic to constructivist philosophy in early childhood education, but it is always astonishing to me when I see it happen. The diversity of problems and solutions within a group of children, the absorption with which they pursue them, and the intriguing tangents that they explore are always surprising, sometimes dazzling.

This probably happens much more often than I realize. But the challenge is to see it, to capture and understand and make visible the learning that occurs in these situations. It requires very close attention on my part, undistracted by other things in the classroom. This is what happens less frequently—not the learning but the witnessing of the learning. And, trickiest of all, it requires the least possible amount of interference from me: too much and the magic is lost.

times, regardless of size, provide the occasion for teachers to encourage children's listening and speaking skills and help them gain the ability to share their thoughts and ideas. Younger children will interrupt the teacher and other children in their excitement or desire to talk. A part of working with a group is helping those children learn to take turns and listen when others are talking. As you observe other teachers conducting group times, you will see that it takes very little to get children involved and ready to talk. Look at how other teachers handle children who have difficulty waiting for their turn.

At some point in your student teaching you will be required to plan and conduct a group time. Start with the developmental level, interests, and skills of the group. When you begin planning, revisit the planning approach outlined in Figure 6.10. Group times can be one of the most enjoyable activities you have as a teacher once you get past your first few attempts. It is one of the areas of teaching that gives you an opportunity to put your personal stamp on an activity and demonstrate your abilities to be creative, think on your feet, and be in charge.

Practicum Activity

Design a lesson plan for the age level you teach. Indicate how each developmental area (physical/motor, cognitive/language, social-emotional, and creative) is being addressed by this activity. Show how the lesson plan could be adapted for the age just above and just below. Bring the lesson plan to class and share it with the group.

Journaling Assignment

What is a developmentally appropriate curriculum to you, and how does your teaching site measure up to developmentally appropriate practice (DAP)? What trouble spots do you see, and what changes would you make in the curriculum to remedy these?

References

Bredekamp, S., & Rosegrant, T. (Eds.). (1995). *Reaching potentials: Transforming early childhood curriculum and assessment* (Vol. 2). Washington, DC: National Association for the Education of Young Children.

Chard, S. (2000). *The project approach.* New York: Scholastic.

Copple, C., & Bredekamp, S. (Eds.). (2006). *Basics of developmentally appropriate practice.* Washington, DC: National Association for the Education of Young Children.

Gardner, H. (1993). *Multiple intelligences.* New York: Basic Books.

Gordon, A. M., & Browne, K. W. (2011). *Beginnings and beyond: Foundations in early childhood education* (8th ed.). Belmont, CA: Wadsworth Cengage Learning.

Gronlund, G. (2006). *Make early learning standards come alive: Connecting your practice and curriculum to state guidelines.* St. Paul, MN: Redleaf Press.

Jones, E., & Nimmo, J. (1994). *Emergent curriculum.* Washington, DC: National Association for the Education of Young Children.

Lam, M., & Wiggins-Dowler, K. (2005). "Project Blueprint: A construction project." Unpublished documentation board, College of San Mateo Child Development Center.

Parten, M. (1932). Social participation among preschool children. *Journal of Abnormal and Social Psychology, 27,* 243–369.

Piaget, J. (1962). *Play, dreams, & imitation in childhood.* New York: Norton.

Web Sites

Association Montessori Internationale
www.montessori-ami.org

Teaching Strategies for Early Childhood
www.TeachingStrategies.com

High/Scope Educational Research Foundation
www.highscope.org

National Association for the Education of Young Children
www.naeyc.org

Project Approach
www.projectapproach.org

Reggio Emilia
www.reggioalliance.org
www.reggiochildren.it/?lang=en

The Division for Learning Disabilities, Council for Exceptional Children
www.teachingld.org

chapter 7

....

Team Teaching

Articulate the essentials of team teaching and the challenges of developing positive working relationships with colleagues.

Team Teaching: Collaboration at Its Best

By virtue of participating in a student practicum, you are a member of a team of people who work together for the children and their families who are enrolled in the center or school. The function of the teaching team is to help the many interested parties involved in children's education relate to each other through a mutually respectful and supportive system.

What Is Team Teaching?

There are always two parts of every educational endeavor, the nonteaching team and those who work directly with the children.

Definitions. The total team consists of everyone who has some role to play in the lives of the children and families. This includes the sponsoring organization (such as a church or synagogue and the board or council); the authorizing or licensing agency; the administration staff; the director of the program; and specialists such as nurses, social workers, nutritionists, doctors, and psychologists. Maintenance personnel, such as the cook and janitor, and the bus driver, fill out the remainder of the nonteaching part of the team. Each person plays a critical role in the effectiveness of the school organization.

Parents and families are an integral part of the team as well. Some families are able to participate in the classroom itself; others may help drive on field trips or pull weeds on family workdays at the school. A growing number of centers encourage families to help set policy by serving on the decision-making committees and boards. Families in which both parents work outside the home do tasks that do not require their presence in the classroom, such as calling other parents to remind them of school events, participating in fund-raising, or contributing to the class newsletter. In any event, every family with a child who is enrolled in the school is considered part of the team.

The classroom team is the day-to-day group of which you are a part. A teaching team is defined as two or more adults working together in one classroom with one group of children. As you have probably noted, the actual number may vary from one day to the next. At any given time, the team may consist of the supervising teacher, teacher's aides and assistants, student teachers, parent volunteer, early childhood specialist, and observers.

Team Size and Composition. The size of the teaching team is determined by the number of children in the classroom. This core group of teachers has the primary responsibility for the program. The number may be mandated by the licensing or accrediting agency, the state, or the school's philosophy. Organized groups for children's education and care may be family, center, or institution based, which will affect group sizes and age ranges. Taking into consideration these groups, we suggest adult–child ratios for different age groups such as the following:

- Infants and toddlers (birth to 30 months) should keep their group size to 12 or fewer children, with ratios ranging from 1:3 up to 1:6 with the oldest children.

- Preschoolers (30+ months to age 5) should keep group sizes to 20 or fewer children, with ratios ranging from 1:6 up to 1:10 with the oldest children.

- School-age children (ages 5 to 8) should keep their group size to 30 or fewer children, although some after-school programs have children up to age 12 and thus increase group size later in the afternoon, with ratios ranging from 1:10 to 1:12.

You can see that the younger the child, the greater the number of adults (teachers, teacher's aides and assistants, and other adults who are regular members of the teaching team) who are needed to support the program. Infants and toddlers require more intense care than do preschoolers who have learned to dress and feed themselves. Each team size reflects the developmental levels of the children in the class and requires fewer teaching staff as children mature and function more independently.

The composition of each team will vary. Each teacher is an individual with different experiences, interests, and abilities. Team members are chosen for the unique blend they add to the team, so that they can use their abilities and teach to their strengths. At the same time, each team member can learn from and teach others on the team.

Teaching teams usually consist of a head or lead teacher, one or more assistant teachers and/or teacher's aides, and sometimes a parent or other volunteer. Student teachers add to the mix in settings that serve as training grounds for early childhood teachers. For family-child care programs, there may be a single caregiver. In laboratory schools, researchers and observers may be present, whereas in schools that include a significant number of children with special needs, consultants and specialists will be part of the team. Special resource teachers in art, music, and physical development can also be part of the staff, meeting with children a few times a week. Substitute teachers and those who are hired to assist with a child with special needs may also be part of the team.

A teacher's position on the team generally depends on the level of education, training, and experience with young children. The head or lead teacher usually has the most education and experience in early childhood education and child development, preferably a bachelor's degree in early childhood education. Assistants and aides usually have less education or experience, and are often taking courses, working toward certification or degrees.

Benefits of Team Teaching

A team of teachers is a standard practice in good early childhood programs for many reasons. Team teaching not only fulfills the appropriate

Team teachers share the responsibilities and provide a wider range of role models for children.

teacher–child ratios necessary for effective interactions with young children but has other benefits as well. Teaching on a team makes it possible to:

- *Provide a wide range of adult role models* as well as diverse attitudes, cultural backgrounds, and social interactions.

- *Be supportive of children.* If staff changes occur, the rest of the team is intact and provides stability through the transition.

- *Share information* about children, families, curriculum, guidance strategies, and professional growth opportunities.

- *Contribute new ideas* on curriculum planning, behavior management, professional growth opportunities, and family–school relationships.

- *Solve problems* as they arise and make mutually acceptable decisions that reflects the best thinking of the team regarding class policy, behavior management, and parent or family issues.

- *Resolve conflicts* that may occur within the team involving differences in opinion, approach, personality, and style.

- *Support other team members* by sharing the workload and providing help and encouragement when needed.

It is easy to see how the program is enriched by a team of people working together, sharing their talents and resources for the benefit of the children and families in their class. Most of the disadvantages of team teaching stem from poor communication styles, issues of power and control, or unclear job descriptions. These issues will be addressed in the "Challenges of Team Teaching" section later in this chapter.

Role Set

Because early childhood programs are busy, people-filled places, teachers come in contact with a multitude of people, as discussed previously. Each person has a set of expectations about what the teacher should do and how to do it. Together, they compose what sociologists call a *role set* (Katz & Kahn, cited in Caruso & Fawcett, 2006). For instance, the head teacher's role set consists of:

Children	Parents and families
Teachers	Volunteers
Teacher assistants and aides	Outside consultants
Director	Health and social services
Student teachers	Local public schools

The members of a role set communicate their expectations to each other based on their understandings and beliefs about the role and their perceptions of how their messages are received. For instance, teachers may feel that the director should give them more help in working with difficult children, whereas the parents may want the teachers to call in a consultant, and the director may want the parents to do more at home. Members of the teacher's role set "push and pull" the teacher, competing for time and attention and creating multiple demands. This pressure is part of any job; those "with clear priorities, goals, and philosophy of education will be better able to formulate realistic expectations" (Caruso & Fawcett, 2006, p. 37).

Unlike elementary classrooms, where there is usually just one teacher, early childhood teams include many partners. Teachers are usually supervised by a head or lead (or mentor) teacher, coordinator, or director. There are assistants (paid or volunteer), student teachers, and parent or adult family members.

Essentials of Team Teaching

How do a group of teachers become a productive and cohesive unit? If you have ever played on a sports team you know that teamwork does not just happen. It takes intention, organization, planning, and practice as well as coordination, communication, and cooperation. Team teaching is successful when each member understands the complexity and challenges, as outlined in Figure 7.1 (adapted from Gordon & Browne, 1985).

Professionalism

In Chapter 2 you learned some of the factors that influence a professional approach to teaching. Teacher preparation and experience, knowledge of

Figure 7.1
Top 10 Benefits of Team Teaching

1. Professionalism
2. A satisfying role
3. Flexibility
4. Open and frequent communication
5. Self-awareness
6. Mutual respect and acceptance
7. Collegiality
8. Willingness to share the spotlight
9. Clearly defined roles and job description
10. Evaluation

ethical guidelines, and effective evaluations are important considerations. Professional attitudes and behaviors can make or break a successful teaching team.

In a team setting it is important to maintain confidentiality. You may be aware of matters within the personal lives of your team members that should remain in confidence, and your knowledge of the intimate details of children and their families should not be discussed outside the professional team setting.

When differences arise with other team members, as they do, the professional teacher attempts to work out the issues with the other person(s) directly and in a timely fashion. Complaining about personal grievances and gossip (see the "My Reaction" feature later in this chapter) undermine the trust and cooperation necessary for a good team relationship.

A Satisfying Role

Each teacher is a unique resource, with individual talents, training, and interests, and likes to be appreciated for that special something he or she brings to the team. It is essential that the assignment for each team member be appropriate to his or her role and abilities. As a team member, you will want to have some understanding of your own talents and experiences and how they might be best used on a teaching team. Look again at your role set where you are student teaching, and think of the roles each person plays.

Flexibility

Effective teachers learn to change and adapt to children's interests and needs. As a team member, you will need to learn to be flexible with your adult colleagues as well. The daily give-and-take among staff members is key to team effort. A team functions well when its members change with the emerging needs of the staff. This is especially critical with a small team, such as in family child care. As a team member, you will want to keep an open mind to ideas presented by co-workers and be able to adapt to changing preset plans or filling in where needed.

Open and Frequent Communication

Interweaving the resources represented by each team is a dynamic process that requires good communication skills from the team members. Some of the techniques for working with other adults were discussed in Chapter 1. It is important to remember that adult relationships within the early childhood setting are as critical as relationships with the children.

Aside from informal communications among the team, there are other reasons for developing strong communication links: sharing information about children and their families or changes in the schedule; contributing new ideas, such as a recent article from *Young Children*, or resources from a recent workshop; and working through differences of opinion that may arise. Open and honest communication is an essential element in teamwork.

Self-Awareness

One of the fundamentals of teaching noted in Chapter 1 discussed the importance of self-reflective teaching. Throughout this text, you have been asked to reflect on various aspects of a student teacher's life within the context of each chapter. Self-awareness is obviously one of the most significant qualifications for a good teacher. This is especially true when you are a member of a teaching team. Student teachers may feel uncomfortable or uneasy in their relationship with other teachers. Once you know more about yourself as a teacher, however, you can apply this self-awareness to your connections with others on the staff.

It is useful to know what your teaching strengths and weaknesses are and how they might complement or conflict with others on the team. As you teach, you will come to understand yourself in new ways, discovering when and where you do—or do not—feel comfortable in certain teaching situations, and how you perceive yourself as a learner. Fortunately, evaluations are a part of the teaching–learning process. Feedback from master to student teacher provides opportunities to learn more about yourself and grow and change with experience.

Mutual Respect and Acceptance

One of the most important roles teachers model for others is the degree to which we accept and respect differences in our fellow humans. Appreciating the individuality of each team member is as important as appreciating the uniqueness of each child we teach.

All members of a teaching team should learn about the people with whom they work. Knowledge of your team's diverse personalities, experiences, strengths and challenges, values, culture, and background leads to greater understanding in the work environment. In the interest of developing a respect for, and acceptance of, the uniqueness of team members, you might look at what you have in common with your co-workers and appreciate what you can learn from your differences. Self-awareness helps you understand what you bring to the team; you will want to know what other team members believe to be their particular gifts. What is it you want the team to respect and accept about you? What is something you can learn from each team member?

Collegiality

Collegiality is the extent to which the team is friendly, supportive, and trusting of one another (Jorde-Bloom, 2005). A sense of collegiality or "teamness" is the result of a conscious effort to share and communicate openly and honestly, to value professional interactions, and to learn to be a cohesive group. When each team member promotes and sustains a high level of sharing and caring, a team spirit develops.

Opportunities for collaboration and teamwork abound in early childhood settings. Teachers can work together on projects for the classroom, share resources and curriculum ideas with the rest of the team, or plan a parent meeting with each other. Depending on the schedule, sharing lunch or break time promotes team spirit, as do monthly birthday celebrations for the staff. A sense of community can be nurtured through structured and unstructured times when teachers are able to have frequent communication with one another. As they share problems and achievements, the team will grow in admiration and respect for one another.

Working collaboratively with another teacher promotes a team spirit and a sense of community.

Confidentiality

Situation: The teaching team has just learned that their student teacher, Maya, is a neighbor of one of the children in the class whose parent is a well-known professional athlete. During the day, different staff members approached Maya and asked her questions about the family, making Maya very uncomfortable and unsure how to answer.

Code of Ethical Conduct Resources:

1-1.3a 2—Share resources with co-workers, collaborating to ensure that the best possible early childhood care and education program is provided.

P-3.a 1—Recognize the contributions of colleagues to our program and not participate in practices that diminish their reputations or impair their effectiveness in working with children and families.

Solution: The next day Maya's practicum class was meeting so she shared her dilemma with her faculty instructor and classmates. They discussed the nature of the teachers' questions and concluded that the information was not relevant to the school community and that Maya should not answer the questions. The faculty instructor then had Maya and another student role-play her responses to teachers who asked inappropriate questions about a family she knew. Maya reported this interaction with her supervising teacher, and they agreed that Maya would refer to the Code of Ethical Conduct in her response to inappropriate questions.

Share the Spotlight

Being a good team member means sharing your strengths in ways that support the rest of the team but do not create a climate of competition. Everyone on the team is good at something, whether it is working with difficult children, creating an outdoor curriculum, or relating to parents and families. We all like to be acknowledged for what we do well and hear from our colleagues that they agree. Differences notwithstanding, all team members are dedicated to their work and deserving of recognition. A supportive and collegial team shares the success when things work well, just as they share the responsibility when problems arise.

Clearly Defined Roles and Job Descriptions

A clear understanding of the roles and unique responsibilities of each team member is essential. Teamwork is more efficient when each teacher's role is outlined and understood by all. Clearly articulated responsibilities also serve as a guard against legal and ethical problems, particularly if a child is injured at school. Knowing the extent of and limits on your role and responsibilities gives you the confidence to act with authority in areas you supervise.

For further in-depth discussion of role definition, see the following section titled "Challenges of Team Teaching."

Evaluation

In Chapter 2 you read about the importance of a regular evaluation process. As members of the staff of the center or school, you will probably participate in an annual evaluation. The goals you set and the feedback you receive influence your role as a member of the teaching team. More than likely, the head or lead teacher participated in your evaluation process and will, with the help of the teaching team, support and encourage you in your progress.

The 10 benefits of team teaching (Figure 7.1) apply to the individual teacher as well as the group. They are also attributes that provide good models for young children through positive adult relationships, embracing differences and sharing the responsibilities.

Challenges of Team Teaching

Team teaching involves those many cooperative efforts that are best done when everyone knows his or her function. "I consider that everybody in my site is on the same side," writes Patricia in her student teaching journal. "We are all there because we love our work, we understand the importance of making a difference in the life of each child enrolled at Wu Yee Center, and we all try to support the families to the best of our abilities, and support each other to make the work less stressful."

Clarifying Roles

The roles and responsibilities of an early childhood teaching team are complex, and teams work best when all members have clear roles. As mentioned earlier in the chapter, the classroom team has the major responsibility for working with children, although role sets outline the secondary obligations of these jobs. In an early study on teaching-team structure, Whitebook (1989) found that head teachers and teacher-directors, teachers, and aides all have the same range of duties about curriculum planning and implementation, meal preparation, and maintenance. Head teachers often have more family communication and administrative work; all classroom teachers plan and carry out the program for children.

The jobs of aide or assistant and student teacher are important. These positions are usually jobs with few qualifications or education requirements. Assisting the teacher may involve performing housekeeping duties as well as teaching children directly, and can include supervising areas when a teacher is called away, or overseeing nap time while others meet. Attending staff meetings, training sessions, and meetings with consultants or parents may be included. Preparing curriculum materials or participating in child assessment might be part of these jobs.

However, there is a wide range of expectations for these positions, and the jobs can be misused and misunderstood. Clarifying what is—and what is not—part of the job is crucial. For instance, a student teacher can be expected to make snacks, mix paint, or set up cots part of the time, but should also get experience assisting in activities, supervising free-play areas, and running planned small or large groups. If student teachers are unclear about what to do, problems occur. This note came from a classroom teacher:

> At my school, there are two practicum student teachers who are not as willing to put in effort to help regular teachers in the classroom. These students sit by themselves away from the children. One even made a comment putting down a teacher's discipline. The situation needed to be resolved; fortunately, the master teacher spoke with them about how one could shadow a difficult child and the other could get busy involving herself without being invited. So far, the two of them have assisted more in the classroom, and we appreciate the efforts and help.

If you are unclear or uncertain about your job, be sure to talk with your supervising teacher right away. Inquire if your fieldwork site uses any of the following items to clarify roles and responsibilities.

Job Descriptions

Specific job descriptions define roles: In some centers, job cards are given to each participating parent, the student teacher, and the head teacher. These cards outline the team member's responsibilities throughout the session (see Figure 7.2 for a sample). "As my mentor says, 'The higher the organizational component, the less stress on both children and staff,'" student teacher Gordon reports. "Teachers and staff are individually responsible for a small group of children; this responsibility includes doing observations, collecting work samples, providing developmentally appropriate small group activities, and managing the children. Then, at staff meetings, everyone is to relate that information—and get advice—back to the rest of the staff."

Team Roles. On a typical team, people will have different roles depending on their position, much like a family or athletic team. Having clearly

Teacher 1:   Art, Snack, and Sand Areas

8:30–9:00 a.m.   *Set up art area:*   Set up easels, help-yourself table, and structured art project. Set up sand area: open shed; put out sample toys.

9:00–10:00 a.m.   *Supervise all art areas:*   Invite children; help them put on smocks; help write names on and pin up work; keep areas more or less organized.

10:00 a.m.   *Assist children in cleaning up areas:*   Put caps on paint jars; set brushes in sink; put materials on shelves; spray and wipe tables.

10:15 a.m.   Set up snack trays for each small group during circle time; place near tables.

10:30 a.m.   *Sit at table for snack:*   Help children settle from handwashing and prepare their own snack space; supervise their passing and serving; read a story or converse; ensure they clean up their own space and stay at table until you can go outside together.

10:45–11:45 a.m.   *Supervise sand area:*   Get out a sample of toys; decide if using water and assist; start cleanup by 11:40 and get children to help.

11:50 a.m.   *Assist at story time:*   Help children settle; sit with wiggly ones.

Noon   *Move to art counter:*   Help children pick up their projects; say good-bye.

12:10–12:30 p.m.   Clean up art and sand areas after everyone has left.

Figure 7.2 Sample Team Teaching Job Card
A job card can clarify what is expected to successfully fulfill the teacher's responsibilities.

defined responsibilities helps all team members understand their designated roles; having fuzzy roles or vague tasks causes confusion, conflict, and dysfunction. Leaders might think of themselves like coaches (who guide but don't actually play the game) or team captains (who give directions while on the floor in the action). Team members may have different talents, even roles to play, yet everyone always contributes and stays focused on the same goals. The scorekeeper role may be given to one or more members, but keeping track of time, goals, and accountability is important.

Basic team roles help all members address challenges that arise. One such team role might be responsibility for handling what is decided during a meeting, who would be best suited to create teacher job cards, and what member would be involved in finding the money to buy a new rug for the classroom. In addition to the official team roles, there are usually informal roles that can be either helpful or harmful. Helpful roles promote communication and smooth achievement of goals; harmful ones keep the team from being successful. We all appreciate someone on the lookout for who needs help, or attempts to help when people are in conflict because this helps keep the team headed in the right direction. If your team seems to have someone who always points out what is wrong with something or labels behaviors without being asked, the morale of the team is at risk. Think about your team and how it operates.

Surveying Your Team. Staff surveys can be used to measure teamwork effectiveness and identify areas for improvement. Although student teachers are not likely to be assessing organizational climate, they may find such work enlightening. Consider your own fieldwork site as you read these aspects of overall staff relations from Jorde-Bloom (2005):

- Cooperative environment has friendly staffers.
- Competition is in the atmosphere
- People are reluctant to express their feelings.
- Teachers are very helpful to new staff.
- Team spirit is good.
- Staff are generally frank and candid.
- Morale is low.
- People socialize outside work.
- People feel isolated.
- People complain a lot.

When responsibilities are clear and roles feel equitable, the interpersonal climate of the team is more likely to be positive, and student teachers will integrate easily into the teaching environment. "I have felt very welcomed and accepted here as a member of this team," comments Gordon. "The teachers and assistants are all responsible for individual areas; those are rotated every three weeks. Staff works hard to coordinate their efforts to help ensure smooth transitions, maintain proper ratio at all times, and deal with safety issues. Everyone is very supportive of one another, and I have been encouraged to become fully integrated and engaged in the team effort. It's going to be hard to say good-bye."

Team Leadership: Power and Hierarchy

Team structure varies from setting to setting. Each school or center has its own hierarchical structure that differentiates the multiple roles of the team. The team leader has a significant role to play in creating a healthy work climate where the staff members are valued and involved. Good leaders provide clear expectations, support, and encouragement to the team, giving honest and open feedback that is respectful and fair (Jorde-Bloom, 2005).

The decision-making process indicates how the power is distributed throughout the team and how much influence each team member has in the program. Team morale is high in programs where the teachers feel the decision-making process is fair; high morale leads to deeper commitment to fulfilling the program goals and greater satisfaction from the job.

Baumrind's classic work (1971) gathered information about parents' child-rearing patterns, which you will read about in Chapter 8 about families. It is also useful to adapt this to team leadership styles.

1. *Authoritative style:* Characterized by acceptance, interaction, patience, warmth, and sensitivity to teachers' needs. Leaders have reasonable expectations of their staff, place a premium on communication, engage in joint decision making, and encourage teachers to express their thoughts and feelings.

2. *Authoritarian style:* Characterized by the need for control and by demands through criticism and command. Leaders rarely listen to another's point of view and make all the decisions for the team.

3. *Permissive style:* Characterized by warmth and acceptance yet also inattention or overindulgence. Clear standards and rules are not set, and those that exist are not reinforced consistently. Leaders appear not to be in control, make few demands on the staff, and allow teachers to make their own decisions, appropriate or not.

Teachers take on different roles in response to the leader's style. As in parenting, each leadership style can work, but has distinct strengths and weaknesses. With *authoritative* leaders, teachers participate in much of the decision making even though this adds to their workload. Teams often feel involved but sometimes overextended in their commitment. Teachers on the team feel good about expressing themselves to each other and the leader. In contrast, an *authoritarian* style is a top-down approach in which teams are not involved in making decisions, but are told what to do. Teachers like the clarity of expectations, but sometimes resent being left out. In a *permissive* team, it is sometimes difficult to understand priorities and rules (see "Reflective Incident"). Although allowed to make decisions on their own, teachers are sometimes confused and feel ignored, though others like the more nebulous boundaries.

Which style do you think your supervising teacher has? How does it affect you? How does it affect the team? As you observe your team leader in action, you can form your own understanding of good team styles.

Team Dynamics

Team relationships and the dynamics among teachers are "the good, the bad, and the ugly," as Roseline's supervising teacher put it. "With every job and situation you have to expect the unexpected, but compromising and problem solving are necessary." As the student teacher, you are coming

Team dynamics involve keeping other adults in mind while conducting a separate activity.

into an ongoing team. As mentioned in Chapter 1, this is a challenge. "It's a strain having to start new," notes Ichun's mentor teacher. "With time, one does learn to work in a team. As we mature, we learn to accommodate, to let go, becoming less critical, more reflective." Many early childhood programs have regular turnover; others use a "continuity of care" philosophy or Waldorf-type system that moves teachers with children so that teaching teams change.

Taking into account one another's personal and professional characteristics, each person's stage of development and of teaching, and everyone's learning style and preferences are a challenge.

> When we talk about staff relationships, we really are talking about how harmoniously we as individuals get along with members of a group—how well we interact with one another; how well we communicate, support, and accept each other's differences, strengths, weaknesses, and points of view. (Zavitkovsky, 1992, p. 14)

"Team relationships at our site are important, and they make an effort to have meetings and share the responsibilities," note student teachers Michelle and Theo. "It seems that they are direct with each other, and the nicest thing we've observed and felt from them is their warmth. They hug each other when one comes into work, and they're diverse both culturally and personality wise."

Reflective Incident "When It Isn't Working"

I've been working at my site for 6 months now, but I still feel like I am new. As I expressed in class, I still feel like we don't work as a team on some days. We never have enough time to plan together, and so a lot of times it depends on someone to take the initiative to plan the lesson for the week. Right now, lesson planning is done by me and another teacher, but we don't really sit down together because our prep/lunch schedules are one after the other. Then, when another teacher doesn't follow it, I get discouraged. I also feel that some of the teachers who have been working at the center longer are spending a lot of time talking with each other. Overall, I feel that the staff is not very organized, and me being the "newbie"—I don't know what to do.

—BARBARA

Your Thoughts

1. How would I feel?

2. What would I do?

3. What might the results be?

As a student teacher, you concentrate your efforts on working with children. However, because early childhood teaching is usually done in team settings, knowing something about stages of development in adults and for teachers is helpful in dealing with team dynamics and conflicts.

Stages of Adult Development. Knowledge of self is fundamental to effective classroom teaching, and it contributes to positive team teaching as well. "By understanding ourselves and the impact of our early life experiences and cultural backgrounds, we increase the control we have over our own behavior and can more easily modify it when necessary" (Caruso & Fawcett, 2006). Understanding adult development increases this level of self-knowledge. Moreover, it will help us understand our co-workers, because teaching teams are usually comprised of adults of all age groups.

Each stage of adult development has certain characteristics and key concerns that affect our work as team members. "At 61, I have many life experiences," states student teacher Pat. "Yet in some ways I have led a sheltered life—I haven't traveled much, and haven't been in school (well, college) for 25 years. I could use some broader experiences. Still, I have a stable self-concept and am responsible and productive in my life. I am good at abstract thinking, but not at expressing it verbally." Think about where you and your teammates are in terms of your stage of adult development:

- Young adults invested in identity and becoming independent?
- Middle adulthood with family obligations, trying to demonstrate stability and competence?
- Later adulthood with increased individuation, modification of dreams, either integrating or regretting accomplishments?

Stages of Teacher Development. Teachers have a developmental sequence in their professional growth patterns as found in Katz's seminal work (1977). Four stages have been outlined, and specific tasks and training needs are associated with each one. Individual teachers may vary greatly in the length of time spent in each of the stages (see Table 7.1 to ascertain where you and your supervising teacher may be). You may be

T a b l e 7 . 1 Stages of Teacher Development

Stage	Developmental Task	Needs
Survival (usually year 1)	"Can I get through the day in one piece? Can I really do this work day after day?" Reality is *not* like theory! Looking for patterns	Support, understanding, encouragement, reassurance, guidance Instruction in specific tasks and skills; needs onsite assistance
Consolidation (often years 2–3)	"I can survive!" Concern with individual children; can identify problem situations; can see variations in patterns	Mutual exploration of a problem on site; extensive give-and-take conversation; has information about specific children or problems; ready for access to specialists and consultants; chances to share feelings with others in this stage
Renewal (may be years 3–5)	"What are new techniques, ways to do things?" Sees self as a teacher; ready for innovations, new ideas	Meet colleagues from different programs, conferences, and workshops; may be ready to look closer at own teaching
Maturity (years 5 plus)	"What is the nature of growth and learning?" Meaningful search for answers	Participate in conferences; lead workshops; become mentor teacher

Source: Data based on Katz (1977).

able to determine the kind of help you need to grow into the next stage. How might this affect the way a team works together?

Conflicts. Whenever there is contact between two or more people, there is likely to be both cooperation and conflict. Conflict can be seen as a predicament or opportunity, although most people see it as problematic rather than as a vehicle for greater understanding or intimacy. Many teachers, even those who handle problems among children with ease, prefer to smooth over conflicts with adults. However, it is a challenge of team teaching that we cannot avoid.

When a disagreement of principle or practice arises, teams must devise ways to resolve their differences. As you read the five common approaches that follow, think about how you—and the teacher on your team—address conflicts.

Approach	Description
No-nonsense or command	I don't give in. I try to be fair and honest. I know what's best. Confronting the issue head on is the way to go.
Problem solving	If there's a conflict, there's a problem, and we all share it. We need to solve it together. This produces creative ideas and stronger relationships.
Compromising	I listen to everyone and support them in listening to me. Then I help each one give in a little. Half a loaf is better than none.
Smoothing	I like things to stay calm and peaceful whenever possible. Most teacher concerns aren't life threatening, so I just direct attention to other things.
Ignoring	I am uneasy dealing with conflict. There is not a whole lot I can do about these situations, so I avoid it.

At one time or another, each of the preceding approaches is appropriate. For example, if a teacher sees children pushing one another off the slide, she must move in swiftly; the *no-nonsense approach* is best, even though the team member at the slide may feel upset at being chastised or brushed aside. If, however, a teacher is unhappy that a co-worker interrupted his circle time, he can use a *problem-solving approach* later, at break time or during the next staff meeting. When student teacher Ellen began to tell Nathan's mother new ways to calm him, her mentor teacher observed the interaction, then took a *compromising approach* when she saw the parent's discomfort, offering a way that both parties could feel heard and satisfied with their viewpoints.

Communicating your thoughts is important; how to do so is challenging. Be a good listener, showing that you are concentrating and asking open-ended questions. Treat your colleagues as you would treat the children you teach. Student teacher Yuji keeps his "eyes on the prize" in the midst of conflict.

> I see sometimes the teachers do not get along about some issues, so I (or another teacher) volunteer to be a bridge between teachers to find a solution. I believe that all humans are different, so it is just a normal thing that some people will disagree. I don't think it is a bad thing that someone makes me upset. When there is a conflict with teachers, I first think that I am here for the children, and what choice should I make with the person to provide a better environment for the children? That way I avoid mixing my own personal feelings in the action. It is sometimes difficult, but I have managed to set my personal feelings aside.

Others get discouraged. For example, frequent interaction and an exchange of information and ideas are important parts of good teamwork, but sometimes difficult. Sau-Kuen faces a different substitute frequently, and there is a language barrier between her and one of the teaching team members. And Paula finds that "there are so many cooks, but we are all cooking up something completely different!" Gossip is another issue (see the following "My Reaction" feature) that often occurs at the workplace.

Many factors contribute to positive conflict resolution. Everyone needs help learning positive approaches to solving interpersonal problems. Refer back to the six steps to problem solving in Chapter 3 (Figure 3.6). At the

---

My Reaction

"Gossip in the Workplace"

I think most teachers at ECE centers are generally really busy and have to stay focused on everything that is going on with the children. They don't have a lot of time to talk to each other—at my place, we don't even have overlapping lunch schedules. It's ironic, then, that the teachers seem to find a way to talk a lot about "things" but not about the program. I get so sick of all the gossiping at the center. If you have an issue with another teacher, then you should go talk to her, right? What's the point of talking *about* her to another teacher? Nothing gets solved and the person just keeps on behaving the same way because no one talks to her. I know that straight communication doesn't come easy to some people (like me, too ☺), but if your goal is to provide the best education for the children, then you should do anything to accomplish that goal.

—Gitel

same time, clear roles and responsibilities, frequent ongoing communication, and an organized framework for discussion help a team bring up important matters. One of the best ways to do this is through staff meetings.

Staff Meetings

Staff meetings offer a place and time for teams to get together "off the floor" of a program. Regular meetings, although often difficult to schedule, provide the best opportunity for team members to talk together, listen, and broaden their own views as they make decisions affecting themselves and the children they teach. In family child care settings, student teachers may be able to talk with their supervising teacher easier than in a larger center. School-age programs are often spread thin, and student teachers may find themselves at the far end of a playground, out of earshot of their supervisor. Meetings can serve many purposes, and clarity of goals helps any meeting run better.

Curriculum is a common focus of staff meetings; student teacher Ming Hong notes that "The teachers always plan together for the weekly theme, and they like to prepare the materials and share their ideas while they do it. I really like their practice because it saves time and they can talk over conflicts while they are doing something together for the program." Meetings also target children; in Tiana's program, weekly staff meetings are a productive means of discussing each child's development, planning for the required assessments, and discussing children before family conferences.

Communicating frequently with each other is an important part of participating on a team.

Whereas organizing the agenda often falls to the team leader, items may be suggested by all members. Formats vary, as does the frequency of meetings. Agenda items include plans for activities, discussion of children, families' issues, strategies for managing behavior and schedules, and conflict resolution as well as more formal training such as CPR or first aid or consultations with specialists. "The more formal ways that my team communicates and plans together are through a monthly shared calendar and a daily list of each teacher's responsibilities," notes Fontana. In addition, many early childhood programs try to include celebrations, fun activities, joint conference or workshop attendance or site visits, even an annual retreat to build a sense of teamwork as well as provide staff training and education.

Some programs do not have regular staff meetings. Without them, creating a shared vision and ensuring smooth operations are difficult to achieve. Weekly meetings are preferable, with more informal check-ins and debriefings throughout the day. Half-day programs usually meet after the class session, and school-age programs can meet before the children arrive. In full-day programs, and those with staggered staff, meetings for everyone are more challenging to schedule. A center that operates from 7:00 a.m. to 6:00 p.m. may meet bimonthly in the evening, or may alternate the meeting times so that an early staff meeting has a team member from the morning staff and the afternoon meeting can get an afternoon teacher during nap time.

> My room's teachers get together once a week for an hour to an hour and a half; they e-mail and communicate in class. They have an in-service day, and quarterly staff meetings for all the school. Then they know what the teachers in the other rooms are doing, and also the children in the other rooms. I think these are some of the reasons that they are very supportive toward each other, not just about children, but taking into account one another's personal well-being.
>
> —JANE

Find out about staff meetings at your fieldwork site, and see if you can attend at least one during your practicum. You will find it interesting to observe and participate in this important part of team teaching.

Betwixt and Between: Student Teachers on an ECE Team

What is the role of the student teacher in a team teaching situation? Ideally, your fieldwork site is ready for you, is looking forward to your participation with a clear plan, and has a supervising teacher who will shepherd you through your practicum experience. There is so much to learn: classroom environments and schedules to understand, team roles and responsibilities to learn, systems to follow, and an organizational culture to understand. One's self-esteem is fragile, and teachers' remarks or looks, even well-intended, can seem critical. Sylvette's comments echo this feeling: "I'm afraid that I am in a new situation where I do not feel I am part of the team. I have been there less than a month, but I only have a semester here. Initially I felt a cool reception and a lack of communication. Sometimes I feel like I am pretty much on my own."

Anxiety is a common experience, and uncertainty brings low initiative. In one study, "92% of beginning teachers did not seek help directly from colleagues. They admitted being afraid of acknowledging uncertainty of problems in their classrooms. At best, new teachers swapped stories about problems informally and attempted to hide weaknesses from colleagues" (Berl, 2004).

To feel part of a teaching team, new and student teachers must focus on getting to know the teachers as well as the children. As mentioned earlier in this chapter (see Figure 7.2), having a clear and meaningful role is important. Observing and taking notes about children and a program should expand to other significant duties. Augusto comments:

> The teachers help student teachers and volunteers feel at home by placing a lot of trust in us to help with activities, interact with the children (including handling their behavior), prepare meals and snacks, and so on. The head teacher is kind enough to check in with me to see if there are any practicum assignments that I have to do, or if I have anything for her to fill out. All in all, I think the outlook of the teachers is that we are part of their family.

As you learn the names of teachers as well as the children, you can greet and speak to each of them, finding out their expertise and educated opinions. It is more likely that you will get included as things happen. Joan notes:

> The other teachers at my site let me try to handle whatever happens at my table. They will help me out if I have trouble, but I think it's a good way to learn by trying to deal with it myself first. If there is a big conflict, they will step in so there are two teachers. They will also call me over, and then I'm that second person.

One way to bring you closer to the team is to be open to feedback to your work. Notice how this student's teaching practice is shaped as her supervisor "catches her at being good":

> When my head teacher is at the table when I am doing a project, he might say to the children, "When Teacher Grace shares with me, it makes me feel good. Isn't that right?" I agree, and it feels like he is putting me on the same level in front of the children.

Another point to remember is that we learn first by doing, by trying things concretely. Only later do we learn the same things conceptually. So, ask for specifics when you are to do something, and offer to help alongside a more experienced teammate. As Marc points out, there are strategies for putting you into the team:

> Because the center gets new student teachers every semester, the teachers try their best to make the transition as easy as possible and make us feel part of the team. One way of doing this is having job cards, and these include step-by-step directions on how to fulfill the duties. Also, student teachers are invited to staff meetings and take part in the discussions.

Figure 7.3 offers ideas for getting involved in teaching teams.

A final note: Team teaching may be challenging, but it is an integral part of teaching in early childhood programs and is an excellent way to find out a lot about yourself (see "Lessons from the Field"). In response to his practicum instructor's assignment to discuss team relationships, student teacher Yuji offers this quote from Joseph Campbell (2008): "If you follow your bliss . . . . you begin to meet people who are in your field of bliss, and they open doors for you."

Figure 7.3 Getting Yourself In: Teamwork as a Student Teacher
Getting yourself into a teaching team requires some key strategies so you feel part of the team.

- Focus discussions on how to understand situations—describe an incident and ask for team members' ideas, their assumptions about how children learn, what works and what doesn't, what they expect of themselves, and what you could have done (or do next time).

- Look for opportunities to offer another teacher what you observed about the children, and how you wonder what it means, or how to help children express ideas and feelings.

- While respecting each team member's privacy, try to relate to each person on a more personal level as well as on a professional level. Teaching teams are made of individuals, and knowing each person will help you understand the dynamics of each unique member.

- Make a list each week of what you have learned, and then practice those skills to refine them the next time you go to your site.

- Nurture your own curiosity, enthusiasm, and eagerness. Try to balance your anxiety with these more positive feelings. Feel free to model the children in this regard.

- Ask for and be open to suggestions from other teachers regarding changes in your approach or behavior.

- Cultivate a habit of suspending judgment of yourself, both when others step in and also if you do not get help in tricky situations.

- Avoid the temptation to find *the one and only right way.* There are many appropriate practices. You will need to develop your own style, but also need to align your work with that of your team.

"Team Teaching"

by Jill Watkins

Mentor Teacher

I've often been asked why I didn't pursue a career in elementary education. Primarily, it's because I so value the experience of team teaching that is typical of the preschool environment.

As a teacher for nearly 20 years, I have benefited immensely from working with some amazing women. I was told early on—and continue to pass on the wisdom to teachers mentoring with me—to be a sponge. These senior teachers genuinely desired to see me succeed and were eager to assist me in acquiring more tools for my belt. I had built-in resources to observe, bounce things off of, and model myself after. I still utilize some of the strategies gleaned from the teachers with whom I first worked.

A definite advantage of the team teaching approach is that we each bring a slightly different set of interests and skills to the table. For instance, while I have a real love for literacy but science doesn't appeal to me too much, one of my co-teachers can compensate. Or, I may respond more easily to the "slow to warm" child whereas my co-teacher connects fabulously with a child who is gregarious or creative.

Similarly, we all have those days when our patience reserves run a little lower. In those times we can rely on our co-teachers to take over in a given negotiation with a child. Ultimately, having this balance serves the children most effectively.

However, the reality is that these aforementioned differences can present challenges in the team dynamic. The most helpful thing I have learned—and this applies to any healthy relationship, really—is communicate, communicate, communicate. It is much better to be able to be open and honest with each other, in an atmosphere of respect. And while you don't always have to see eye to eye, the bottom line is a foundation of mutual caring and support.

Practicum Activity

Using the Role Set model described on pages 163–164, sketch a role set for yourself as a student teacher. List the expectations you have for each member of your role set, and their expectations of you. Next, go through each list, marking which expectations are reasonable and which are not. What adjustments can be made for more sensible targets?

Journaling Assignment

Discuss team relationships at your practicum site. How do teachers work together? Resolve conflicts? Build a team?

References

Baumrind, D. (1971). Current patterns of parental authority. *Developmental Psychology Monograph, 4*(1), Pt. 2.

Berl, P. (2004, January/February). Insights into teacher development: Part 1. The emergent teacher. *Child Care Exchange* (www.childcareexchange.com).

Campbell, J. (2008). *Hero with a thousand faces* (collected works of Joseph Campbell, 3rd ed.). Novato, CA: New World Library.

Caruso, J. J., & Fawcett, M. T. (2006). *Supervision in early childhood education: A developmental perspective.* New York: Teachers College Press.

Gordon, A. M., & Browne, K. W. (1985). *Beginnings and beyond: Foundations in early childhood education.* Albany, NY: Delmar Publishers.

Jorde-Bloom, P. (2005). *Blueprint for action: Achieving center-based change through staff development* (2nd ed.). Lake Forest, IL: New Horizons.

Katz, L. (1977) *Talks with teachers: Reflections on early childhood education.* Washington, DC: National Association for the Education of Young Children.

Whitebook, M. (1989). *Who cares? Child care teachers and the quality of child care in America.* (Final Report, National Child Care Staffing Study.) Oakland, CA: Center for the Child Care Workforce.

Zavitkovsky, D. (1992, January). Docia shares a story about staff relationships. *Child Care Exchange.* Retrieved June 5, 2012, at www.childcareexchange.com/library/5013982.pdf

Web Sites

Association for Supervision and Curriculum Development
www.ascd.org

Center for the Child Care Workforce
www.ccw.org

Early Childhood Research & Practice
www.ecrp.uiuc.edu

Exchange Press (Child Care Exchange)
www.childcareexchange.com

The National Teaching & Learning Forum
www.ntlf.com

c h a p t e r   8

Collaborating with Families

LEARNING OUTCOME

Demonstrate an awareness of the diversity of families and family-school connections, and evaluate how teachers communicate with families about their children's development and learning.

Who Is the Family?

Today's families are widely defined, reflecting the sociological changes of the past 50 years, when the "nuclear family" consisting of a mother, father, and two children was the prevailing model. A family unit today may consist of parents (who may or may not be married to one another or who may be adoptive or foster parents) and other family members, such as grandparents, aunts, and uncles, as well as step- or half-brothers and -sisters. Two people can consider themselves a family, as can a collective or commune of greater numbers of people. These characteristics of families may be very different from the way your parents and grandparents were raised, or they may be similar to your next-door neighbors. These are the kinds of families you meet as you enter the field of early childhood education. A student teacher reflects on her own family of origin in the following "Reflective Incident."

In your student teaching experience, you may have noticed that teachers often refer to families, rather than just "parents." Increasingly, we have become more aware of the influence of not only the child's immediate family but also the extended family and community. In today's world a significant number of people take care of children, and we want them all to feel included, for through these family networks we gain greater knowledge and understanding of the child.

Parent is a word that has expanded to fit a variety of relationships—not just people who have the legal status of mother or father. The definition of a parent has broadened to include not only those individuals who

Reflective Incident "Growing Up in My Family"

When I was born my parents had an educational plan for me. Because my mother did not attend college and my father only finished vocational training, they wanted better for me. My parents taught me that education is very important. Then my father passed away when I was 10 and my mother remarried when I was 12. I had a new father and 2 step-sisters, so I went from being the only one to being the youngest. My stepfather was very strict about not leaving a mess around the house. His rule was "If I find something littering or out of place I will throw it away," so I learned to clean up after myself pretty quick. Today I am a bit of a neat freak, probably because of that.

Growing up in this family was an experience (Isn't everyone's?), and I believe that my family structure and values that were instilled in me truly built the person I am today. I am the first one to go to college in my family. Seeing how proud my family is of me motivates me to continue to go to school and receive my degree. Also I wanted to be a role model for my younger cousins and show them that they have equal opportunities to go to college and become successful.

When I observe children at school (and also my own) I often compare their behavior to mine when I was a child. In particular, I notice the stubbornness, rebellion and persistence in my 3-year-old daughter and wonder if it all comes from me or if my wife had something to do with it as well. If I continue to look at my own experiences as a child and a teenager I might get a little worried about what to expect from my children as they grow up, but then I think of how I survived and made the right decisions in the end and I feel less concerned.

—Gianfrancesco

Your Thoughts

1. How would I feel?

2. What would I do?

3. What might the results be?

are raising their own biological children, but also those who are raising foster children, adopted children, and children of other family members or friends. The complexity and number of today's varying lifestyles cause us to continue to look at how we define the parents and families of the children we teach.

The Diversity of American Families

Changing sociological patterns have given rise to a number of families with unique needs. Economics, immigration, medical technology, divorce rates, career commitments, lifestyle changes, demographics, and gender issues are some of the influences that are reshaping family structure. Some family situations are more challenging for parents and teachers, and the early childhood educator must be prepared to work with the diversity that is typical today. This includes the following:

- Families with children with developmental delays and disabilities
- Adoptive and foster parent families
- Single-parent families
- Blended families
- Families in which both parents work outside the home
- Multiracial families
- Families raising children in a culture not their own and where English is not their primary language
- Grandparents who are raising grandchildren
- First-time older-parent families
- Gay and lesbian families
- Homeless families
- Teenage-parent families

Families help build strong communication links to their children's teachers to foster trust and understanding.

As you read through the preceding list you might think about some of the families you are meeting through your student teaching. How many of them fit one or more of these categories? What are some of the difficulties these families face? In what ways do the teachers and the school support these families?

Valuing Home Culture

Child-rearing practices are culturally based, so it follows that understanding a family's culture is an essential element in building strong family–school relationships. Children's growth and development can be understood only within their cultural context. Each culture has its own values and attitudes that must be recognized and respected by the teaching staff as they share their strengths with families for the benefit of each child.

To be successful, teachers must first reflect on their own cultural heritage, experience, and attitudes. Teachers must examine any prejudice and bias they may have toward cultural groups different from their own that would prevent them from connecting with families in the school. Different perspectives on eating, sleeping, toileting, disciplining, and showing respect, for instance, could be barriers to working together in a child's best interest. When viewed in a cultural context, these differences can become understood and respected as the teacher and the family work toward mutually acceptable resolutions.

Children learn best in a setting that reflects and supports their families. Families are more comfortable in school settings where they and their cultural influences are acknowledged and understood (see the section titled "Family Involvement" later in this chapter). Children gain when there is some similarity between their home and their school. Cultural congruency suggests that a sensitivity to diversity includes understanding individual histories, families of origin, and ethnic family cultures to help blend home and family. We then see what makes us similar to as well as different from one another.

Bradley and Kibera (2007) cite four important characteristics of culture to consider when working with families of diverse backgrounds (see Table 8.1). Each of the questions concerning a cultural characteristic encourages further exploration of the cultures you find in your classroom.

Understanding Parenthood

As families and teachers work together, the assumption is that we are all working for what is best for the child, yet there is often a difference of opinion about what "best" is and whose "best" will prevail. Parents and

Table 8.1 Cultural Characteristics and Diversity
The questions that are posed may help you reflect on how powerful culture is in shaping children's development and our teaching.

Cultural Dimensions of Families	Questions for Reflection
Values and beliefs	How is *family* defined? What roles do adults and children play? How does the family make sense of the child's behavioral difficulties? How does culture inform the family's view of appropriate and inappropriate ways of dealing with problem behavior and child guidance? What is most important to the family?
Historical and social influences	What strengths and stressors does the family identify? What barriers does it experience?
Communication	What is the family's primary language? What support is required to enable communication? How are needs and wants expressed? How are unhappiness, dissatisfaction, or distress experienced and expressed?
Attitudes toward seeking help	How does the family seek help and from whom? How do members view professionals, and how do professionals view members?

Source: From "Closing the Gap: Culture and the Promotion of Inclusion in Child Care," by J. Bradley and P. Kibera, 2007, in D. Koralek (Ed.) *Spotlight on Young Children and Families.* Washington, DC: National Association for the Education of Young Children. Adapted with permission from the National Association for the Education of Young Children.

teachers come together with different viewpoints, different needs, and different experiences. Each has a point of view that enlightens the other; in this spirit we look at two areas of parenting with implications for working with parents: stages of parent development and patterns of child rearing.

Stages of Parent Development. The parents you meet are in various stages of development, just like their children. A first-time parent has different experiences and feelings than does a parent with three older children, or older parents of an only child. Galinsky's exemplary work on stages of parenthood (1987) found that the role of the parent changes in various ways as the parents and children grow old together.

In the earliest of the six stages, beginning with pregnancy, parents fantasize about what kind of parents they would like to be and prepare for the inclusion of a child in their lives. During the first 2 years attachment is a primary concern, as is matching their fantasy of child rearing with the actual experience.

From toddlerhood to adolescence, family rules are clarified and the parent's authority style is established. During the same time period parents interpret themselves and the world to their children through the values, knowledge, and skills they pass on.

The teenage years are a time for renegotiating family rules and authority and creating new relationships between parents and child. As the child matures and leaves home, the parents examine their sense of accomplishment and again redefine the relationship with their now adult child.

The six stages describe how parents change and grow in response to having children and how they alter their own behavior and attitudes to the reality of child rearing. In larger families, many parents go through several stages at once; with a single child or the oldest one, parental feelings may be intensified. Just as we look at the developmental needs and stages of children, we can be aware that parents also have unique developmental tasks. Do you recognize if any of the parents you know are going through these stages?

Patterns of Child Rearing. In Chapter 7, Baumrind's seminal work on authority styles (1972) were discussed under the topic of team leadership. Now we will look at the study as it relates to parental styles of behavior because children are affected by the way their parents treat them. Teachers find their role with each family becomes clear as they learn more about parental styles of behavior. The three parental styles and their effect on children are shown in Table 8.2.

Table 8.2 Parental Child-Rearing Styles
These have a powerful effect on how children behave.

Parental Style	Characteristics	Effect on Children
Authoritative	Warm, responsive, attentive to child's needs; moderate and consistent in enforcing rules, with much discussion; moderate expectations and high communication that allows child to make reasonable decisions	High self-esteem, articulate; self-control; happy with themselves; persistent with tasks; cooperative and generous with others, usually liked by teachers and peers
Authoritarian	Focuses on control; low warmth, strict, often physical discipline; high demand and expectations; makes decisions for the child; high communication to child but low from child	Likely to be conscientious, obedient, and quiet but not especially happy; may internalize frustrations and blame self; sometimes rebels in adolescence
Permissive	Warm but overindulgent; low discipline and low expectations; accepting but often inattentive; usually high communication from children but few demands of them	Impulsive, disobedient, rebellious; inadequate emotional regulation may result in difficulties with authority or give-and-take of peers; overly demanding and dependent on adults

Research has continued to support Baumrind's findings that there are more positive outcomes for children when parents use an authoritative style, although temperament and culture are also strong influences (Galambos et al., 2003). How does this study help you relate to the families in your student teaching setting? What does the study tell you about your own childhood?

When teachers understand the parental styles of child rearing, they are better able to help families learn more appropriate and effective ways to raise their children. Because child rearing is culture bound, teachers must always be sensitive to each family's cultural values when discussing child-rearing issues.

The Importance of Family–School Connections

How do teachers create partnerships with parents? Three basic guidelines apply:

- Establish an open, friendly, and cooperative relationship with each child's family.
- Encourage family involvement in the program in many ways.
- Support the child's relationship with their family and vice versa.

From the first contact with a prospective family, early childhood teachers are developing a relationship.

Why Relationships Matter

Whether the young child is an infant entering child care for the first time, a preschooler ready to try nursery school, or a third-grader attending the after-school club, he or she is faced with the challenge of adapting to a strange environment, different routines, and new relationships. Families must make adjustments, too, because they are sharing the care of their child with someone outside the family. The changes are more likely to be positive and happen smoothly if teachers can develop a cooperative relationship on the child's behalf.

"Working with families gives me a better understanding of the children," notes student teacher Sylvette. "I then have better insights on how to deal with them than I might not know otherwise." Life for young children is shaped by many experiences, and having caring and attentive relationships is crucial to their growth. "Adults really count in a young child's life. . . . Research only confirms what we know from experience: children thrive when they are surrounded by people who are crazy about them" (Baker & Manfredi-Petitt, 2004, p. 2).

Creating a Caring Community

All national standards of excellence recognize the importance of the parent–caregiver relationship. Creating a caring community of learners is a key indicator of quality early education, as identified by the National Association for the Education of Young Children (Copple & Bredekamp, 2009). The quality of a caregiver's approach to families is emphasized in the accreditation process of the National Association for Family Child Care. Head Start involves families as partners by providing a family advocate, having home visits, and involving parents in reviewing program effectiveness. The environmental rating scales for all age groups (see Chapter 5) include family involvement.

This community should include everyone who is fulfilling the role of parent. Regardless of family structure (see the previous section "Who Is the Family?"), the one unifying theme is that all adult family members are stressed by their obligations in the workplace, wishes for healthy relationships with significant people in their lives, and dreams of raising their children well. As we address the challenges of meeting our mutual obligations for children, we must create a community of members who care for one another.

Common Goals, Different Perspectives

At first glance, teachers and families have similar goals. They both want the child to be safe, to learn, and to thrive. Both school and home are places of learning for the young child, so adults in both locations have the common goal of educating young children. Still, families and teachers have different perspectives on the child and on the enterprise. Katz's original work on the distinctions between mothering and teaching (1980) is adapted in Table 8.3.

Families and teachers should have different perspectives; after all, their relationship to the child, their function in the educational setting, and their areas of expertise do differ. For example, working with infants and toddlers usually includes dealing with conflicts, and student teachers find themselves challenged by the contest of wills that

No one knows a child better than his or her own family members.

Table 8.3 Families and Teachers: Different Perspectives

Key Dimension	Families	Teachers
On connection to child	Optimum attachment: emotionally intense, even unrealistically optimistic	Detached concern: emotionally warm but more objective
In viewing the classroom	Individual, from my child's perspective, partial	Whole group, from the group or team's perspective, impartial
With a rational role	Optimally irrational: "in the service of the heart," "crazy about that kid"	Optimally rational: careful analysis, use of research and knowledge
On spontaneity	More impulsive, responsive, casual	More intentional, rational

Source: Based on Katz (1980).

often occurs. This is intensified by the relationships with families, and the importance of finding common goals even with differing perspectives. The advent of siblings is such a situation.

For the child who is born into a family with other children, having siblings is a preexisting condition. For the toddler who has spent 2 years being a single child, the arrival of his younger sibling is another change, and not an altogether welcome one. The fact that parents want and bring in another child makes the first child feel jealous and pushed out. All family members are affected by a new baby, and fatigue is just one of the many factors with which parents must deal.

Teachers can expect negative reactions to both the news and, more important, the reality. Some children have a mild reaction to a newborn, but they begin to bristle when the baby becomes mobile; others want the baby to return to the hospital as quickly as a library book. Not all toddlers exhibit all of these behaviors, but all of them are common:

- Increased clinginess to parent upon separation
- Increased temper tantrums and low frustration tolerance
- More "babyish" behavior
- Less interest in toileting; if started, some regression
- Defiance of parent and caregiver, sulkiness or withdrawal

Parents and older adult family members often have a different perspective. Mathew's mother was struggling to make ends meet; as a single parent living with her mother again, the new baby was a cause for conflict and strife. Jenna's grandfather, on the other hand, was thrilled to have another little one around; it was Jenna's tantrums he didn't care for, and let her know in no uncertain terms. In both cases, nobody was thinking much about the toddlers' reactions. Student teachers can help toddlers and their families through this time by offering a few practical ideas for use at home and doing a few extra things at school.

To help families, work with your supervising teacher to encourage toddler independence and skill development before the baby arrives. Suggest ways they can continue to do things with the toddler, such as reading while nursing or doing a puzzle on the floor while rocking the baby. Developing an attitude of "benign superiority" can help a child overcome the feelings of displacement.

For the child, be a rock at the center, consistently available and positive and deliberately noticing skills and activities. Without overdoing it, allow the child to express feelings of jealousy or loneliness, and be accepting of those common reactions. Remember that cooperative, gentle behavior is a challenge to *all* toddlers and will be especially so for the stressed sibling of a new baby.

Parents are experts on one child (or a few) in an intimate, primary way, whereas teacher expertise lies in experience with many children and more studied knowledge. As student teacher Grace puts it:

> Working with families provides rich information about the child's background, culture, et cetera—basically everything that's been going on in the child's life since birth. Despite our knowledge of early childhood development, as educators we must remember that nobody knows a child like his family. If you just put yourself in the parents' shoes, working with them becomes easier.

The roles of parents and teachers are complementary but distinctive. If it seems that parents expect you to teach only *their* child, it may be an expression of the perspective of "optimal attachment." You can help by acknowledging how important their child is while still asserting your more detached, but warm, concern: for example, "You're right; she *is* a pistol and does need help getting on her shoes. At the same time, when she needs to wait while I help someone else first, she learns about the give-and-take in a group that sometimes includes waiting."

Family Involvement

Both families and teachers indicate they think family involvement in their children's education is beneficial (Diffily, 2004). Families usually start their involvement because of a specific request or at the invitation of a teacher.

Low--Moderate--------------------------------------High

Take leadership position
Support parent leaders

Participate weekly in classroom
Prepare, observe, and *support*

Create class newsletter
Jointly publish newsletter

Work in the office or library
Visit when parent is there

Help with school events
Send appreciation notes, assist parent

Collect or make materials for class
Have "helping hands" meetings

Participate in parent–teacher conferences
Plan conferences carefully, send follow-up note

Attend class or school events
Plan welcoming, send home appreciation notes

Visit the class or help with an activity
Invite to work alongside you; offer feasible tasks

Stay to observe on arrival or before departure
Be available and talk with them

Figure 8.1
Kinds of Family Involvement
From low to high levels of involvement, teachers [*in italics*] support families' involvement [in regular type] by scaffolding their participation.

Involvement takes many forms, as seen in Figure 8.1. When parents have a positive experience the first time they attend an event or volunteer at school, they are likely to repeat those experiences. Beginnings are critical: Many families feel tentative in school settings with teachers who they fear may be critical, and teachers must work gently and carefully to nurture the relationship in order to get involvement.

A single negative experience may decrease the family's interest in staying involved, so teachers—and their students—must be sensitive and alert to how to be welcoming and clear. Family feelings and attitudes can undermine their involvement with teachers or a center. Parents may have conflicted feelings about leaving children in care. Moreover, time with their children can feel rushed or restricted because of the demands of school or the workplace, which cause cranky or resentful feelings. Some families worry that they will be displaced by teachers in the eyes of their children; indeed, often children seem more cooperative, even happier, in child care. A parent with a balky child at pickup time may wonder what's happening to the family. Occasionally families and schools seem to vie for authority over a child; Brazelton and Sparrow (2006) call this "gatekeeping": competitive urges among adults to protect and care for children. Finally, families often feel exposed and uncomfortable sharing private information. This reluctance has complex cultural and personal roots.

For example, student teacher Raquel noted that families often get defensive when being told about their children's misbehavior. She gets nervous herself, and ends up avoiding talking to those families at pickup time. To encourage a stronger bond and thus deeper family involvement, Raquel needs to initiate informal conversations with exactly those families. At arrival time, she can communicate in positive ways by greeting the child and family and inviting them to her table. Then she can offer an explanation about the activity, and ask the family what they do at home that is similar. The joint focus on the child's learning builds camaraderie and common purpose, and makes a later conversation about a child's difficulties in other areas a bit easier to have.

Establishing frequent, ongoing interactions helps families and teachers become comfortable with each other. Phone calls, e-mails, notes, home visits, conferences, and the daily connection at the beginning or end of school are some of the ways to keep in contact. With the vast array of possibilities and family configurations, cultures, and styles, cultivating family involvement is a complex and time-consuming task.

Some teachers are reluctant to involve families, and student teachers often feel ill equipped to work with parents. Some think their job is to teach children, not parents. Many feel uncomfortable with someone watching them teach, fearing the same criticism families may feel when entering a classroom. Teachers who are not parents themselves worry that parents will dismiss them as inexperienced. Others are uncertain how to involve family members, seeing the class as the teacher's territory.

Overcoming these barriers is essential, because families are often hesitant and will withdraw if feeling unwelcome. Teachers are responsible for reaching out to families. If you are uncomfortable with parents and other family members, talk with your supervising teacher. Find out what teachers do to establish a relaxed rapport and, if you can, observe or participate in some of the activities that include families. Figure 8.2 describes 10 steps to creating positive family relationships.

Figure 8.2
Top 10 Tips for
Positive Family–School
Relationships

1. Treat each family with dignity and respect.
2. Listen and learn.
3. Have clear expectations of one another.
4. Share the responsibility and the power.
5. Understand each family's culture and values.
6. Encourage participation at any level.
7. Teach families what they need to know.
8. Keep informed: It works both ways.
9. Provide families with support.
10. Promote interactions among families.

The same skills for creating an inviting environment for children can be applied to families. Student teacher Ellen noticed this:

> In our room I feel that the "open-door policy" is fully operational and there is a sense of partnership between the parents and staff. Teachers are so warm and inviting that "the moms" feel both welcome and at ease, so they spend time in the place where their babies spend so much of *their* day, to get a feel for the surroundings. Moms also introduce themselves to each other, learn about the other babies, and frequently greet other babies by name. And I feel at the end of the day that this positive experience has rubbed off on me, too. I am starting to talk with them and add some things I've been seeing with their babies.

Strategies for Collaboration

All families are interested in the education and well-being of their children. Good family–school relationships encourage a strong partnership that benefits everyone. Student teachers are to follow the lead of their supervising teacher and the program's policies. Although there are many strategies for family–school collaboration, what follows are those that affect the student teacher.

- Respect families' religious, cultural, social, and ethnic backgrounds. Respect their right to disagree, and respect their privacy.
- Listen without judging. Accept parents as they are.
- Enhance the family's perception of their child by telling them something positive about their child's day.

See the top 10 tips for positive family–school relationships in Figure 8.2.

Sharing a child's classroom success with parents enhances the family's perception of their child.

Person-to-Person Communications

Some of the many informal ways that the school and the family maintain contact with each other were discussed in the previous section. More formal contacts are made through meetings, events, and conferences that allow for greater personal interaction between the teaching staff and the family. Student teacher involvement with families varies widely; ask your lead teacher how you should interact.

Meetings and Events

Parent meetings can have any number of functions. The teaching staff may develop workshop topics designed to teach parenting skills or introduce a home literacy program. These meetings are scheduled at times when working parents can participate, and child care is often provided. Some meetings are social events, just for enjoyment, such as a potluck dinner at the school where parents can mingle with teachers and other families and take time to look through the classroom where their children spend so much time. Parent workdays are scheduled on weekends so that parents can share in the upkeep of the school and grounds. In some school settings, the parents are in charge of the fund-raising activities and plan festivals, auctions, and other activities to support the school's budget (see

Figure 8.1). Ask your supervising teacher if you are expected to attend any of these events.

Conferences

Family–teacher conferences are the backbone of any good family–school relationship and one of the most important links for a successful partnership. They should be a regular part of the communication process in all early childhood programs. In some settings, a conference is scheduled soon after the child begins for the purpose of getting to know the child and family. Important information such as health issues and family concerns may be discussed. Later on, the family–teacher conferences focus on communicating teachers' observations and assessments of children, building mutual goals for them, and creating mutual trust and respect. Individual conferences, called by the family or the teacher, are used to share knowledge and information, resolve conflicts and solve problems together, and set goals for the child that can be reinforced at home and at school.

As a practicum student, you will probably not have to conduct a family–teacher conference on your own. It would be to your advantage if you ask to participate in one to experience this important teaching responsibility. Your supervising teacher can share the preparation process with you and ask the family for permission for you to attend. You will see firsthand how sharing information and observations of the child help draw the teacher and family into deeper discussion and dialogue.

To ensure a successful family–teacher conference, a quiet space, sufficient time, comfortable seating, and adequate planning are necessary. Figure 8.3 highlights some of the ways to make sure the family–teacher conference works well.

Conferencing with a family can be challenging, yet it offers some of the most personal insights into the life of the child. The following section presents ways to handle some of the difficult situations that may arise during a family–teacher conference.

When Difficulties Arise

When asked what was difficult about working with families, the group of student teachers clamored to respond:

"Parents are often so busy."

"They are so picky."

"Sometimes they aren't interested in what we tell them."

Figure 8.3 Three Steps for a Productive Family/Teacher Conference

Source: Based on Gordon/Browne, *Beginnings and Beyond: Foundations in Early Childhood Education, 9e.* Wadsworth, a part of Cengage Learning, Inc.

Before the Meeting

1. Establish a clear purpose: Is this a progress report? A meeting called by the family? By the teachers? Have concerns been raised by either?

2. Create a short agenda. List a few points to cover during the meeting. Ask the family for their suggestions.

3. Gather current data, including examples of the child's progress, interests, and abilities.

4. Secure permission from the family. If a student teacher, colleague, or director will be attending the meeting with you, be sure the family is comfortable with having another person present.

5. Secure a comfortable room with good meeting space. Be sure you have scheduled enough time for the conference.

During the Meeting

1. Greet the family warmly and thank them for coming. Begin by telling them something special and positive about their child: "Katie was a real friend today. One of the children forgot to bring a snack today and Katie offered to share hers with her friend. We all thought that was very thoughtful of her."

2. Recognize the family's important role in their child's education. "Katie tells me that you have a book night every Friday evening. That sounds like a fun family activity and a wonderful way to reinforce Katie's reading skills." When parents love to read, children pick up on the importance of reading and that it can be fun."

3. Be aware of any cultural nuances. Ask the family to help you understand any cultural issues of which you may not be aware. "How else might we work together to help the other students understand what Flora brings for lunch?"

4. Listen to what the family members say. Respond with open-ended questions, such as, "What else can you tell me about that?" "What do you think about that?" Try not to tell the family what you think; ask them to help you understand what they are saying.

5. Center the discussion around the shared concerns. Connect with the family by keeping the main focus on the child's needs. "I understand that it is hard for you to always attend to Katie when you have two more little ones at home and you say that makes you feel guilty. Do you think it would help if could arrange a "special Katie time" with her once a week?"

6. For problems that need solving, create a plan together. "We will continue to help Katie work on her writing here at school. And if you continue to work with her at home by sitting with her while she writes out her spelling words, that will be helpful as well. You might also have her write notes to people she cares about, such as her grandparents or friends. Leave little notes for her that ask a question that she needs to answer in writing. Try to encourage writing without it becoming a negative experience."

7. Define dates for a follow up conversation. Agree that you will check in with each other about Katie's spelling progress at the end of two weeks.

After the Meeting

1. Write a brief note about the meeting. Include any strategies suggested, concerns of the family, solutions agreed upon, and the follow-up dates.

2. Inform the rest of the staff. Tell them about the meeting and what responsibilities the teaching staff has in regard to Katie and her family.

"They get defensive when you have to tell them about misbehavior."

"It seems like they're always two steps behind the child's development."

"Some are not open to teachers' views."

"They are uncomfortable with us."

"The teachers don't speak the same language as the parents."

"They expect you to teach just *their* child."

"They smother their child."

"Parents gossip or complain to each other and don't tell us teachers."

"The teachers and families [may] come from different cultures."

"There just isn't enough time each day to really talk to each one individually."

When families withdraw, disagree, or have issues that we don't know about or understand, problems arise. As student teacher Denise puts it:

> When working with parents it is important to remember where the person is coming from—not only on a daily basis, such as a rough day at work, but also from a cultural, personality, and family life standpoint. This takes time and patience and can be difficult at times.

We will discuss these difficulties in two areas: problems between the program and the child, and conflicts between the family and the program.

Problems Between the Program and the Child

Dealing with children's behavior is challenging (see Chapter 3)!

Even when behavior is typical, situations in the classroom can be problematic for teachers and families. "This week we had a serious situation in my room due to a bite," writes student teacher Ani:

> One of our children bit another, and it left a big mark on the back of his "victim." It was very tense when I was giving the bitee's mother the report. Of course she was upset, but she asked me to promise that her child will never

Parents may hear about a conflict from their child and want to be reassured that it was handled ethically and with respect for the child's self-worth.

get another bite. I needed to tell her that I am unable to make that promise, although I can do many things to try to prevent it. Both parents came the next day and talked to the master teacher. The father asked to exclude the biter from the program. They even went to the director!

The student teacher made the appropriate response, yet because the family was still upset, they took their concerns to other authorities. It is important to realize that parents need to have a clear chain of command to use when dealing with problems about their child. After hearing the same response for the third time, the family came to understand that a bite did not constitute expulsion, but also that the program would offer a parent workshop about biting, and would work to shadow both children. "For a few weeks, the parents still looked upset, and they did not talk much with the staff," continues Ani. "But their child did not get bitten again; we treated the family with the same friendliness as before the incident, and slowly things warmed up."

A parent may walk into a situation, not understand the whole picture, and form a negative opinion. Tobi mentioned one child at her fieldwork site who hit other children and pulled hair. Teachers needed firm intervention, often putting themselves between the child and others, using a strong tone of voice in telling the child to stop. An arriving father was alarmed at the teacher's behavior, and told parents in the parking lot that the teachers were picking on the child. What could Tobi do when the next three parents came to her about the situation?

For ethical reasons, Tobi needed to respect the dignity of each individual and keep professional confidentiality by not talking about the child in question. At the same time, she could explain to those concerned parents that each child develops and learns social skills in unique ways. Children whose home language differs from what is used in the classroom need clear nonverbal communication. Ani can also show them the picture cards she keeps with her that help all children understand and start to communicate their wishes in nonviolent ways.

Delivering complaints or bad news is one of the most difficult kinds of communication for most of us. Families are sensitive to how teachers tell them about their children. "If a professional says, 'in my professional opinion,' a parent hears 'This is what I'm telling you to do, and I have the power to say so'" (Tomko, 2010). When you deliver information that is hard to receive, try to think through what you want to say and not have the conversation occur in an intense or public manner. "Gunther had some problems at group time today," student teacher Fadwa tells the child's uncle before he greets the child. "I know you two need to get home, but do you have a few minutes now, or would you rather talk on the telephone this evening?" The message is clear and complete, but it does allow Uncle Dioli to decide on the time and place for the conversation. He decides to step outside and hear Fadwa describe how Gunther kept playing with Jessica's braids and had to be moved. The teacher's calm and honest description helps both adults discuss the situation.

Making professional referrals is one of the toughest issues. Student teachers new to their practicum setting or in an assistant position are unlikely to be in this position. However, it is important to note that this is an especially delicate situation, as in the following situation:

> Daniela is a puzzle. From the day last Spring when she visited kindergarten, she was full of curiosity and excitement. She came in so bubbly in September; now she droops her way into the class and often fusses about circle time. The child who was first to dance in front of the preschool class now frowns at story time and won't say her line in some rhyming chants. The teacher sees all this negative behavior, and finds it escalating even as it is dealt with daily.

Daniela's contrary behavior could have been mistaken as that of a wayward child in need of sterner discipline. An upset family might have decided the problem was a bad teacher who asked too much of kindergartners. A worried teacher might have misjudged nervous parents as neglectful ones who didn't expect enough. Instead, they talk together about their mutual concerns. Student teacher Sam is asked for his observations; the parents and uncle who lives with the family agree that Daniela has changed dramatically in just a couple of months.

The teacher suggests a visit to the pediatrician, but Daniela's mother points out she had just gone there 2 weeks ago. The family reluctantly agrees to have Daniela observed by the school speech and language specialist, who recommends vision and hearing tests. It was determined that Daniela has a moderate vision problem: She cannot distinguish the words that the teacher asks beginners to "read" in a picture book, and the chart is blurry from the back of the class. She is fitted with glasses and, once again, is enthusiastic, participates, and leads the group on the reading chart for the holiday song they are to perform.

Making referrals is not easy, and often families are not ready to take action at the first suggestion. However, it is the professional responsibility of teachers to notice and report their observations to parents if they see something that alerts them to a possible developmental or learning problem. As with any conflict, a systematic problem-solving approach is called for (see Chapter 7). In addition, it is critical that teachers have specific anecdotes and evidence and do not pass judgment on what they hear. It is likely that parents will feel upset; teachers should try to accept those

Collaborating with Families

feelings and what is said without getting defensive. Every so often, notes Stone (2001), a teacher faces a child

> so troubled, so embattled by circumstance that he cannot find a way to live with others in the classroom. If, after an enormous effort along with ongoing consultation with his family, this child is unable to make progress, the teacher may have to suggest referral not only for special help but for placement in a different setting. The hope is that the child and family will find the help that is so urgently needed. This can be a difficult and sad time for everyone. However, the concern for the health and safety of all the children in the class must be first above all. (p. 51)

Conflicts Between the Family and the Program

Families sometimes have a disagreement about the program, feel uncomfortable about differences with the staff, or do not follow policy and procedures. "No matter how nice a teacher is or how much she reaches out to families, there will inevitably be time when she misunderstands a parent or a parent misunderstands her" (Diffily, 2004). Two common areas of conflict are cultural differences and policy disagreements.

Cultural differences occur frequently in early childhood programs. Culture includes ethnicity, racial identity, economic level, family structure, language, and religious and political beliefs. With that complexity, differences between the teaching staff and families are likely. It is not possible to describe here all the many cultural values and habits of every family or of each teacher. However, teachers need to be aware of their own cultures, gain an understanding of other cultures, and learn about the particular constellation of the life habits, traditions, and beliefs of the particular families in their current center.

> **Student teacher Ping:** Gina is almost three years old, and I don't know what to do. She gets into a power struggle every day when her father comes to pick her up. It is so disrespectful, but he does nothing. It looks like he lets her walk all over him but won't take any suggestions or offers of help from me.
>
> **Parent Gil:** I am tired of Gina's teacher. She hovers over Gina and me whenever I come to pick her up, which isn't that often because I get her only every other weekend. I wish she'd just back off and give us some space; eventually Gina will get tired of running around, and then I'll just sweep her up and get out of there.

Family structure and different cultural expectations make this conflict uncomfortable for both teacher and parent. If Ping thinks further about her own upbringing, she may see that there are many ways to interact and raise children. Finding out more about joint custody challenges may also help Ping understand Gina's father.

Differences in school culture also occur. Gordon found himself in a conflict with a parent when she decided to stay for his small-group activity:

> The mom came in and started directing her child, trying to help her get the "right answers." It really changed the dynamic of the activity and threw me off course. She began to ask me exactly what we were doing—in this case, identifying the letter names of musical notes on the scale. She then turned to the small group of five kids and showed one of them "the mistakes" on her little wipe-off board. I casually explained to her that they didn't have to get it right, and that the idea was not to get all (or any!) of the notes correctly identified, but rather to get the kids familiar with what notes look like and that the sounds have names like letters of the alphabet. She got real quiet, and I was wondering if I was out of place telling her that. When I asked my mentor teacher, she told me it was all right to let the mom know what I was and wasn't trying to do, but also that the mom has three kids in elementary school. Oh, she's kind of into that study-test-grade mindset!

Early childhood educators should remember that they, too, have a school culture that not all families know, understand, or even agree with. It can make for tricky situations.

Working with families is a complicated and essential part of being an early childhood professional. Whether you are working in a family child care home, providing center-based care, or working with school-age children elsewhere, you are teaching both the child and the family. In the following "Lessons from the Field," the director of a parent co-op nursery school offers her suggestions for successful parent–school relations.

ethical dilemma

Why Don't You Help Her Make Friends?

Four-year-old Melissa reported to her family that the other children wouldn't let her play, and that when she told on them to student teacher Jerry, he said they didn't have to let her play if they really didn't want to. When Melissa's mother brings her to school the next day, she goes to head teacher Mai and complains about Jerry's handling of the situation. "Why aren't you helping her make friends?" she says. "How can you just let Melissa be left out like that?"

At the end of class that day Mai tells Jerry about the conversation. He feels terrible, somewhat "tattled on," and slighted that the parents didn't come to him first. After all,

Jerry had been together with Mai in the last parent–teacher conference, which included the recommendation that Melissa develop more social skills.

Code References: *Standard II, Ideal 1-2.2—* To develop relationships of mutual trust and create partnerships with the families we serve.

Standard II Ideal 1-2.8—To help family members enhance their understanding of their children, as staff are enhancing their understanding of each child through communications with families, and support family members in the continuing development of their skills as parents.

Resolution: As Mai and Jerry talk, Jerry explains that what Melissa's parents didn't know was that he had tried to work with Melissa that day. She had already disrupted the play twice and didn't respond to his overtures to talk things out. Finally, Jerry did say that the others wouldn't be forced to include Melissa if she wouldn't go along with what they were already playing. He asked Mai, "How should I respond to her parents now?" Mai suggested the two of them talk with her parents together, so everyone would know the details and work to keep communication direct and open. While Jerry felt uncomfortable at first—as did Melissa's parents—in that conversation Mai endorsed Jerry's attempts and also offered her observations about Melissa's need for more "coaching" on getting included. They agreed that Jerry would give Melissa's parents suggested children for play dates, and they would report on the results by the end of the month. All agreed to practice conflict resolution with Melissa. This constructive approach served to keep the family–school partnership healthy.

Policy disagreement is another area of conflict between families and programs. Figure 8.4 shows a handbook introduction that outlines the center's philosophy and approach to families. The handbook also lists guidelines for how to handle arrival and departure, clothing, health and safety, billing, and complaints. It is important for families to have this information; still, it is unrealistic to assume that the handbook is as well known to families as it should be to teachers.

As you read the "My Reaction" feature, think about what your center's policy is and how you might handle the situation.

Figure 8.4
A Family Handbook: Our Commitment to You

A family handbook is a helpful guide to a center's policies and procedures, and student teachers should be familiar with its contents.

Our policies and practices are designed to:

Create a place where everyone feels welcome anytime and is respected.

Have classrooms that reflect and celebrate the life of every child's family.

Respect the cultural, racial, and linguistic diversity of the children and their families.

Understand, respect, and support the values and goals of each family.

Communicate with parents in positive ways and with confidentiality.

Help parents understand and appreciate the value of developmentally appropriate programs.

Encourage parent participation in the classroom.

Invite parent involvement in the development of policies and curricula that are culturally sensitive.

Help strengthen the bond between child and parents.

Provide community resources and/or professional services that support families.

My Reaction

"Megan's Blanket"

For over a week, the teachers at our child care center were having trouble getting 2½-year-old Megan to take a nap. Megan was usually good about finding a book to look at and getting on her cot and falling asleep quickly. But that all stopped, and nothing the teachers did seemed to make a difference. Megan was told she could "just rest" and not sleep. That didn't work. She was told she could keep the book with her during her rest, and that didn't work either. One of the teachers sat by Megan's cot, rubbing her back to help her relax and go to sleep. That didn't work either.

The head teacher told Megan's father when he picked up Megan about the difficulty with napping. The next day, he came back and asked if it would be okay for Megan to bring a favorite blanket to school with her to use at nap time. He was concerned about the school policy of not bringing special things from home. The teacher told him it would be fine, so he went out to the car and brought in her blanket. Megan put it in her cubby and ran off to play. Megan sleeps well at nap time again.

—ANDY

lessons from the field

"Working with Families: The More, the Better"

by Jeanne Lindberg

Director-Teacher, United Methodist Co-op Nursery School, Burlingame, CA

Children and Parents. Our school is a parent co-operative. That means the parents participate both in the classroom and in the operation of the school. Because the parents are often on site, it is easy to get to know them. If you only see the parents at drop-off and pick-up times, it is no doubt more difficult to establish a relationship. Still, it is well worth the extra effort. One of the most important things you can do for the success of your program is to work with children in the context of their families.

Communication. Informal, in-person interchanges are probably the best ways to communicate, but time is limited for that. Drop-off and pick-up are busy times. Be sure to make some contact—a few words about the day, what is happening in their lives, or even just warm eye contact and a wave from across the room are valuable bits of communication.

Written communication is also important. We put out a monthly schoolwide newsletter, and each teacher writes a monthly class bulletin. E-mail makes communication a lot easier. The information gets to everyone, and e-mail allows private communication with individual parents. Of course, phone calls are still sometimes necessary and appreciated. Remember to communicate positive things as well as negative. You don't want parents cringing when they get a call from you!

Parent conferences are a good way to ensure that each family has set time aside to talk with you about their child. A little advance planning is important. You want to make sure the time is well spent. The most important thing is to establish an atmosphere of partnership with the parents—you are working together for the good of their child.

Families need to be able to trust you, not only with the care of their child, but also with information about their families that they may not want others to know. If a parent confides in you, remember that information is confidential. Be careful how and why you share it with other staff members.

Attitude. The regard you have for children—the respect and appreciation of each child's unique qualities—is the same regard you should have for parents. Sometimes this can be harder with parents because adults are usually not as open as children. Some people are slow to warm by nature. Be patient. You are the one who will have to be open. Guard against being defensive. Assume that they will like you. The most valuable tool you have is your own attitude.

Train yourself to put aside the all-too-human tendency to judge others. After all, we cannot know what each person's life is really like. We can try to see things from what we imagine is their perspective, but we can never really know. I have learned that, despite appearances, no one's life is trouble free. Try to truly appreciate the good you see in each person. It will be reflected back to you.

Dealing with Problems. If you have a problem with a parent, or the parent has a problem with you, first examine your own attitude and then try to see things from their perspective. People need to be heard, especially if they are upset; so be sure to look in their eyes and listen carefully for their feelings as well as their words. While you are listening, reflect on something positive about that person. Acknowledge their feelings and take the time to think carefully before responding. You may be amazed by the creative solutions and the increased understanding that can result from such conversations. There is very seldom just one right way to do things—we do not need to be rigid in our expectations regarding families.

Appreciation. A mutual appreciation for the talents and contributions of all the members is what makes a community strong. Each person truly does have something important to contribute. You need to be on the lookout for it. Once you get to know the families in your program, you will be delighted by what they have to offer.

Practicum Activity

How is your center family friendly? Ask your supervising teacher to list the ways that the program encourages family involvement. Add your own ideas to that list, and bring it to your college class.

Journaling Assignment

What are my feelings about working with families? What parent(s) am I most comfortable with and why? What families do I have difficulties with and why? What do I hope to learn that will help me feel more comfortable and more effective?

References

Baker, A. C., & Manfredi-Petitt, L. A. (2004). *Relationships: The heart of quality care.* Washington, DC: National Association for the Education of Young Children.

Baumrind, D. (1972). Current patterns of parental authority. *Developmental Psychology Monograph, 4*(1), Pt. 2.

Bradley, J., & Kibera, P. (2007). Closing the gap: Culture and the promotion of inclusion in child care. In D. Koralek (Ed.), *Spotlight on young children and families.* Washington, DC: National Association for the Education of Young Children.

Brazelton, T. B., & Sparrow, J. D. (2006). *Touchpoints: Three to six* (2nd ed.). Cambridge, MA: Perseus Books Group.

Copple, C., & Bredekamp, S. (Eds.). (2009). *Developmentally appropriate practice* (3rd ed.). Washington, DC: NAEYC.

Diffily, D. (2004). *Teachers and families working together.* Upper Saddle River, NJ: Allyn & Bacon/Pearson.

Galambos, N. L., Barker, E. T., & Almeida, D. M. (2003). Parents do matter: Trajectories of change in externalizing and internalizing problems in early adolescence. *Child Development, 74,* 578–594.

Galinsky, E. (1987). *Six stages of parenthood.* Cambridge, MA: Perseus Books.

Katz, L. G. (1980). Mothering and teaching: Some significant distinctions. In L. G. Katz (Ed.), *Current topics in early childhood education* (Vol. 3). Norwood, NJ: Ablex.

Stone, J. G. (2001). *Building classroom community: The early childhood teacher's role.* Washington, DC: National Association for the Education of Young Children.

Tomko, C. T. (2010). *When a professional says.* … Retrieved June 7, 2011, from www.kidstogether.org/perspectives/whenaprofessionalsays.htm

Web Sites

Families and Work Institute
www.familiesandwork.org

National Coalition for Parent Involvement in Education
www.ncpie.org

National Parent–Teacher Association
www.pta.org

Parents Without Partners
www.parentswithoutpartners.org

Partnership for Family Involvement in Education
www.pfie.ed.gov

Partnership for Learning
www.partnershipforlearning.org

The Dynamics of Diversity

Demonstrate an understanding of the many facets of diversity and the skills for interacting collaboratively with children and adults of various cultures, languages, and abilities in group care and education settings.

Reflections on Diversity

The middle-aged Caucasian White woman with a bachelor's degree and teaching certificate is no longer the prototype for today's early childhood teacher. Although it is true that women make up most of the workforce in early education, their race and ethnicity, age, and educational level have changed dramatically. The same is true for the children you teach. Classrooms are a "salad bowl" of people, each one a wonderfully diverse flavor that, when added to the whole, creates something unique.

Today's Context

Twenty-first-century teachers are working across cultures with children, families, and colleagues in an early childhood setting. No matter what culture you were raised in, you will need to adapt to others with diverse backgrounds. Census reports (U.S. Census Bureau, 2010) indicate that all five of the categories of racial groups increased in population between 2000 and 2010, with the largest increases in Hispanic, Asian, and Pacific Islander. Moreover, nearly one-third of Americans reported an identification with two or more racial groups. Other changes in the United States bring greater diversity to the population as well. Parents who are gay or lesbian, the mandated inclusion of children with a variety of disabilities, and the influx of world religions add to the classroom mix.

This chapter focuses on many facets of diversity to help student teachers achieve a level of competence in working with children and families

Teachers, like children, vary in educational background, age, gender, culture/ethnicity, and ability.

whose background and culture may be different from their own. Our intention is to shift the focus from just cultural diversity to that of *human* diversity. To do so requires responding to differences with a broad viewpoint, incorporating what we know about the wide range of human experience as it is expressed in children and in families.

To reflect on diversity means making a second paradigm shift, this time in our identity as teachers. Teachers are often considered experts in education, but to work in today's diverse classrooms, teachers must become learners, a concept stressed throughout this text. We have to redefine the nature of teaching and learn to say "I don't know." Our sources of information will be the children, their families, colleagues, the media, and the Internet. All information will have to be screened for bias and stereotypes.

The aim of this chapter is to explore the many aspects of diversity—culture/ethnicity/race, gender, religion, age, ability, language, social class and income, and temperament—as components that influence children's behavior and identity. As a teacher, you will be able to go forward in your own learning as you work with actual children. A working knowledge of the issues facing the families you teach is an important element in creating a responsive and inclusive environment.

Culture

The blueprint for human development is the culture in which a person is raised. Gonzalez-Mena (2007) suggests looking at culture as a framework that is influenced by race, gender, ability, social class, status, income, sexual orientation, religion, and age. Like growth and development in the whole child, cultures are integrated systems that must be viewed in their entirety, not as discrete and isolated parts. Change in one component will

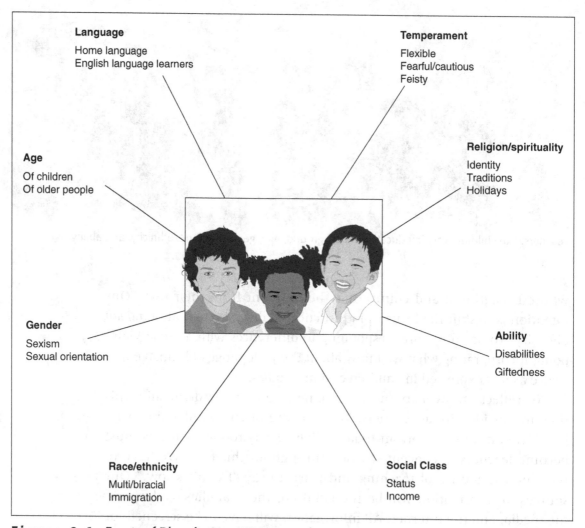

Language
Home language
English language learners

Temperament
Flexible
Fearful/cautious
Feisty

Age
Of children
Of older people

Religion/spirituality
Identity
Traditions
Holidays

Gender
Sexism
Sexual orientation

Ability
Disabilities
Giftedness

Race/ethnicity
Multi/biracial
Immigration

Social Class
Status
Income

Figure 9.1 Facets of Diversity Must Be Honored

The components of human diversity interact and influence children's well-being, behavior, attitudes, and growth.

affect the rest of the system (Banks, 2005). Figure 9.1 illustrates the components that interact to influence who we are. In the following sections, each of these elements will be discussed individually.

Culture is a set of rules we learn from birth onward that tell us how to behave in ways that are similar to our family and larger community. The extensive work on culture and its influence on development (Lynch & Hanson, 2004; Phillips, 1995) describe how cultural rules dictate our behavior—for instance, whether we bow or shake hands when greeting someone, or what we feed our children. The rules are sometimes articulated ("Don't put your elbows on the table when you eat") and often demonstrated (men holding doors open for women).

Depending on the family in which you grew up, you may behave according to rules from more than one culture. A Japanese mother and

> ### My Reaction
>
> **"A First Impression"**
>
> My first impression of the school was that there were different cultures, which I love greatly! The staff were all so kind. I noticed that all the teachers were either of Latin descent or Caucasian but the supervisor was African American. I thought, "How am I going to fit in?" I would be the only African/Filipino teacher there; will the children be scared? But then I said to myself, I am going to be a beautiful addition to the preschool because of my love for children and my hardworking ability. My main focus is to be the best observer, learner, and teacher I can be! I look forward now to start working with the children at the site and experience new teaching skills!
>
> —RAQUEL

African American father each bring their own cultural rules to their family. If they raise their children in London or Los Angeles, a third set of cultural rules may be added. Often cultures share the same rules yet exhibit different practices. People may speak the same language, for instance, but have widely different child-rearing views. Shanghainese parents are likely to raise their children differently from those in Hunan province, though they both identify as Han Chinese and their children are taught in Mandarin.

The rules governing our behavior are culture bound, but not everyone maintains the rules to the same degree. Some people are immersed in their culture, and others have a lesser degree of involvement. This may explain why a friend of yours who is Italian may not know anything about cooking a good pasta sauce.

Culture is shaped by the group and is passed down from one generation to another. We all develop within a cultural context, exhibiting behaviors appropriate to that cultural group. What cultural experiences do you remember that are important to your family? In the "My Reaction" feature, a student teacher reflects on her cultural contributions to her teaching.

The Many Facets of Diversity

As humans, we are deeply influenced by the cultural socialization we experience, and our attitudes and behavior reflect the values we are taught. As educators, we work in institutions that are dedicated to educating each individual child and also helping all children learn to live together.

The Dynamics of Diversity

As a developing professional, you know that children are best understood in the context of their families, and that you pledge to adhere to a code of ethical conduct to respect the dignity and worth of each family. The following components of culture challenge teachers in their relationships with children and families.

Race/Ethnicity

Race and ethnicity, as used in this text, refer to a shared common ancestry, history, traditions, behavioral characteristics, culture, and a sense of identification. The U.S. Census of 2010 used five race categories—White, Black/African American, American Indian/Alaska Native, Asian, Native Hawaiian/Other Pacific Islander—as defined by the Office of Management and Budget as well as a category that allowed the option to self-identify (for the first time since its inception in 1790) that included Hispanic/Latino, multiracial/mixed, and so on. Categories generally reflect a social definition of race recognized in the United States and are not an attempt to define race biologically or genetically. Some social scientists say that race is designated by genetic heritage (Banks, 2005), whereas some have other views (Phillips, 1995).

In any case, ethnic/racial diversity in the United States has changed dramatically over the past decade. Between 2000 and 2010, the Hispanic/Latino population increased 43%, the Asian population grew by 43%, Pacific Islanders by 35%, and the Black/African American population by 12%, while the White population increased by nearly 6%. Those who claim two or more races increased by 32% (U.S. Census Bureau, 2010). Unlike the great European immigration pattern of a hundred years ago, most of the recent immigrants are from Asia and South and Central America.

These demographic changes in the United States have several implications for teachers. There will be more cultures to learn about in order to gain a sense of a family's cultural values. There are still problems of racial bias that impact children and families of color. We know that as early as 2 years of age children notice physical differences, by 4 years they may have a sense of their ethnic identity, and by primary school they begin to assess value to different cultural groups (Trawick-Smith, 2009). Teachers need to develop strategies for ensuring that all children receive an equal and bias-free education. Later in this chapter (and in Chapter 6) you will learn about the anti-bias approach that will introduce you to some of the techniques you can use to fight bias.

Gender

The behavior of males and females is influenced by culture, and every culture has its own gender stereotypes (Trawick-Smith, 2009). By the time children are in preschool, they begin to acquire and understand their gender identity, and in the early elementary years children have a sense that certain behaviors and attitudes are expected of them because they are boys or girls. It is not uncommon to hear children say "You can't play ball—you're a girl" or "Boys don't cook." Erasing sexual stereotypes is not simply a matter of having books that show boys cooking or helping girls gain a place in the playground. You must also look at family patterns of gender roles and the cultural values that support the behavior.

Many educational settings continue to reflect gender stereotypes in their choice of books and literature, toys, displays of photographs and pictures, and their acceptance of rigid role definitions. Teachers can expand children's experiences in more equitable learning activities that help eliminate stereotypes. Group games, activities, and projects can break down gender barriers by encouraging mixed-gender play and positive interactions between boys and girls. It is a more complex task to work with families around gender stereotyping; ask your supervising teacher about what your program does to address gender bias.

For children of gay and lesbian parents, it is important to ensure a safe environment where family structure and sexual orientation are respected. Clay (2004) describes four areas of concern for gay and lesbian parents. They want (a) emotional safety from homophobia, (b) visible diversity throughout the school environment so that their child is not considered "unique", (c) staff who are comfortable with and have experience with gay and lesbian people, and (d) to feel part of the whole community, not be treated as "outsiders." Gay and lesbian parents also feel that adoption issues are more critical to them than issues of sexual orientation. It is only through open, honest, and trusting relationships with families that teachers can learn what families need most from the school experience.

Language

Maintaining the home language is an important aspect of family culture and identity. Respecting home languages in the school setting enhances family pride in their unique heritage.

Several communication challenges are possible with a multilinguistic clientele. Some families may be fluent in both English and their native language, whereas others know little or no English. Many may have receptive skills in the dominant language but be less confident in speaking, and may not be literate. Building bridges to cross the language barrier will help families feel less isolated and establish a relationship of equality and respect. Using translators in communicating verbally and in print tells families that you want to involve them in their children's education.

Preserving a child's home language is important.

For children whose first language is not English, the situation can be complicated. Families vary in their desire for how much home language and English they want their children to hear and use. Find out the home languages of the children in your care, and learn some key words and phrases (see the "Putting Diversity into Action" section). This way you can offer children reassurance that they will be understood and demonstrate your appreciation of what they already know well.

In responding to linguistic and cultural diversity, NAEYC (2009) states that for optimal development, "educators must accept the legitimacy of children's home language," and further recommends that early childhood programs recruit teachers who are trained in languages other than English.

Abilities

Children with special needs come in all sizes, colors, and shapes, and their disabilities cover a wide range of characteristics. There are two types of children with special needs: those who have some sort of disability and those who are gifted. Allen and Cowdery (2011) suggest that children are considered disabled if their normal growth and development are delayed, abnormal, or severely affected in their mental, social, emotional, physical, and social developmental domains. A gifted student is one who has an exceptional ability in one or more areas of development.

The number of programs that enroll children with disabilities has risen dramatically due to federal legislation that mandates equal educational opportunities for children with disabilities (P.L. 94-142 and P.L. 99-457; idea.ed.gov). From infancy through age 21, people with disabilities are included in regular classrooms whenever possible, in the least restrictive environment, and with an individualized plan. In many cases, the family will have an individualized family service plan (IFSP) if their child is younger than 3 years or an individualized education plan (IEP) if their child is 3 years or older. The two plans are mandated by law to help families and specialists work together to identify priorities, resources, and concerns, and to become the guidelines for providing appropriate intervention services and teaching strategies, as in the following example.

To fully include a child who has an identified special need in a regular classroom, teachers must educate themselves about the disorder as well as work with the family and specialists to implement the child's IEP. For example, first-grader Conrad has been assessed for attention deficit disorder and has been found to have moderate ADHD-1, a subtype of attention deficit with hyperactivity disorder that presents as predominantly inattentive (NRC/ADHD, 2009). He does not pay close attention to details and is easily distracted, so it is hard for him to maintain attention in a large group or in active free play indoors. Student teacher Janelle is challenged in the busy school-age center, where children are coming and going on their own. Conrad's best time is at the homework corner, where movement is restricted and it is quiet. His IEP suggests she make contact when giving directions using clear and simple explanations, and allow time for transitions by giving a plan for the next step. She makes sure she sits next to him as he gets started with homework, and then shadows him when he leaves to put away his things. She gets him to select jobs, such as setting the snack table or helping her feed the animals outdoors, in which he will be successful. She can thus recognize his accomplishments, as there are plenty of challenges for him (circle time, outdoor sports choice) in the normal routines of the afternoon

As an early childhood educator you will meet and teach children with a variety of disabilities. Figure 9.2 lists some of the conditions you may experience. Hopefully, you have completed a course about children with special needs to prepare you to teach in the early childhood field. Your primary concern as a teacher is to plan programs that are adaptable to a wide range of developmental differences of the children in the class. In Chapter 6, Figure 6.6 is an example of how to adapt an art project for children with special needs.

There are two important aspects about working with children with special needs. The first is about language: *Put children first*. As you speak or write about a child with a disability, you mention the child, followed by the specific disorder. For example, you say "Tito, a *child with* Down syndrome, is in my class," not "Tito is a Down syndrome child." It will take practice to speak of a *child who is blind* rather than a blind child. The

Figure 9.2
Special Needs
That Teachers May
Encounter

These disabilities may
range from mild to severe
and vary widely with
individual children.

Source: Based on information
from *Children with Special
Needs in Early Childhood
Settings* by Carol L. Paasche,
Lola Gorrill, and Bev Strom.
(2003). Thomson/Delmar
Learning: Clifton Park, NY.

Allergies: itching, hives, eczema, runny and swollen eyes, stuffy/runny nose, plugged ears, breathing through mouth, sneezing., nausea, constipation, fever, excessive sweating, headaches, poor appetite, fatigues.

Asthma: breathing difficulties, gasping for air, cough wheezing.

Behavioral/Social/Emotional Problems: disruptive, impulsive, restless, temper tantrums, lack concentration, uncooperative or withdrawn, clingy, solitary avoids eye contact, fearful.

Failure to Thrive: underweight, motor, language, and social delays, withdrawn, does not smile, ongoing respiratory infections, resists being comforted, poor appetite.

Fetal Alcohol Syndrome: small head and brain, low birth weight, facial abnormalities, mental retardation, irregular body proportions, poor motor skills, developmental delays, lack of social skills.

Hearing Impairments: poor articulation & grammar, asks for instructions to be repeated, does not follow directions or seem to pay attention, poor social skills, poor balance.

HIV/AIDs: low resistance to all viruses, colds, infections, chronic fatigue, developmental delays, frequent infections, kidney and/or heart problems.

Intellectual Disabilities: delayed developmental milestones, cognitive function significantly below age level, unable to follow simple routines, short attention span, limited communication skills, lacks age-appropriate self-help skills, motor skills and problem-solving skills, rarely contributes new ideas.

Motor Problems: appears clumsy, awkward, poor balance, difficulty in climbing, jumping, hopping, unable to bounce, catch balls, tires easily, seems accident prone, difficulty picking up small objects and in balancing a stack of blocks, difficulty with turning and manipulating objects.

Oppositional Defiant Disorder: consistently negative, disobedient, hostile, angry, argumentative, stubborn, spiteful.

Speech and Language Problems: substitute one sound for another, voice may be monotone, nasal, or too soft/loud, poor motor coordination, attention span, listening skills, short attention span, delayed language development, difficulty classifying objects and remembering personal information (address, phone number), difficulty with phonetic skills, not comprehend what is read, problems with spelling, limited vocabulary, difficulty with expressing ideas, does not initiate conversation or ideas, poor peer interactions.

Specific Learning Disorders: problems with acquiring, processing, and retaining information, difficulties with reading, writing, spelling and math, delayed motor skills, often not apparent until school age.

Visual Impairment: rubs, shuts or covers eyes frequently, tilts head forward, dizziness, headaches, nausea, stumbles over small objects, cognitive, motor, social, and language delays, holds objects close/far away, difficulties with beginning reading and math, may not distinguish between colors.

difference may be subtle but critical to enhancing a child's self-respect. Putting the child first helps you remember that children are defined by an abundance of adjectives, not by their abilities.

The second key factor is to remember the phrase *more alike than different*. The children are more like normally developing children than they are different from them. You will want to look at the similarities children with special needs have with other children, not just at their specific disability.

In the "Lessons from the Field" feature at the end of this chapter, mentor teacher Elaine Francisco describes this factor in personal terms.

Working with families whose children have special needs can be challenging. Your initial role may be to help identify areas of concern through observations and assessments (see Chapter 4). You may also be part of a team of teachers who implement the plan and are links between classroom practice and treatment recommendations.

Religion or Spirituality

Along with other cultural values, it is important for teachers to respect the religious heritage and customs of children and their families. Immigration patterns have brought increasingly diverse models of religious expression into communities and classrooms today.

Saxton (2004) notes that some people may feel a sense of identification within a community of faith more than their membership in a racial or ethnic group. We know that children are spiritual beings and will talk with their teachers anytime about God, a brother's bar mitzvah, or their grandmother's hijab. Student teachers often wonder how to respond to children's comments and questions. For example, what should student teacher Sylvia do when Joseph tells her, "If you don't go to church, you can't go to heaven." Her response should be twofold: First, she is mindful of her school's policy about the separation of church and state, so she refrains from speaking about church doctrine. Second, she is respectful, so she shows interest in what he is sharing by asking him some questions, such as when he does there and with whom he goes.

Holidays often bring religious differences to light because there is great diversity in which holidays and celebrations are important to different religious groups. If these are celebrated in the classroom, the question becomes one of excluding children because of their families' religious beliefs or not celebrating holidays at all, as in the following "Ethical Dilemma." How is this handled in the setting where you practice teach?

Age

Issues around ageism primarily relate to older people. The media often stereotypes older people as physically and mentally inferior, useless, and unwanted (Wolpert, 2005). This picture of our aging population is unfortunate, especially at a time when many senior citizens are enjoying full and useful lives for a very long time. Older people do face issues of fixed incomes and declining health, but that should not prevent a more equitable portrayal of their strengths and level of activity. Many seniors find

---

"What—and How—Shall We Celebrate?"

Rachael is a Jewish woman who is student teaching in a nondenominational preschool housed in a church basement. It is nearly December, and the staff begins to plan activities about the Christmas holidays, focusing on the school traditions of having a father or grandfather visit the classroom as Santa Claus and the class decorating a tree. Rachael considers whether or not to say anything. Do others notice she is not Christian, and should she point that out? Are other non-Christians in the school feeling isolated or offended by these plans?

Code References: *Core Values:* We have made a commitment to respect the dignity, worth, and uniqueness of each individual (child, family member, colleague) and to respect diversity in children, families, and colleagues.

Section III, Ethical Responsibilities to Colleagues, P-3A-4: We shall not participate in practices that discriminate against a co-worker because of sex, race, national origin, religious beliefs or other affiliations, age, marital status/family structure, disability, or sexual orientation

Resolution: Rachael consults with her faculty adviser, and then takes the issue and the Code to her Head Teacher, who puts this on the next week's staff meeting agenda. The school staff is taken aback; they have not considered this viewpoint before. Everyone feels uncomfortable, not knowing what to do. The director suggests using the month to explore the many ways people celebrate this time of year. All classrooms agree and brainstorm the curriculum potential this offers. Rachael offers to do activities around Hanukkah, two families who are Muslim will talk about Islamic New Year, and a British family volunteers to work with their child's teacher about Boxing Day. Moreover, three families approach Rachael and ask if she will visit their children's classroom, as they are not comfortable speaking in front of the class but would like their children's family culture to be celebrated.

---

new careers after retirement and are involved in extensive volunteer work within their communities.

Social injustice is the real cause of discrimination of older citizens; factors include poverty and discrimination policies such as enforced retirement at a certain age. The same type of bias surrounding people with disabilities also applies to older people who use wheelchairs, canes, or walkers. Children need models of older citizens who display the whole range of human abilities and who delight in sharing their lives with people of all ages.

Social Class, Status, or Income

A family's socioeconomic status is determined by level of education, income, place of residence, and occupation of the primary wage earners (Trawick-Smith, 2009). Families of wealth and families of poverty come to school with different perspectives, needs, and resources. For children raised in poverty, issues of health and nutrition are of concern. Working with families of privilege raises different issues. For example, these children may be developing a sense of superiority and entitlement or have a strong focus on material things.

Derman-Sparks, Ramsey, and Olsen Edwards (2006) suggest some ways teachers can address the inequalities of class distinctions:

- Make frequent observations about how children are identifying themselves; use self-portraits to stimulate conversation.
- To discover more about children's self-image, note which activities they prefer and/or avoid.
- Listen to children's conversations as they play to ascertain any feelings they may have about the race and ethnicity of themselves or others; pay close attention to any sense of superiority or entitlement.
- Check to see if the social or racial/ethnic differences influence children's choice of friends.
- Identify the overall tone of the classroom to see if children are sensitive, empathetic, inclusive, negative, or full of conflict.

Through these and other strategies you will uncover a lot of information about how children see themselves and others. The judicious use of curriculum, materials, and activities will help them understand their own identities and appreciate the differences in other people.

Temperament

From birth, a child's temperamental characteristics are observable through their attention span, general mood, activity level, and the regularity of their routines such as eating, sleeping, and digestion. Classic research by Thomas and Chess (1977) identified nine characteristics of temperaments and noted that many children have one of three types: easy, slow to warm, and difficult. Today they are often referred to as follows:

1. The *flexible* child (about 40% of all children) is adaptable, optimistic, cheerful, and easily trained in eating, sleeping, and toileting; has mild reactions to frustration.
2. The *fearful* child (about 15%) seems shy and, although uncomfortable with new situations, adapts slowly if allowed to observe and watch; needs to go at own pace and expresses negative mood slowly.
3. The *feisty* child (about 10%) is the opposite of the flexible child: has irregular sleeping and eating habits; is fussy about new situations; is often disagreeable and prone to temper tantrums; and adapts slowly.

As you come to know and understand the diverse reactions of the children you teach, you will gain insights into their behavior and find strategies that suit their innate temperament.

Figure 9.3
Top 10 Strategies for
Addressing Diversity

1. Know that it begins with you.
2. Realize that there is not only one best or right way.
3. Move from an "either/or" to a "both/and" perspective.
4. Foster a climate of acceptance.
5. Recognize bias in yourself, others, and institutions.
6. Become competent in issues of diversity.
7. Create inclusive classrooms and programs.
8. Expand your teaching strategies.
9. Promote equity in teaching teams.
10. Invite families into the process.

Putting Diversity into Action

To help children develop a solid sense of self, teachers need to incorporate the kaleidoscope of identities the students bring into the classroom. Putting diversity into action can be done, and done well (see Figure 9.3).

Becoming Competent

Many of us grew up with the contradictions of race, gender, and class. We may have been segregated from people with differing abilities, or raised with biases about differing languages or religious practices. Many of us grew up hearing statements that stereotyped people by their age or even temperament, often in negative tones.

Looking Within. To become sensitive to issues of diversity, student teachers start by looking within. You are developing a teaching style and need to understand your own roots and habits first. At the same time, your style evolves over many years; as you gain experience, you will form your own unique personal and professional approach. Build on solid ground by examining your own attitudes; only then can you proceed. You can add your experience to new knowledge and apply what you are learning. Start by asking yourself the questions in Figure 9.4.

Figure 9.4
Uncover Your Beliefs

When putting diversity into action, start with yourself.

1. What is your ethnic group or cultural identity? What has it meant to belong to your ethnic group?
2. What are your earliest images of color and race?
3. Have you ever had the experience of feeling different? If so, what was your first experience?
4. Have you ever experienced a feeling of powerlessness in relation to your ethnic, class, gender, or sexual identity? What was it like?
5. What values, history, or traditions of your group identities have been sources of strength?

Moreover, self-awareness begins with an exploration of your own background and beginnings. Place of origin, time of and reasons for immigration, the languages spoken by the family, and even where the family first settles all influences one's cultural identification. This leads to an examination of the values, behaviors, beliefs, and customs in your own cultural heritage. As student teacher Ellyn relates:

I was thinking about my own English and Danish background when I was reading to the children in the center from a book of nursery rhymes. Cutting off the three blind mice's tails with a carving knife! How horridly cruel—what were my relatives thinking? What kind of life did they live that mice were so threatening? I start to catch myself, when I sing a song to one of the babies: "Are these lyrics okay? What exactly is a "Knick-knack" or "Paddy-whack"? Is this a slam against the Irish? And how does this connect to giving a dog a bone?

Moreover, remember that you bring so much to your program in yourself. Mentor teacher Venecia offered this example:

Charlene was different from anyone I'd known, with a Filipino and Chinese cultural background. Her relationships with the other staff and children fit in right away. Maybe this was because the children and staff had diverse cultural backgrounds as well. As a Venezuelan and a seasoned teacher, I had certain ideas about things. My relationship with Charlene helped me learn to step back and observe more closely how Charlene spoke to and played with children and how she redirected any negative behaviors that might have occurred. I learned new ways for myself!

Gaining Knowledge. Student teaching and becoming culturally competent go hand in hand. Through your own cultural exploration you are finding out the impact that culture has on the individual. Look for cultural information about others; there is an abundance of material available about diversity and difference in our field (see the References and Web Sites sections at the end of this chapter). There is not only one right way to do things. The world in which you were born is only one model of reality: Rather than seeing things as "either my way *or* not," think about adding another way so that your thinking becomes both yours and another's. Lynch and Hanson (2004) outline four effective ways to learn about other cultures:

1. Learning through studying and reading about the culture
2. Talking and working with individuals from the culture who can act as cultural guides or mediators
3. Participating in the daily life of another culture
4. Learning the language of the other culture

The Dynamics of Diversity

Applying What I Learn. Communicating across cultures is challenging. We interpret the meaning of behavior based on our own culture. Each of us has a set of familiar body language, facial expressions, and voice tone that convey a variety of messages to us. Others, however, may see things differently:

> I once sat by a window looking out across the street at a man who was acting very strange. He was making extraordinary gestures and facial expressions. The words coming out of his mouth were in a language I didn't understand. I had decided he was crazy and had begun to feel afraid when finally I stood up and saw the whole picture. There at the man's heels was a dog. Immediately everything made sense. Aha, he's training a dog. (Gonzalez-Mena, 2007, p. 35)

Applying what we learn can be difficult; learning the meaning of behavior from other perspectives will help keep biases in check and expand our own view of the world. For example, nonverbal communication is important to observe and act on with very young children, who are not yet fluent in verbal language. What about immigrant families in your care? Some examples of nonverbal behavior that are accepted and understood in many cultures are burping (an indication that the food was good), not making eye contact (a sign that an elder is respected), and bowing (a form of greeting another person). How can you become more fluent in the nonverbal ways of your children and connect to them? Student teacher Monica describes what it takes to apply what you learn:

> How I wish I could communicate in other languages! I find that I try to be aware of the limitations when "talking" with English learners, and I use lots of gestures and lots of full sentences. Somehow that is working; I get kids nodding their heads that they understand. Today I had the greatest experience when a young boy who speaks only Cambodian made it a point to run to the fence as I walked by toward a college class. He was waving and smiling and gesturing and saying good-bye in English. It has been 4 weeks of being there for him, and smiling and gesturing and talking with his parents and getting him included in activities with others. I felt so high from his running across the playground and waving and speaking to me. I wish I had a photo to match the mental picture I will always carry!

Using what you have learned helps you become culturally competent. Be aware, however, that culture is only one aspect of personal identity. Proceed with caution as you learn new ways of cross-cultural communication. Acknowledging and respecting differences rather than minimizing them will go a long way.

R	**React/*Reaccionar*** Recognize your initial feelings and thoughts about the situation.
E	**Examine/*Examinar*** Think about your reactions. Identify any beliefs you hold that may be affecting your response. Are there any biases that might be shaping your feelings and thoughts?
A	**Ask/*Preguntar*** Look for multiple perspectives. Look for other perspectives to expand and deepen your own understanding.
C	**Consider/*Considerar*** Generate multiple strategies. Look deeply into the situation and explore those strategies that help address the situation in ways that are culturally and linguistically respectful of others and have the best potential for positive results.
H	**Handle/*Manejar*** Look at the situation with respect and honor. Implement the strategies that you select, being vigilant of the reactions of others in order to make adjustments to your approach when warranted.

Figure 9.5
Reach/*Alcanzar*

Follow a process for creating dialogue, reflection, and action, and for addressing the many challenges we face in diversity work.

Source: From *Reaching for Answers: Forum on Diversity in Early Childhood Education,* by BANDTEC (Bay Area Network for Diversity Training: Building Equity and Social Justice for Children and Families), 2006, San Mateo, CA: San Mateo County Office of Education. Used with permission.

Learning to REACH. It is likely that today's children in the world of child care are learning diversity firsthand, differently than many of their teachers did. So it is important that their teachers see diversity in its many forms and develop cross-cultural competence. Figure 9.5 offers a way student teachers can reach for answers.

Recognizing Bias

A second step in cultural competence is recognizing bias in ourselves and others and taking appropriate action. This is a crucial aspect of the *anti-bias curriculum* (described in Chapter 6) and is essential to the process of becoming a competent educator. The goal of anti-bias work is inclusion. Teachers do this work so that children develop empathy and can experience what it means to be active in the face of injustice. If we start seeing the meaning of diversity, we need to examine our own biases. We can then see bias in others, listen to voices traditionally silenced, and incorporate what we learn into our teaching (Carter, Curtis, & Jones, 2002).

Personal Biases. Sometimes we surprise ourselves. Teaching young children brings us face to face with new experiences and feelings. Kate writes:

> As a new teacher in a university lab school, I was nervous but excited about teaching there. This school incorporated children with special needs, which was new for me, but I was looking forward to being in a place that welcomed everyone. One day Jonathan—one of the youngest in our room—was toddling into the bathroom; 6-year-old Dawn, with Down syndrome, came barreling behind him and pushed him down.

The Dynamics of Diversity

Understanding diversity means getting to know the diversity within each child.

Running over to Dawn, I took her by the arm and made her help me pick up Jonathan and get him a tissue. I was shaking inside: "They shouldn't let these kids be here!" I seethed. Later, I was embarrassed to even write those words. How could I be so prejudiced?

Over time in the learning process, we come to see how bias can shape our lives without our awareness. As we identify our own feelings, we can work to find our own voices.

Biases of Others. It is often easier to spot bias or prejudice in others than it is to see it in ourselves. Use your observation skills well: First, you can see yourself in a different light and, second, you can develop strategies for addressing the biases you may encounter. For example, Jimenez (2002) recounts an experience in a teacher support group:

I was frightened and intimidated by some of the participants. Later, I would find out they felt the same way. When Rosa, another Chicana in the group, would question Louise, I would think to myself, "What a troublemaker." Now, as I look back, I realize I wouldn't have labeled her a troublemaker if she had been white. (p. 36)

Over time, the process of incorporating a broader perspective can help educators become more honest about who they are, and allow them to grow. Discovering messages of inferiority or superiority you internalized while growing up can help you build a knowledgeable, confident sense of yourself. Again, Jimenez (2002) states: "Shutting people out just keeps you from being able to peel back through all the layers of bias and misunderstanding" (p. 36).

As a student teacher, your work in the program and with the children is your first priority. Having a strategy to respond to biased behavior will support your efforts. Figure 9.6 lists questions you should ask yourself when you encounter bias.

Notice how student teacher Ellina tries to process a typical situation she encounters. In her journal she writes:

One of my worst moments was with a child who is hard of hearing, so he has trouble speaking. During lunchtime, one of the teachers said to

1. What happened?
   a. What issues of bias are involved?
   b. What is your bias in this situation?
   c. How does the situation make you feel?
   d. Is there a conflict between your own beliefs and those of other adults involved or those of the families of the children involved?

2. Why did it happen?
   a. Why do the people involved have the ideas they have?
   b. What societal images and messages are influencing them?

3. What is the impact of what happened?
   a. What is the impact on people directly involved?
   b. What is the impact on others who overhear?

4. What intervention can change what happened?
   a. What do you want to accomplish?
   b. If there is a conflict between your own beliefs and those of other adults or the families of children involved, how will you be respectful of those beliefs?
   c. What developmental issues will influence your response?
   d. What can be said to affirm the feelings and identity of each person?
   e. What questions will model investigation and encourage critical thinking rather than interrogation that will embarrass or shame?

Figure 9.6
When You Encounter Bias: Feel-Think-Respond
Practice responding to incidents involving bias using these think-feel-respond questions.
Source: From *Start Seeing Diversity: The Basic Guide to an Anti-Bias Classroom,* by Ellen Wolpert for the committee for Boston Public Housing. Copyright © 2005 by Ellen Wolpert for the Committee for Boston Public Housing. Reprinted by permission of Redleaf Press, St. Paul, MN, www.redleafpress.org

the boy, "Say 'Teacher.'" When he couldn't, the rest of the table starting saying "Say Teacher, Say Teacher." I was waiting for the teacher to tell the children to stop, and then explain to them. But nothing happened, and the boy didn't talk for the rest of the day.

1. *What happened:* The bias was the teacher's assumption that exposing the child was okay. Mine is that you should never embarrass a child, and it reminds me of how people treated me with my polio since I couldn't walk or run as well as everyone else.

2. *Why it happened:* That teacher probably has never been in that position. She doesn't see people with hearing impairment as any different or sensitive to being pointed out.

3. *The impact of what happened:* The child stopped talking—it affected him all day and who knows how long. The kids who overheard behaved badly, teasing and practicing how to be bullies, not how to have empathy.

4. *Intervention that could change what happened:* I want the child to be protected from meanness; maybe that's not realistic. I want the kids to understand how their teasing hurt him—how do I do that with preschoolers? "Did that hurt your feelings?"—then what? "When you tease people about something they can't help, it's not okay"—what else? Maybe I need to ask the children individually. Stop the teasing; then ask "How did that make you feel?" of all the kids.

Taking Action. The biases we find in society are reflected early in school life. Student teachers who choose to address these inequalities when they arise in their programs are taking an active stance in promoting tolerance. This is not always comfortable, as evidenced by the following Reflective Incident. Yet by understanding the complexity of our diverse society, you come closer to providing an equitable educational experience for all children. As Tatum (2003) states:

> We all have a sphere of influence. Each of us needs to find our own sources of courage so that we will begin to speak. There are many problems to address, and we cannot avoid them indefinitely. . . . I have seen that meaningful dialogue can lead to effective action. Change is possible. (p. xii)

Reflective Incident "Gordon and the Pumpkin Eater"

I had an interesting experience around Halloween at the center. I downloaded an activity that included the Peter Piper poem and a cutout project. When I read the classic poem, I realized I needed to change it. I still started it "Peter, Peter, Pumpkin Eater," but then changed the rest of it.

Instead of . . .	I changed it to . . .
"Had a wife and couldn't keep her"	"Had a wife but couldn't see her"
"Put her in a pumpkin shell and"	"Looked into a pumpkin shell and"
"There he kept her very well."	"There he saw her very well."

I was proud of myself for keeping the rhythm but getting rid of the sexist tone. I thought I had covered all the bases, but I had not. The Peter and Wife cutouts were dressed as Pilgrims. I did not consider that, but several parents did and were vocal in their complaints to the director and my head teacher. They informed me that the school policy, formed in cooperation with parental input, was to not use anything "pilgrim" because of the barbaric practices pilgrims and missionaries perpetuated against Native Americans. I was aghast at my gaffe. I should have recognized Peter as a Pilgrim rather than a Pumpkin Eater with bad fashion sense.

—GORDON

Your Thoughts

1. How would I feel?

2. What would I do?

3. What might the results be?

Creating a Climate of Acceptance

Student teachers can initiate several concrete actions to create a climate of acceptance in their fieldwork sites. Several of these focus on aspects of student teaching already introduced in this book, such as the environment (Chapter 5), the curriculum (Chapter 6), teaching strategies (Chapter 3), your site or team (Chapter 7), and families (Chapter 8). We weave these ideas into all we do; at the same time, using diversity as the focal point underscores both a multicultural focus and an anti-bias perspective.

Preparing a Diverse Environment. As a student teacher, you know that a key part of teaching is to prepare an appropriate environment for children (see Chapter 5). How do we provide for diversity? Think about the children in your program, and ensure that every one is represented visually. Next, consider the diversity of the planet and bring that into the classroom. Finally, check for stereotyped images. Environments that are developmentally appropriate will be rich in a variety of materials; those that are also diversity responsive will ensure that materials and activities successfully address the previous list.

Of course, no one is perfect, but it is important to be vigilant about what is used in the learning environment (refer back to the "Reflective Incident"). Be sure to look at the total environment; learning through outdoor play, for instance, is important for all children, and may need individual adaptations to include those with special needs. A child with autism may need a physical boundary around a garden area or a specific area to dig and plant, whereas one who is blind might need an adapted ball with an active beeper inside.

Integrating Diversity into the Curriculum. Once space and materials are organized, teachers prepare the curriculum (see Chapter 6). Table 9.1 gives examples; in addition, remember that children's curiosity and questions about the differences they see (language, hair texture, lunch boxes and their contents) can trigger curriculum that emerges from their interests.

Student teacher Miho was at a loss about what to do when Diaz's grandfather died unexpectedly in the fall. Supervising teacher Karen asked her to research how to talk to children about death, then conferred with Diaz's mother, Maria, about the family's plans. The next month, Maria offered to speak with the children about El Día de los Muertos, and Diaz brought in photos of the altar

Student teachers experience hands-on learning when families share their interests and culture with the class.

Table 9.1 Multicultural Goals Transformed into Curriculum for Diversity
The goals of multicultural education can aid in developing a curriculum for diversity.

Goal	Curriculum Example
Teach children to respect others' cultures and values as well as their own.	With the children, cook a dish from each child's culture and serve it for snack.
Help all children function successfully in a multicultural, multiracial society.	Make people-colored fans with skin-colored paint on index cards that get fastened together with brads.
Develop a positive self-concept in those children most affected by racism, such as children of color.	Using persona dolls, do storytelling about someone being teased about their hair texture or style.
Help all children experience their differences as culturally diverse people and their similarities as human beings in positive ways.	In developing a unit on "heroes and sheroes," introduce children to the concepts of personal shields and have each make a powerful and safe one to use and share.
Encourage children to see that people of diverse cultures work together, making the unique parts of a community whole.	Make sequence cards to illustrate food chains in their community. Then visit those places or invite people in to show and tell what they do as part of the food chain.

Source: Based on York (2002).

they had at home. The children were fascinated and wanted to build boxes for their loved ones (including pets). An informational meeting was held and a packet was prepared for the families, and Miho learned how to make *calaveras* (sugar skulls) and to cook *chayotes* (a type of Mexican squash), while Karen worked with the children to make a "special place" for the boxes. Each step was documented in the entry hall, and the culminating event was a "Sharing Celebration" in which several families and teachers offered flowers, photos, and memories of their beloved dead. This example is integrated curriculum at its best, starting with individual need, emerging into cultural diversity, involving many families, and concluding with a project of great interest and meaning to all.

Developing Teaching Strategies for Diversity. The strategies around teaching diversity parallel what good teachers use with children every day. Observing, guiding, facilitating, and intervening carefully are all techniques that the effective teacher uses in developing relationships and handling children's behavior (see Chapter 3). Student teachers often feel overwhelmed by the daily interactions with young children, and the thought of adding more "tools to the kit" seems impossible. Fortunately, you will not need to master a completely new set of skills; rather, you will need to focus your efforts in some special ways.

"Can I p'ay wif you?" Nieta asks Lourdes and Sarah who are in the play-house. "No, it's already full here," Lourdes replies. "Yeah, and we don't need anyone else," adds Sarah, while they both turn their backs on her. Student teacher Fiona has seen this happen before with Nieta and is concerned that the child is being excluded because of her language skills. In fact, Fiona notices that all the English language learners are isolated from the "power players," more so on the playground than during indoor activity time.

What can Fiona do? She is wise to attend to this issue; in an English-language classroom, the child who does not yet understand or speak English may find it difficult to interact appropriately with children and may be treated as invisible or marginalized by others. The same can be said about any child who is not of the dominant language, culture, gen-der, religion, or ability of the group as a whole. Several strategies may help (Derman-Sparks et al., 2010):

- *Help children develop authentic identities based on personal abilities and interests, family history, and culture rather than on notions of inferiority or superiority.* If it is okay for Nieta to be left out, then all three girls experience the results of exclusion and may come to accept it as a reasonable, common strategy for play. Fiona intervenes by say-ing "It looks like you need some shoppers in your store, Lourdes. Nieta and I have some money. Do you have anything for us to buy today?" Nieta becomes a powerful figure in the play without need-ing words, while Lourdes and Sarah get the experience of inclusion.

- *Know, respect, and value the range of diversity of physical and social attributes among people.* By tracking what activities interest Nieta, Fiona can help her learn some vocabulary that would help her be more successful and see how she can contribute. Fiona modifies the environment by adding several tools and clothing familiar to Nieta (and not to the oth-ers). Later, she invites Nieta to start the play with her. When Lourdes and Sarah approach as newcomers, Nieta can show *them* how to play.

- *Build the capacity for caring, cooperative, and equitable interactions with oth-ers.* By observing the overall social tone of the classroom, Fiona sees that the White children seem to have a sense of entitlement that emphasizes children outdoing each other. For circle time she starts a discussion about what activities the children like to do with fam-ily and friends that show caring ("I help Mom wash the car"), then organizes a game to act out those activities with partners chosen from names in a hat. Lourdes and Nieta are partners "helping Dad give the baby a bath," and everyone laughs when Nieta splashes Lourdes!

As you work and play with the children at your site, you will find that the observing and interacting you start with (see Chapter 1) will help you

---

My Reaction

"Me and the Shu"

I was so happy Thursday that the little boy who speaks Cantonese has started speaking and laughing with me. It was so heartwarming! The center just hired a teaching assistant who speaks Cantonese, so I asked her to teach me some words. We were having broccoli for lunch and the boy said "Shu," which I knew is the word for "tree." I pantomimed getting under the "shu" and everyone at the table thought it was a riot. We all did it, saying "tree-shu." We had so much fun!

—TIANA

---

develop teaching strategies for diversity, as in the "My Reaction" feature that follows.

Promoting Equity with the Team. As mentioned in Chapter 1, placements in a practicum vary widely, particularly in the role the student teacher may play in the teaching team. Many of you will be new to your site, and so your primary connection may be to your supervising teacher, rather than to the whole team. Some of you may already be working at the fieldwork site. In that case, you may have a larger role to play on your team. In any case, do what you can to build a sense of community among the teaching team (see Chapter 7). This increases the level of communication and trust, which helps create a dialogue about diversity.

Working with Families. The first component in working with families around issues of diversity is convincing them that their home's cultural values and norms are honored (see Chapter 8). Involving families in the program in many ways helps you incorporate a range of activities and ways of doing things into the life of the center. "My fellow teachers and myself always talk to the parents and find out what's going on in the home life," offers student teacher Lenoir. "I use their food sometimes because at lunch they send food I haven't seen. So at the end of the day I will ask them, 'What was the food you sent? Is it from your culture or just something you like?' It really is a conversation starter, and I have learned a lot about families, where they are from, and what they do at home."

You do not need to know everything beforehand about every child or his or her culture. Rather, you need to learn how to *find out* what you need to know to be sensitive and responsive to every child.

Each of us is a unique manifestation of the human spirit; teaching with diversity as a cornerstone allows each child to express this spirit while also bringing everyone together in community. (See "Lessons from the Field.")

"Opportunities for Every Ability"

by Elaine Francisco

Mentor/Preschool Special Needs Teacher

During my classroom's free-choice period, I observe John walk straight to the sandbox, scoop up a handful of sand, and throw it on the floor. At the same time, Erica picks up the broom and dustpan, and randomly sweeps the grains of sand as they fall to the ground. These two students have been doing this same activity for over a month. It heartens me that John, who was diagnosed with autism, and Erica, a child who has a severe language impairment, are engaging in near cooperative play. It was not long ago that both students started in my class as mere onlookers who were not interested in any type of play interaction.

Although I was an early childhood teacher for 10 years when I began to teach special education, I thought that I needed to implement a different approach in my teaching methods. Knowing that a special education environment is supposedly a "restrictive" environment, I decided I must restrict many of the hands-on, child-initiated, and discovery learning strategies that I had always believed in. I started shelving many of my classroom toys and took to designing specific goal-focused play activities for my students without considering the choices they could have made independently. This implementation deprived the children of the opportunity to engage in spontaneous play at their own pace, since I literally "dictated" what they could and could not do.

As my classroom began to look like a highly structured, well-defined environment that encouraged teacher-initiated activities, I often had moments of guilt but always reminded myself that my class dealt with special education and should therefore be different from general education. Despite my own doubts, student teachers in early childhood special education who spent entire semesters with me observed that I did implement "best practices" in special education. They mentioned that I effectively connected with parents, addressed individual goals, was able to collaborate effectively with the IEP team, and had implemented activity-based interventions, the majority of which, unfortunately, were strictly teacher directed.

By my third year of teaching special education, I unknowingly became a focused "interventionist," and began to emphasize my student's disabilities rather than viewing each as a "whole" child. With this newly adapted mind-set, I had a true restrictive environment. I focused on planned work between an adult and child rather than promoting spontaneous child play as I aimed to promote language and social cognition.

Then I was invited to apply to an ECE mentor teacher program. Part of the application process was a self-assessment and classroom environmental rating, after which evaluators would visit my classroom. I was fortunate to be given honest feedback by the evaluators as they used the tool to assess my classroom. I passed many areas of the rating, but the findings were a wake-up call for me. I did not have enough toys out, my classroom materials did not represent the diversity of my student population, and my outdoor play activities failed to provide choices for my students. Even my sandbox was not part of everyday play!

To make it short and simple, I had lost sight of my own early childhood "roots" in the quest to be a competent teacher in special education. I had forgotten how promoting spontaneous child's play is crucial to the development of *every* child. In my focus on planned adult–child interactions, I had moved toward an idea of isolated play with such limited choices that the children's "diversity" of special needs was overriding their "universality" of being children. I mistakenly judged their abilities prior to giving them opportunities.

Now, as I observe John and Erica play in the sandbox area, I am inspired by the conviction that someday both will advance their play as I consistently give them multiple opportunities to interact with materials and with their peers throughout the day. I feel relieved that once again I regard spontaneous play as a fundamental element in an early childhood classroom without which learning becomes an adult's prescription rather than a child's personal discovery. They can do more, I can do better, and we all can grow together.

Practicum Activity

Examine the toys and interest areas in your program: Are there any forms of bias present? Which materials would you eliminate (and why) and what might you want to add?

Journaling Assignment

How aware are you of your own identity (culture, race/ethnicity, gender, language, ability, religion, age, social class, temperament)? What experiences have you had with feeling excluded because of your background?

References

Allen, K. E., & Cowdery, G. E. (2011). *The exceptional child: Inclusion in early childhood education* (7th ed.). Belmont, CA: Wadsworth Publishing.

BANDTEC (Bay Area Network for Diversity Training: Building Equity and Social Justice for Children and Families. (2006). *Reaching for Answers: Forum on Diversity in Early Childhood Education.* San Mateo, CA: San Mateo County Office of Education.

Banks, J. A. (2005). *Cultural diversity and education: Foundations, curriculum, and teaching* (5th ed.). Boston: Allyn & Bacon.

Carter, M., Curtis, D., & Jones, E. (2002). *Training teachers: A harvest of theory and practice* (2nd ed.). St. Paul, MN: Redleaf Press.

Clay, J. W. (2004, November). Creating safe, just places to learn for children of lesbian and gay parents: The NAEYC code of ethics in action. *Young Children, 59*(6), 34–38.

Derman-Sparks, L., & Olsen Edwards, L. (2010). *Anti-bias education for children and ourselves.* Washington, DC: National Association for the Education of Young Children.

Derman-Sparks, L., Ramsey, P. G., & Olsen Edwards, J. (2006). *What if all the kids are white?* New York: Teachers College Press.

Gonzalez-Mena, J. (2007). *Diversity in early care and education: Honoring differences* (5th ed.). Boston: McGraw-Hill.

Jimenez, L. I. (2002). Finding a voice. In C. Alvarado et al. (Eds.), *In our own way: How anti-bias work shapes our lives.* St. Paul, MN: Redleaf Press.

Lynch, E. W., & Hanson, M. J. (2004). *Developing cross-cultural competence: A guide for working with young children and their families* (3rd ed.). Baltimore: Paul H. Brookes.

National Association for the Education of Young Children. (2009). *Where we stand: On responding to linguistic and cultural diversity.* Retrieved June 8, 2012, from www.naeyc. org/files/naeyc/file/positions/diversity.pdf

National Association for the Education of Young Children. (2011). Code of Ethical Conduct and Statement of Commitment. Washington, DC: NAEYC.

NRC/ADHD. (2009). Welcome to the National Resource Center on ADHD. Retrieved June 10, 2012, from www.help4adhd.org

Phillips, C. (1995). Culture: A process that empowers. In P. Mangione (Ed.), *Infant/toddler caregiving: A guide to culturally sensitive care.* Sacramento, CA: California Department of Education Press.

Saxton, R. (2004). A place for faith. In A. M. Gordon & K. W. Browne (Eds.), *Beginnings and beyond: Foundations in early childhood education* (6th ed.). Clifton Park, NY: Thomson Delmar Learning.

Tatum, B. D. (2003). *Why are all the Black kids sitting together in the cafeteria? and other conversations about race* (rev. ed.). New York: Basic Books.

Thomas, A., & Chess, S. (1977). *Temperament and development.* New York: Brunner/Mazel.

Trawick-Smith, J. (2009). *Early childhood development: A multi-cultural perspective* (5th ed.). Upper Saddle River, NJ: Merrill/Pearson.

U.S. Census Bureau. (2009). *Foreign born population.* Retrieved June 8, 2012, from www.census.gov/population/www/socdemo/foreign/cps2009

U.S. Census Bureau. (2010). *2010 Census Bureau Data.* Retrieved June 8, 2012, from http://2010.census.gov/2010census/data

York, S. (2002). *Big as life: The everyday inclusive curriculum* (vol. 2). St. Paul, MN: Redleaf Press.

Wolpert, E. (2005). *Start Seeing Diversity: The Basic Guide to an Anti-Bias Classroom.* St. Paul, MN: Redleaf Press.

Web Sites

Culturally and Linguistically Appropriate Services
http://clas.uiuc.edu

Individuals with Disabilities Education Act
idea.ed.gov

National Association for Bilingual Education
www.nabe.org

National Association for Multicultural Education
www.nameorg.org

National Association for the Education of Young Children
www.naeyc.org

National Black Child Development Institute
www.nbcdi.org

index